TIM CAHILL'S

A WOLVERINE IS EATING MY LEG

"It is like no night on the face of the earth: in this cave the darkness is palpable and it physically swallows the brightest light. The air underground smells clean, damp, curiously sterile. It feels thick, like freshly washed still-damp velvet, and I am about to rappel down a long single strand of rope into the heart of all that heavy darkness. This is the second deepest cave pit in America: the drop is four hundred and forty feet, about what you'd experience from the top of a forty-story building. If you took the shaft in free-fall you'd accelerate to one hundred and some miles an hour and then—about six seconds into the experience—instantly decelerate to zero miles an hour. And die. Wah-hoo-hoo over and out. With six bad seconds to think about it."

Also by Tim Cahill

Buried Dreams: Inside the Mind
of a Serial Killer
Jaguars Ripped My Flesh

A
WOLVERINE
IS
EATING
MY LEG

Tim Cahill

VINTAGE DEPARTURES

TIM CAHILL

A WOLVERINE IS EATING MY LEG

VINTAGE BOOKS

A DIVISION OF RANDOM HOUSE   NEW YORK

A Vintage Departures Original, First Edition
February 1989

Copyright © 1973, 1979, 1981, 1983, 1984, 1985, 1986, 1989 by Tim
Cahill

Portions of this text were originally published in *Outside, Powder, Rolling
Stone, The San Francisco Examiner,* and *Sport Diver.*

Library of Congress Cataloging-in-Publication Data
Cahill, Tim.
A wolverine is eating my leg.
"A Vintage original."
1. Adventure stories, American. I. Title.
PS3553.A365W65   1989   910.4'53   88-40122
ISBN 0-679-72026-X (pbk.)

Design: Blackpool Design

Manufactured in the United States of America
10 9 8 7 6

Grateful acknowledgment is made to the following for permission to re-
print previously published material:

Islands Magazine: "The Marquesas" by Tim Cahill. Copyright © 1985 by
Islands Publishing Company. Reprinted with permission.
Far Musikverlag GmbH: excerpt from the lyrics to "Rasputin" by George Reyam,
Frank Farian and Fred Jay. Copyright © 1978 by Far Musikverlag GmbH.

For the Board of Directors

CONTENTS

INTRODUCTION

The following stories, I see, span a sixteen-year period. Rereading all these pieces—especially the less-recent efforts—was like encountering good friends, old army buddies, for instance, after many years. I had a sense that it might be fun to take a few of these stories out for a drink, bring them home to dinner. What a bunch of guys.

Some of them are simply good-time stories, fun-time stories, stories that are going to find the humor in any situation. These are the guys who want to make us laugh, who will help us keep our perspective during dinner. Because other guests are obsessed with the tether line, that razored precipice separating rational behavior from irrational, good from evil, heroism from sainthood.

A very few of the more somber guests are vaguely haunted individuals. They are obsessed with the darker regions of the soul, with frightening places on the earth or in the mind. They seem to feel a discordant resonance and appear to see the darkness of the physical world reflected in the psychological.

Healthier, perhaps, to find beauty in the physical world and feel it expand inside of us. We call that feeling paradise. Certain of our guests are seekers, and they have suffered varying degrees of success in their quests. I'm sure they'll want to talk about it, maybe over dessert.

A couple of the partygoers will regale us with long, convoluted stories that build to the outrage of a bad pun or a good hoax. We will likely groan in a kind of pain that is very close to laughter sometime during dinner.

The last group to join the party will come swaggering in late, just in time for a few glasses of cognac. Some of them may be limping just a bit or have an arm in a cast. These are guys who have been lost in the desert, who have had a crisis of courage in some underground cavern, who have been beaten up by sacred Himalayan rivers. They seem like daredevils, this group that rides the raggedy edge of risk. And they are problematic individuals, these fellows. Some of them drink a little too much or laugh too loud. They are in entirely too good a mood.

Over the years, a lot of people have asked why I've invited them to any parties at all. I suppose I owe these old friends some explanation.

Look at them from my point of view:

They are, to be sure, often an embarrassment. The subject matter—adventure travel—is sometimes considered fodder for the old Action for Men type of magazine, the kind with articles that take place in the present tense, right now, as you are reading them: "A Wolverine Is Eating My Leg!"

The adventure story—or, more properly, the impulse that drives it—is often difficult to describe. A few years ago, I spent some time trying to explain myself to the media. I didn't do that hot of a job. "Various insane adventures in the out-of-doors have helped me preserve my sanity," I pointed out, "during a time in which my sanity was at substantial risk." Or somewhat less-precise words to that effect.

I was supposed to be promoting a book I'd written about a serial killer, a book that takes the reader on a tour through the twisted sewers of the monster's mind. My publisher had scheduled me to appear on a lot of radio talk shows. ("The caller is either misinformed or a moron, Jim.") I chatted with print reporters ("Let's get another round; publisher pays") and appeared on several local TV talk shows: Good Morning Detroit and Chicago and Cleveland and Toronto and Boston and Los Angeles. The subject matter required that I dress in a funereal fashion, so the audience saw a large bearded man who, I'm sure, didn't seem entirely comfortable wearing a suit and tie. I looked like a gorilla in a tuxedo.

Worse, I found that the bright lights of a television studio seemed to have a paralyzing effect on my body and my powers of speech. There was a stiffness in my performance on these shows that I am sure was not lost on the viewer. "This guy wrote a book? He can't even talk."

The question most asked by those reviewers who had read the book and comprehended its psychological nuances was: "Tim Cahill (they always use your full name), how did you maintain your own sanity during the four years it took you to write *Buried Dreams*?"

The temptation to drool and gibber was always very great at this point; to say, quite seriously, that the constant litany of horror "never bothered me, bothered me, bothered me, bothered me. . . ."

In fact, looking inside the mind of a murderer was terrifying, and it did bother me. It bothered me a lot. It played on my mind during racquetball games; it hit me halfway through short treks in the mountains. There was really no release from the dark parade of horrors that marched over the pages of my research. I was enduring a kind of psychological Chinese water torture. In those bad, shaky times, when I realized that one more morbid detail, one more sordid fact, would send me screaming around the bend, I knew it was time to go out and risk my life for no very good reason.

So I told interviewers across the country that I sought psychological relief in risk-sport. Actually, I've been flirting with serious risk for just over a decade, and when the "wuffos" (wuffo you jump out of an airplane?) have asked me in the past why I choose, say, to climb mountains, I have generally denied that there is any risk at all. Sometimes numbers help: in an old issue of *Science 85*, for instance, experts and lay people were asked to rank the risk of dying from thirty activities. The experts' ranking closely matched known fatality statistics, which showed that more people die yearly from activities the public considers innocuous (using home appliances, power mowers, spray cans, food colorings, food preservatives, and contraceptives) than die climbing mountains (rated twenty-ninth in terms of death risk by experts; skiing was thirtieth).

No one with any sense believes statistics, however, and

an argument can be made that fewer people die climbing mountains because fewer people climb mountains than use spray cans. The law of averages legislates against the users of spray cans. More to the point, most of us perceive mountain climbing as a dangerous activity, and we take precautions precisely so we won't go plunging to our deaths. The question then arises: why do something you perceive as dangerous, even if the numbers suggest it isn't? Why go out and purposefully scare yourself silly?

Well (I should have said), there are some emotional and even biochemical rewards. Danger, or the perception of danger, releases opiate-type natural drugs into the nervous system. Endorphins still sloshing about in the brain after the first skydive complement the sense of accomplishment: people often mention an overwhelming sense of euphoria.

Ralph Keyes, in his book *Chancing It: Why We Take Risks*, mentions this euphoria along with a feeling of control. The skydiver, for instance, is the only one who can pull his own ripcord. The skydiver controls his or her own destiny and, according to Keyes, "those who feel more control over their lives are less likely to have accidents, commit suicide. . . . Taking extreme and even death-defying risks can actually reduce one's sense of being at risk because it increases a sense of control over one's destiny. . . . Fear is sought because (unlike anxiety) it feels as if it is subject to our will. In islands of created danger, the danger creator is king."

A third benefit of perceived jeopardy is total concentration. Quoting Mihaly Csikszentmihalyi, a psychologist who has studied risk-takers from professional dancers to rock climbers, Keyes says that "concentration could become so total that it resembled a state of religious transcendence."

Following the moments of transcendent concentration and the resultant endorphin-fueled euphoria is a calm so serene that Keyes believes the term stress seeker is "a misnomer. One of the main reasons for seeking stress is to enjoy the subsequent tranquility."

All this is said with a good deal more poetry in Diane Ackerman's book, *On Extended Wings*. Ackerman, a pilot, scuba diver, and horsewoman, writes that she likes "that moment central to danger . . . when you become so thoroughly concerned with acting deftly, in order to be safe, that only reaction is possible, not analysis. You shed the centuries and feel creatural. Of course you do have to scan, assess, and make constant minute decisions. But there is nothing like thinking in the usual methodical way. What takes its place is more akin to informed instinct. For a compulsively pensive person, to be fully alert but free of thought is a form of ecstasy."

I suppose those salient factors—concentration, control, ecstasy, and tranquility—go a long way toward explaining the desire to scare oneself badly. They are, of course, the very sensations a man whose work has become a psychologically dangerous obsession needs to experience. If the work in question is a study in human evil, as mine was, the claustrophobia can become intense, the obsession soul-threatening. Reason demands that the escape must be equally intense.

And so it was that I came to understand that risk is a form of therapy. That's what I'll tell the interviewers next time around. The stories I've written about various adventures are among my favorites. In them, I've discovered you can put your life on the line in order to save your soul.

Which is why I want these loud, goofy, boisterous fellows at my party.

Tim Cahill, Montana

JUNGLES
OF THE
MIND

N
W E
S

AN
ECOLOGY
OF
SECRETS

Being a Consideration
of the Real Laws of the Jungle
Complete with Diamonds, Madmen, and Gold

N
W —◇— E
S

There is something a bit *humid* about the picture, something moist and mysterious, something vaguely erotic and tangled and malarial. It is a picture taken somewhere in a South American jungle: a white woman, naked but for what appears to be a pair of panty hose, and three male Indians decked out in Stone Age regalia.

I found it quite by accident about five years ago while poring over the files at the South American Explorers Club in Lima, Peru. It fell out from between two folders. No one at the club knew where it had come from or what it meant. And I guess you might say I sort of stole it.

In the years since then, I've traveled regularly to various Central and South American jungles. They scare me, these jungles. I find them dark and mythic, and I keep returning to them in the way that one returns to a disturbing nightmare. They are, finally, inexplicable in their chaos, but there is meaning in that, just as there is meaning in the picture.

Gold and diamonds draw men of varying degrees of desperation into the jungles of South America. Some of these men, old-timers for the most part, can be found in and around Canaima. Formerly the exclusive haunt of adventurers, bush pilots, prospectors, and explorers, Canaima is, these days, a modern resort. Set deep in a Venezuelan jungle known as the Lost World, Canaima is only a day or two's journey by outboard-powered dugout from Angel Falls, at the base of Auyan-Tepui, the devil mountain. The resort itself is situated on an immense lagoon formed by the Rio Carrao and fringed by soft, pink sand.

Everywhere there are orchids, and the fecund, slightly sweet odor of the jungle is amiable and caressing. At its deepest, the lagoon is black, somehow metallic, and great clouds float across it in reflection. Where it's shallow, the water is clear and clean and brown, the color of strong tea or good bourbon. Such dark jungle rivers and lagoons carry organic acids and do not provide a good place for insects to breed. Piranha are seldom found, since they tend to live in slow, swollen, sediment-rich rivers, such as the Orinoco, whose surface is the color of lead. I have seen men fishing for piranha on the Orinoco banks, fishing for the sheer joy of killing. They would pull the piranha in and let them flop to death on the bank. The little fish looked like vampire sunperch.

But there are no piranha or insects at Canaima, and the tourists, especially the well-to-do Venezuelans, tend to wear those abbreviated swimsuits associated with Rio de Janeiro. For many North Americans, Canaima is a first taste of the jungle, and in the bar overlooking the lagoon, they may meet some of the old-timers and this is where the trouble sometimes starts. Legitimate businessmen in Canaima complain that it is almost impossible to get wealthy tourists to invest in aviation services or other necessary concessions. Instead, people want to drop their money into unlikely gold- and diamond-mining ventures.

And the tale is told of a bush pilot I'll call Norman. Norman shouldn't have been anywhere in Venezuela. His visa had been revoked over some serious financial misunderstandings, but he was in Canaima when two brothers from Houston arrived. Somehow, probably over drinks at the lagoon bar, Norman discovered that these two big, good-hearted old boys owned a machine shop in Houston, and that they were doing very well. Norman decided to tell them about the diamonds. The stones were there for the taking, buried in the coarse, sandy banks of a river that flowed along the flat top of Auyan-Tepui.

Norman had bought the diamonds from a drunken miner near the Luepa army base. They were poor stones, small, discolored, and virtually worthless. Norman salted the sand with them on the devil mountain, and when he flew the brothers up there and showed them where to dig, each came up with a couple of the dark little stones.

The brothers went back to Houston, borrowed all they could on the machine shop, and sent Norman $25,000 to get started on their newly acquired diamond mine. Norman took the money and flew off in the general direction of Brazil. Now, in this area of Venezuela, isolated landing strips are everywhere, and many of them are uncharted except by those who conduct extralegal business. Norman had hired a couple of men to stock one of those strips with drums of fuel. Unfortunately for Norman, he hadn't been paying his bills, and when he put down on the rutted, red-dirt strip in the middle of the jungle, he discovered there was no fuel. Because of his visa difficulties, he couldn't land anywhere where fuel was legitimately sold, and so he decided to try for Brazil on what he had left in his tank.

It is a ticklish matter, crash landing a light plane in a jungle. You want to glide down as slowly as possible; you want to snag your plane in one of the trees that rise like monstrous stalks of broccoli above the lesser vegetation. These trees can be more than one hundred and fifty feet high, and most bush pilots carry a rope for the final descent.

Norman ran out of fuel near Santa Elena, a town about twelve miles short of the Brazilian border, and he was taken into custody. Meanwhile, the brothers were back in Canaima, asking around about Norman, and they didn't seem so good-hearted anymore. Just big. And determined.

That's the end of the story, as the old-timers tell it. No one saw the brothers again. Several years later, Norman showed up in Canaima. The old-timers couldn't help but notice that he had no fingers on his right hand. They were all gone, cut off neat and clean, just as if the job had been done in a machine shop.

Most stories involving precious stones and jungles end poorly. The Muzo mine, about one hundred miles north of Bogotá, Colombia, is the source of 80 percent of the emeralds sold on the world market. Bulldozers strip the hillsides while about twenty thousand prospectors wade through the river below, panning for emeralds loosened by the machines above. The prospectors are not allowed to move above the riverbanks, and armed guards on the hillside fire at them if they do.

After years of gangland slayings in the jungle, the Colombian government has rented the mine to "the Heavy Gang," which won control of the mine from "the Goose Gang" after at least one massacre and uncounted assassinations. The government's lucrative decision to cooperate with the gangsters has eliminated much of the violence associated with Muzo. Officials recently told Warren Hoge of the *New York Times* that the mine has been "pacified," but Hoge quoted an outside observer who said he had counted twenty-four corpses in twenty-one days at Muzo. The observer said that some prospectors had taken to swallowing their emeralds when confronted by thieves, and some thieves had taken to disemboweling their victims.

Two of the most popular bars in the area are called the Seven Knife Stabs and Where Life Is Worth Nothing.

The law of the jungle seems to be this: there is no law in the jungle. Which isn't to suggest that there aren't a lot of policemen and soldiers around. There are, and one reason for this is that boundaries are difficult to establish. There are border disputes everywhere: Peru and Ecuador, Belize and Guatemala, Guyana and Venezuela. The less populated an area becomes and the deeper into the jungle one goes, the more forms there are to fill out and checkpoints to go through. One may be obliged to show a passport, a visa, or permits; to state age, marital status, occupation, reason for being in the area; to explain one's very existence.

In certain areas of Peru, one may have to first report to the Peruvian Investigative Police (PIP) before checking into a hotel. Miguel Zamora, the man who heads up PIP in the northeastern town of Chachapoyas, did not seem to trust the three of us. The expedition had been launched in search of a pre-Incan culture known as the Chachas. We were also making our own maps, and these, Zamora decided, might be of assistance to, say, an Ecuadorian military expedition. Every other day that we were in town, Zamora called us in for another little talk.

On the other hand, the chief of police, the commandant, seemed to like and trust us. He had sent his daughter to a school in Lima, where she studied English, and she had taught him an American song.

"Heengalay bales, heengalay bales . . ."

We figured it out more from the tune than the words, and so, on a hot July afternoon in Chachapoyas, which is located in the eastern foothills of the Andes, on a plateau that drops off into three thousand miles of jungle, we joined in with the commandant.

". . . jingle all the way, oh what fun it is to ride in a one-horse open sleigh . . ."

Every time we saw the commandant, he reminded us of the fun we had singing "Heengalay Bales" together. He wore a hat something like an American policeman's, except it was three times as high and had gold braids on it. It looked like a hat that a loony dictator would wear in a slapstick film. The commandant learned more about our reasons for being in Chachapoyas in one hour than Zamora did in the half-dozen chats he had with us.

As it turned out, we found a number of forts and stone cities of the Chachas. They were set deep in the forests in a mountainous region known as Ceja de Selva ("eyebrow of the jungle"). We had used a sixteenth-century Spanish text as a guide, and the cities were as described in *The Royal Commentaries of the Incas*. We camped for days in some of those vegetation-choked ruins and tried to imagine the lives of a people long gone. I suspect these should have been humbling days, but an intense euphoria overwhelmed all other emotions.

It was as if the jungle had drawn its breath and sucked these people back into its darkness. There were ceramic artifacts one thousand years old and more, and the potsherds sometimes lay in company with human remains. We left this evidence for the archaeologists and marveled at the power of the forest. It had sent roots snaking through the interstices of the great stone forts and had swallowed the culture whole. Standing in the ruins, I imagined uncontrolled natural forces at work: it was like walking through the rubble of a hurricane-ravaged shoreline. The ruins had taken on the syrupy odor of all that triumphant vegetation. I was standing on the scene of some slow, choking horror, and I was alive, I would survive, and these thoughts left me feeling blessed and giddy.

sat next to an investment counselor on a recent flight from Miami to a jungle island off the coast of the Yucatan peninsula. I told him about the picture—the white woman in panty hose, the three impassive Indians—and what it meant to me. We worked our way around that meaning, just as I am doing here, by swapping jungle tales. The man told me this story:

"I have a friend who is a very successful contractor, and his wife is what you might call an adventurer. She's a pilot and has been all over the world. Well, she heard about some gold mines up one of the rivers of Brazil and wanted me to see if I could find investors. It looked a little too iffy for me, so she went ahead and raised the money on her own. She got all the permits and certifications that you need and hired two Vietnam vets to help her work the site.

"One day, a government plane set down on their landing strip and they were arrested. The charge was murder—multiple counts. It seems there was another operation in progress in the area. The guy who headed the thing was hiring criminals, escaped convicts and various other unsavory types who might feel comfortable in the jungle, away from any legal agencies. These fellows would work a site, and each of them, I suppose, had a percentage of the take. The fellow who was running the operation would fly to the site with a couple of thugs and shoot the miners, take the gold, and save the percentage.

"This must have gone on for quite some time. Few of the dead men had family or friends who would worry about them or even know where they were. Anyway, the Brazilian government finally caught on to the operation. My friend was charged in connection with seventy-eight murders.

"She and the two vets were tossed into jail in Manaus along with seven other men. One man, who wore a two-pound gold medallion around his neck, got bail the next day. It turned out that he was running the mining-and-murder operation. My friend was left in the cell with six thugs. She slept against the wall. One of the vets slept beside her while the other kept watch. The other six never made a move.

"Well, you can imagine the field day the Brazilian press had with the case. They found out that my friend had a small canister of Mace in an oversized belt buckle. One headline went something like: AMERICAN AVIATRIX, ALLEGED MASS MURDERESS, IN POSSESSION OF DEADLY NERVE GAS.

"After three weeks, it became apparent that she could not have committed those murders, and she was released."

"Did they ever catch the guy with the medallion?" I asked.

"I don't know. But my friend still has all the permits, and she's going back."

"She's going back?"

"Gold's up over six hundred dollars an ounce again."

 ome poor guy was sobbing in the next room, and I was just coming off another case of dysentery, swigging paregoric and thinking about that damned picture again. The picture and the jungle. The hotel was located just outside Flores, a town in the northern Guatemalan state of El Peten. It was a civilized sort of place, with clean beds, running water, and flush toilets. But it was in the jungle, after all, and the elements had conspired to sabotage the hotel's pretensions. Several months before, the hotel had been situated on the shore of Lake Peten Itza. Now it was *in* Lake Peten Itza.

The lake had been mysteriously rising for more than a year, and the steady, unseasonable rains of the past few weeks had been disastrous. The swimming pool, in what had been the courtyard, was underwater, and a foot or more of Lake Peten Itza lapped up against the building. Flocks of tropical water birds floated by the windows, glanced inside, and blurted out horrid little croaks.

The ceiling of my room was wire mesh. Ten feet above

that was sloping, thatched roof. Air circulated nicely, but you could hear people in other rooms as if they were standing next to you, and a man in the adjacent room seemed to be lifting weights. There was the sound of heavy exertion—*mmm-phuph, mmm-phuph*—followed by several quick breaths—*whee-who, whee-who.*

A young American woman was speaking to the man. "So they're ruined. A pair of jogging shoes. Big deal, thirty bucks. Jeeze. Please, Larry, don't do this to yourself. We can get the camera reconditioned. Jeeze. We have eight more days, and it just can't keep raining like this. Really."

Clearly, Larry was not lifting weights. He was suffering a common sort of allergic reaction to jungle travel. "Larry," the woman said, "now you just stop it. I think the Mayan ruins are beautiful, even in the rain. So it got a little muddy, and there were a few mosquitos, and we had some bad luck. So what? Larry, you're thirty-two years old. Will you please stop crying?"

I had just spent a couple of weeks at the more remote ruins, stumbling around in the same rain and mud. All archaeological evidence suggests that the Mayans, in what we now think of as their classic period, were the most advanced people of pre-Columbian America. They developed accurate calendars and hieroglyphic writing; they built massive stone cities and ceremonial pyramids. About 900 A.D., the race fell into an inexplicable decline. There are any number of theories about what happened: famine, flood, disease, revolt, invasion. My own idea is patently incorrect and stubbornly wrongheaded, but I cling to it because it terrifies me. I like to think that the jungle simply swallowed up the culture.

El Peten has not always been heavily forested. Analysis of windblown pollen that was recovered from a long core drilled into the bottom of a centrally located lake shows that, in about 2000 B.C., El Peten was a land of broad savannas. The dominance of jungle over grassland began early in the classic period. Archaeologists believe that in the post-classic period, a poorer sort of folk moved into the temples and lived there until the jungle engulfed the buildings. Perhaps, as the jungle advanced, they prayed to the carved stone images of their ancestors.

"It was clearing up when we came in," the woman in the next room said.

"We waded in," Larry moaned.

"And there's probably a beautiful sunset going on right now." I heard the sound of drapes being opened, and I looked out my own window. Rain was falling in sheets. It was the same leaden color as the lake. A huge waterfowl drifted by, and, directly under my neighbors' window, it said "*Gawaahhqk.*" There was silence in the room, then Larry began lifting his weights again, much faster this time.

Joseph Conrad, in his brilliant evocations of the jungles of Africa and the Far East, used and perhaps overused the word *impenetrable.* In truth, those jungles, and the lowland jungles of Central and South America, only seem impenetrable from a road or river or trail or clearing. In those places where sunlight is allowed to reach the ground, a tangled wall erupts out of the earth, a dense green wall that protects the jungle from civilization and can easily be seen as a warning.

In the forest proper, under the endless, broad-leaved canopy, direct rays of the sun seldom reach the earth. What light there is seems tired, heavy, turgid—a flaccid twilight. The floor between the tree trunks is largely bare. But the jungle supports an abundance of life. The majority of invertebrate organisms in the Amazon basin have yet to be named, and generations' worth of botanical research has yet to be done. Above, arboreal frogs with adhesive pads on their feet creep over the dripping leaves. Hordes of bats pollinate the colorful flowers sprouting on tree trunks rather than attempt the tangle of greenery. Aquatic flatworms live in the perpetual moistness of the forest floor. There are tapirs and jaguars, spider and howler monkeys, amphibians, ants and anteaters. There are spiders that drop from the canopy above and eat birds, and there are more birds in the jungle than anywhere else on earth.

In the jungle rivers, one-hundred-pound rodents graze on reeds, and anacondas, those twenty- to thirty-foot-long green-and-white snakes, lie in wait for pigs and small deer that they will kill by constriction and eat whole. The jungle generates persistent reports of forty-foot anacondas, and one miner swears he's seen such a reptile, sunning itself on a riverbank, with the antlers of a deer protruding from its open mouth. "The snake was going to have to wait for the head to decompose before it could spit out those horns," the miner told me.

Despite the telling and retelling of such tales, despite the abundance of animal life—the shrieks and barks and howls one hears—it is the forest itself that captures the mind and sometimes ensnares the soul. "Contact with pure, unmitigated savagery," Conrad wrote, "with primitive nature and primitive man, brings sudden and profound trouble into the heart." For Conrad, civilization was not a matter of flush toilets and paved roads. In his jungle tales, good men, left in the isolation of the forest, became slave traders, murderers, less than men. The jungle provides "a suggestion of things vague, uncontrollable, and repulsive, whose discomposing intrusion excites the imagination and tries the civilized nerves of the foolish and the wise alike." I have felt these sensations, and have translated them as fear. Especially when lost in that troubling darkness, I have felt the sheer weight of indifferent animosity, of some vast, humid hatred.

In the jungle, a lost man feels driven by a desire to plunge ahead, while the hanging vines slap at his face and roots rise up to tangle his feet. Better to stop; sit, think. And that is when the green hostility begins to smother the soul. The mind's eye sees the forest as if it were a time-lapse film. Trees twist into grotesque shapes, the better to steal the sun. Parasites erupt out of healthy organisms. Creepers lash out to strangle lesser plants. Lianas—long, woody vines— drop from branches like thick ropes and root at the base of the host tree, choking off its life so that they themselves stand as a new tree with the dead one inside.

The jungle is moist and warm, and living things may grow and reproduce all year long. Competition comes not from the elements but from the volume of life. A lost man, sitting, thinking, perceives that every living thing longs for the death of every other living thing. He understands "the ever-ready suspicion of evil" Conrad wrote about, "the placid and impenetrable mass of an unjustifiable violence."

These thoughts took on a special clarity when, in the company of other reporters, I visited the necropolis of Jonestown, where the stench of decomposing bodies sent bile rising into my throat. I had already spent days talking with survivors, and I knew that Jim Jones had been deluded, probably addicted to drugs, and clinically paranoid even before he moved to the jungle. But the jungle tore at his mind and fed his paranoia: when the rains came early and the crops failed, it was because the CIA had seeded the clouds. In the jungle compound, from the wooden chair he called his throne, Jones passed on his paranoia to the people of Jonestown, for paranoia is a contagious disease. They saw soldiers in the bush beyond the clearing, and they could hear the growling of vehicles as these shadow forces massed for attack. It was a debilitating siege, and in the end, like the heroes of Masada, who killed themselves nearly two millenniums ago rather than surrender to the Romans, most of them committed suicide rather than submit to the shadow forces that lay in wait, out there in the jungle.

I'm not suggesting that the tragedy happened because Jonestown lay in the jungle. Still, it is impossible to conceive of a similar occurrence in Indianapolis or San Francisco. The madness, the *danse macabre* of suicide and murder, could have happened no place else but in the dark vastness of the jungle.

have sat around fires with people others might describe as primitive, even savage. We have shared food. And I have been places where there is no evidence that man exists. I find an inexplicable delight in that, in the sure knowledge that, throughout all of time, no other human being has stood on the same spot. It is, finally, a fragile emotion, something not easily recollected in more temperate climes, where man has stripped the earth of darkness. Still, I find a flicker of that lustrous delight, of lunacy and darkness, in the idea of a white woman in panty hose posing before three unimpressed Indians.

Stare at the picture long enough, knowing that it is a story that will never be told, and you realize that the jungle is an ecology of secrets, that in the jungle, more than any other place on earth, there is the conservation of mystery.

The white woman sits in her panty hose, and the welts on her back tell us the jungle is eating her alive. Long after she is gone—after she has screamed her last curse at the photographer and the whole idiotic project, whatever it may have been—one feels the Indians will still be there, sturdy and placid. And that is the final meaning of the picture: as civilization schemes to violate the jungle, the jungle conspires to brutalize civilization.

LOVE
AND
DEATH
IN
GORILLA COUNTRY

C all it science, I know gossip when I hear gossip. Dr. Kelly Stewart was standing up on the stage in the auditorium at the Academy of Science on Wednesday night; she was standing right there in front of a paying audience talking boldly about who was sleeping with whom and about which females had left which males; she was talking about everyone's favorite, that old rapscallion Nunkie, the opportunistic bachelor who started off alone and ended up with a harem of six females and a family of at least nine healthy infants. Dr. Stewart even had a chart showing Nunkie's rather incredible success in acquiring females and siring infants in the decade before his death.

Nunkie was a mountain gorilla, and his death is mourned. He was one of only 250 to 260 mountain gorillas left in the world. Most live on the high forested slopes of a chain of extinct and dormant volcanoes in central equatorial Africa. Stewart's firsthand account of the gorillas was couched in dispassionate scientific terms—cross-over, interaction, estrous, di-morphism—but the larger subject of her talk was unstated. It was no less than the survival of a species. Her lecture was titled "Friends and Foes in Gorilla Society."

In the question-and-answer period following her lecture, someone asked if she wouldn't be afraid to return to Rwanda in the wake of Dian Fossey's brutal murder at the Karisoke Research Center there. Kelly Stewart said no, she wouldn't be afraid. The tragic violence seemed to be directed against one person only.

No one asked what would happen to the last mountain gorillas on the face of the earth now that Fossey was dead. Many people believe that in the aftermath of Dian Fossey's death, the gorillas' future is bleak. They are, fortunately, wrong.

n the spring of 1980, after thirteen years at Karisoke, Dian Fossey left Volcano Park (Parc National des Volcans) in Rwanda to take a position at Cornell University. A year later, my partner, Berkeley photographer Nick Nichols, wrote to ask her permission to go to Karisoke.

Nichols and I both considered Fossey a hero. In her years at Karisoke, she had amassed an incredible quantity of data about gorillas. She had courageously taken on the poachers who killed gorillas for profit—men who cut off the head and hands of the animals, boiled away the meat, and sold the skeletal remains to tourists. Fossey's antipoaching patrols in the seventies may have actually saved a species. Additionally, she had spent years learning the intricate rules of gorilla behavior and habituating the animals to her presence. Photos and films of Fossey sitting in the midst of a gorilla group, of Fossey being touched—lightly, quizzically—by four-hundred-pound silverbacks (mature males), struck a chord in the viewer's mind, something that echoed with the divinity of Michelangelo's work in the Sistine Chapel: God and man, reaching out to touch one another, to understand one another. It was Dian Fossey—through her writing, through these films and photos—who singlehandedly changed the public's perception of gorillas. The King Kong image gave way to Fossey's formulation: the mountain gorillas were "gentle giants."

It was a remarkable record of lonely courage and achievement. The word "single-handedly" seemed appropriate. Nichols and I, quite frankly, were in awe of Dian Fossey, and the letter Nick wrote to her was humble, respectful. It fell a yard or two short of outright cringing.

Fossey must have fired off the telegram within hours of reading that letter. "Proposed visit of yourself and Cahill for Karisoke filming and writing permission emphatically denied," it read, "letter following."

The letter arrived two days later and it was very nearly scalding: "It is quite impossible for you and/or your colleague, Tim Cahill, to 'go to Karisoke and work with some of the researchers.' " Fossey made it clear that "the Karisoke Research Center is a scientifically oriented institution maintained and supported under my direction" and "is not open to the public for purposes of tourism and/or photography." A bit harshly put, I thought, but fair enough.

The last paragraph, however, was an insult no matter how I read it. "Numerous people are on ego trips concerned with mountain gorilla conservation, a very popular pastime at present. On this end of the ocean, such interest is called 'Comic Book Conservation.' It might be advisable if you did not add your name to the list."

What I had had in mind was a celebration of Fossey's work with the gorillas: something that might end with a plea for more funding for her project. But, it seemed, Fossey would do that herself. Single-handedly.

I suppose Fossey thought Nick and I would blunder around disturbing the gorillas and end up writing an article based on her research anyway. Maybe it had happened like that before. Maybe she was right: perhaps my simple interest in the subject amounted to no more than comic book conservation. Even so, there was a demonstrable lack of tact involved. That last paragraph felt like a slap in the face. Every time I read it, I felt like something the dog left on the lawn.

"**P**ermission emphatically denied" are probably not words one should use to working journalists. Two months after receiving Fossey's letter, Nick and I were in Rwanda. The acting director of the Karisoke, in Fossey's absence—it was thought she wasn't coming back—was Dr. A. H. "Sandy" Harcourt, who was living there with his wife, Kelly Stewart. Stewart and Harcourt introduced me to a British couple, Drs. Conrad and Rosalind Aveling, who lived well below Karisoke, at the boundary of the park. We sat in the Avelings' cabin, where the assembled scientists succinctly listed the inaccuracies and idiocies committed by previous visiting journalists. There had been promises made and broken. Journalists were only looking for a story, only looking to advance their careers. They weren't interested in facts, only controversy. The scientists said they hoped I might be different. Their expressions said they didn't hold out much hope.

Later, after this disagreeable session, I trudged an hour downhill to the nearest village. There, in a wooden hut with a dirt floor, was a place where *pombe* was sold. This is an immensely disgusting alcoholic beverage made from fermented bananas, and drinking it is almost as unpleasant as being scolded by scientists. But not quite.

Sometime after the second quart I believe I expressed a bit of anger about the scientists above. Oh no, I was given to understand, the new ones were friendly. Not that Fossey—the old woman who lives alone—hadn't been friendly. She was very nice. Yes. No trouble.

I bought some *pombe* for my new friends. No trouble, huh? Well . . . And the stories came out, in whispers, with much looking about for eavesdroppers. They were filtered through various translations, and some of them were told in body language, but I could piece one incident together well enough. It seemed that trackers working for the old woman had captured a poacher. The man was detained at

Karisoke, where he was stripped and tied to a tree. There he was whipped with stinging nettles; whipped, I was given to understand, specifically on the genitals. Pictures of the man's humiliation were distributed to the villages below the park. This, the message of the photos was, is what happens to people who kill gorillas.

Could anyone show me those photographs? No. Who would keep such pictures?

Later I checked the story out with Conrad and Rosalind Aveling. Yes, they had heard of the incident: it was being talked about in all the villages. They didn't know if it was true. They hadn't been in Rwanda at the time.

Whether the story is true or not—I like to believe it is not—the fact that it was being told, and frequently told, suggested to me a sure diplomatic failure between Karisoke and the villages below.

In the five weeks that followed, Nick and I learned, first-hand, the inflexible etiquette of gorilla conduct. Volcano Park is a dense forest on the upper slopes of a line of extinct and dormant volcanoes that separates Rwanda from Zaire and Uganda. The undergrowth is often wet, waist high, and hideously tangled. Gorilla trails seem easy enough to follow—a family of ten moving through such foliage will flatten a path in such a way that it looks as if a five-hundred-pound boulder had been rolled through the jungle. The problem is that these trails peter out, they double back on themselves, or they just seem to end out in the middle of some idyllic gorillaless meadow. To find the gorillas, Nick and I hired trained Rwandan trackers.

After a time, I found that I could separate the odors of the jungle from the smell of gorillas, and that I could often smell the animals before I saw them. The odor was sharp, musky, somewhat skunky with a splash of vinegar to it and not nearly as unpleasant as that may sound.

The smell was an obvious clue, and it was sometimes possible to sneak up on a group which, typically, might consist of a dominant male (the silverback), several females, infants, and a couple of sub-dominant males called black-backs. Sneaking up on a group, however, is an outstandingly dumb idea: you don't want to startle a family of apes who may feel the need to, well, nip at you precisely because they have been startled. Instead, it is best to attract the attention of the dominant silverback, whose job it is to protect those he dominates. Make a little noise. And don't ever get between the silverback and an infant.

Once you are certain that the silverback knows you are present on the periphery of his group, it is polite to signal your intention to move in. A throat clearing sound—two raspy exhalations called a DBV or "double belch vocalization"—signals a lack of aggressive intent. If the silverback replies, it is time to begin inching forward.

Watch the silverback's face to see if you are being accepted. Gorilla faces read like human faces: the animals smile when they are happy, frown when they are upset, and often look slightly puzzled. This last expression is the one I most frequently encountered when approaching a silverback. It is the sort of expression you feel on your face when you are sitting alone in your house and there's a noise in the kitchen.

You can move in a bit on a slightly puzzled silverback, but in all cases you must begin to crawl. Your head should always be lower than that of the silverback. This is a submissive posture, and it convinces the dominant gorilla that you are reasonably tractable—no challenge—so he will not feel compelled to rip you to shreds. Do not stare directly into the gorilla's eyes for more than a few seconds at a time as this is interpreted as a challenge and will irritate him. You may smile at him, but do not show your teeth, which is an aggressive and impolite thing to do.

A good time to visit gorillas would be just after noon on a sunny day when the animals are drowsy from their morning feed and ready for a short nap. If you approach carefully, politely, the silverback will watch for a time, then, with a figurative shrug, begin to accept your presence. He may roll over onto his back and yawn. The silverback's teeth are a revelation: here is a strict vegetarian with a set of canine teeth the size of carrots. Gorillas do not—as many people suppose—pound, stomp, punch, or crush their enemies. Instead, they bite. A silverback skull was once found in the jungle, and embedded in the heavy ridge of bone was another silverback's tooth.

Generally, after some period of lying still, the family group will virtually ignore you. There is the occasional glance in your direction, but the animals will go about their daily business. They will groom one another, the children will tussle—their play chuckles are so infectious you want to smile (but don't show your teeth)—the blackbacks nap, the silverback may copulate with one of the females. One bright afternoon, I watched Mrithi, a good-sized silverback, mate with a young female, Ichingo, in the strange, subaqueous light of a meadow in the midst of a bamboo grove.

In observing the various groups, I came to understand that gorilla life, like a daily soap opera, is incredibly slow moving. You can see what is likely to happen before the characters themselves know it. You can identify those characters most likely to fall in love (or at least copulate); you can see groups ranging closer together and know that there will, one day soon, be a fight (or at least "an interaction") between rival silverbacks; you can see that a silverback is getting old and is about to be deposed. You could even miss a few days, then tune in on, say, group thirteen, and pick up the continuing story in about ten minutes. It's like "Dallas" on downers.

The scientists in the park were very professional. They strictly avoided anthropomorphism in their scholarly works, but I can tell you that they often applied human qualities and the faint thrust of human emotions to gorillas when speaking about them in private. There isn't much to do at night under the Virunga volcanoes, and an evening's entertainment is often an evening spent gossiping about gorillas.

I approached the scientists—Harcourt and Stewart, the

Avelings—in much the same way I approached the gorillas: head down, submissive, respectful. Instead of DBVs, I found myself saying words like *interaction* and *display*. The scientists replied in kind and, it seemed, slowly became habituated to my presence. Sometimes one or the other of them might even scribble down a quick note about something I had seen in the field. They were entirely sincere, and I began to like them.

One day I watched Sandy Harcourt in the field. He was studying Beethoven's group, one of the families Dian Fossey had habituated. Dian had worked with them so long and so well, Harcourt didn't need to crawl and show cringing submission. He simply stood near an animal, stood perfectly erect, perfectly still—the man has exquisite posture—and took notes on a reporter's pad. Harcourt recorded what the gorilla ate, the vocalizations it made, the way it interacted with other gorillas. After an hour on one animal, Harcourt moved on to another.

The gorillas were so used to this behavior that Harcourt was absolutely ignored by them. He might have been a ghost in their midst.

Kelly Stewart and the doctors Aveling worked in much the same way. Rosalind Aveling, Nick, and I once were lounging in the bamboo, at the periphery of Mrithi's group, when Mtoto, a three-year-old female, took a sudden interest in us. She performed what is called a "display," the gorilla dance of intimidation, which consists of standing upright and beating the chest, of jumping up and down and throwing vegetation. Mtoto weighed all of twenty-five pounds.

Clearly, the animal was playing. She stared at us for a moment with a mischievous smile, then started for Rosalind, her arms held out in front of her. Mtoto, I was sure, wanted to be held. Rosalind began a locomotive cough, which is a series of small slightly swinish-sounding grunts that mean "you're too close," or "go away," or "keep doing that and there'll be trouble." Mtoto retreated to the silverback, Mrithi, who was lounging on his back in a field of thistles. There, she bounced up and down on her father's ample belly.

Later, I asked Rosalind why she had discouraged Mtoto.

"You don't want them to take you for an object of curiosity," she told me. "You don't want the children to look at you as someone to play with." The goal was to be the ghost in their midst, a thing no more interesting than a tree. That way, habituated gorillas might behave more like wild groups.

"But I've seen pictures of Dian holding baby gorillas," I said. "I've seen photos of her touching silverbacks."

Well, yes, all that had happened.

"And those photos, those films, they're what changed the public's view of gorillas," I said. "After that it was 'gentle giant' time."

True enough. But now, Rosalind thought, it was time for another approach. She thought Dian would be in full agreement with her on this.

"But don't you want to touch them, don't you want them to touch you?"

"No," Rosalind said.

"C'mon. I feel it. You're telling me you don't? What, do you turn in your membership to the human race when you become a scientist?"

"Okay," Rosalind said, "I admit, it's a temptation. A big temptation."

"So you really did want to hold Mtoto."

"Of course I did," Rosalind Aveling said, "God, I wanted to hold her."

The gorillas let you know when you have overstayed your welcome. They let you know with frowns, locomotive coughs, the beginnings of displays. Even so, there was a sense of enormous privilege just sitting with them; privilege felt in their acceptance, no matter what its duration. Once, on the lower slopes of Visoke, one of the volcanoes, a silverback named Ndume woke up from his nap, saw me, and ambled close to the place where I lay. Ponderously, he sat down, yawned, stretched, then reached down to my knee, where he took the

material of my red rain pants between his thumb and fore-
finger and rolled it back and forth like a knowledgeable
garment buyer. Ndume cocked his head to the side. His eyes
were soft, golden brown, and he wore that familiar slightly
puzzled expressed.

"Gore-Tex," I wanted to say. Instead, I grunted twice.
Ndume returned the DBV. There was some genuine in-
terspecies communication going on, and it felt like a fan-
tasy, like one of those strange wondrous dreams in which
you can talk to the animals, to all of creation, and creation
itself responds with approval. There was no science involved in this encounter. It was all emotion.

I felt a kind of unspecified glow, something within that
was very much like love, and it came to me then that for the
past fourteen years Dian Fossey had literally lived in that
glow.

ost of the gorilla families I met had already been
habituated to humans. There was one researcher,
Ann Pierce, who kept tabs on the wild groups that
ranged near the Zaire border. A visit to those
groups was more than a stiff hike: it was an expedition. Once Ann and I, along with a Rwandan
tracker, climbed Visoke, an extinct volcano, where we
camped at 11,000 feet, on the rim of the crater lake. The next
day we were up at dawn, and we trudged through the
tangled vegetation down the west side of the mountain,
toward Zaire. It took a little more than five hours, and I was
exhausted by the time we began finding fresh dung along
the gorillas' trail.

I could smell them then, somewhere across the vegetation-choked flat. Ann fell to her stomach and I crawled
along after her. They were about fifty yards away. The trees
broke the light, which fell through thick branches in El
Greco shafts. I could see dark shapes, like bears, moving
slowly through those purely religious shafts, and then the
silverback saw us.

He charged perhaps five yards. His roar started at a high register then dropped, as a donkey's bray will. It was hard to see him through the vegetation, but he was standing, beating his chest, and the slapping thuds seemed impossibly loud. The rest of the family was moving over a small hillock, and the silverback—I assumed he was the silverback—was covering their retreat. He tore a branch from a tree—a branch the size of a fullback's thigh—and threw it to the ground. He jumped up and down. He hooted at us. I suppose, if I were sitting home watching that display on videotape, it might seem humorous, like a child's temper tantrum. In the jungle, it was terrifying.

I knew, from reading George Schaller's pioneering work on gorillas, that a silverback will display and make a bluff charge, but will not attack a man who holds his ground. I knew that intellectually. Intellect does not inform the scream-and-gibber mechanism.

Nevertheless, we held our ground, Ann and I. We did not advance. After five more minutes of display and bluff charges, the supposed silverback turned to follow his family over the hillock.

"Let's go," Ann Pierce said. "We've disturbed them enough for today."

I thought about Dian Fossey during the seven-hour walk back to our camp overlooking the crater lake. She had read Schaller; she knew that gorillas could be habituated to the presence of humans, that a silverback would not attack if she held her ground. But what courage it must have taken, what incredible courage, to stand firm in the face of so many silverback charges.

Late that afternoon, about halfway back up Visoke, a cold rain began to fall. The temperature stood at about 45 degrees. I was sweating heavily inside my rain jacket so that every time I stopped to rest the chill began working at me until, shivering uncontrollably, I began walking again. We had come through fields of waist-high nettles, acres of them it seemed, and my hands stung from their touch. They felt as if they were on fire.

All this, I thought, for a five-minute encounter. Dian

Fossey had started with wild groups and just such encounters: twelve hours of hard walking for five minutes of rejection. Never mind Fossey's courage: the physical aspects of the woman's achievement, her stamina and commitment, amazed me.

I f anyone on earth had earned the right to speak for the mountain gorillas of Rwanda, it was Dian Fossey. In 1978, an unimaginable tragedy brought her work again to the attention of the world. The silverback Digit was attacked and killed by poachers. Dian had known the animal since he was two and half: a "playful little ball of disorganized black fluff," was how she described him then, "from which protruded two buttonlike velvet brown eyes full of mischief and curiosity." In a report written for the *International Primate Protection League Newsletter*, Dian, working from evidence found at the death scene, described what must have happened. Digit was not the dominant male of the group. He was a peripheral silverback, charged with the responsibility of "assisting the dominant male in the protection of the more defenseless members of their group.

"It was in this service that Digit was killed by poachers on December 31, 1977. On that day, Digit took five mortal spear wounds into his own body, held off six poachers and their dogs, allowing the entire family group to flee four kilometers away to safety. Digit's last lonely battle was a valiant and courageous one in which he managed to kill one of the poachers' dogs before dying. I cannot allow myself to think of his anguish, his pain, and the total comprehension he suffered of knowing what humans were doing to him."

Could anyone really understand the horror of Digit's murder? Dian suggested the *Newsletter* run photos of the death scene, ghastly black-and-white pictures of Digit slumped against a tree, decapitated. Where his hands should have been, there were bloody stumps. One could only compare this horror with film of the living Digit: scenes of the

nearly mature gorilla and Fossey together; of Digit examin-
ing her notebook and pen with that endearing, slightly
puzzled expression; of Digit rolling over to sleep by Dian's
side. "That was the nature of Digit," Dian wrote, "gentle,
inquisitive, trusting."

The tragedy played on Dian's mind. It affected her work,
her relationship with the animals she loved. "I am still
allowed to share their proximity," she wrote, "but it is an
honor and gift that I feel I no longer deserve."

In the wake of Digit's death, Dian established the Digit
Fund, a charitable organization dedicated to the protection
of mountain gorillas. She was joined in this effort by the
African Wildlife Leadership Foundation (now called the
African Wildlife Foundation).

The association lasted a year, then AWF pulled out. No
one wanted to say that they disagreed with Dian's confron-
tational style, her strategy of intimidation, her lack of tact
and diplomacy. "That would be wrong," Diana McMeekin,
deputy director of the AWF, says, "and what's more, it's
unfair to Dian." McMeekin said that AWF set up its own
charity "because we felt that all the gorillas needed protection. Dian was concerned, quite rightly I think, about protecting her research groups. We wanted to establish a
program that would deal with mountain gorilla conservation overall."

AWF joined with a consortium of the Rwandan Office of
Tourism and National Parks, the Fauna Preservation Society, the World Wildlife Fund, and the Peoples Trust for
Endangered Species to sponsor the Mountain Gorilla Project. There were several successful fund drives. Dian felt
that the Project, and specifically AWF, was taking money
that should have gone into her work, that "Digit's blood
money" was being used for an ineffective and potentially
dangerous program.

Especially galling to Dian was the Mountain Gorilla
Project's policy of developing tourism. The idea that tourists could be brought into the park to view habituated
groups of gorillas seemed hazardous to her. Reproductive
cycles could be disrupted by the stress such visits would

cause. Diseases could be passed to the gorillas. The whole
concept was emotionally unacceptable: gorillas should be
granted their privacy, she told a friend. They should be left
alone. Their world should be pristine, not soiled with click-
ing cameras, with loud and curious louts, with people who
had no knowledge or respect for these animals she loved. In
an article published in the April 1981 *National Geographic*
she listed the "tourist presence" among the factors that
would lead to the demise of the mountain gorilla.

ountain gorilla conservation is a multifaceted
problem. Poachers have killed gorillas for their
skulls and hands, but this has always been rare.
Perhaps more threatening to the population as a
whole is the potential trade in baby mountain
gorillas for private collections and zoos.

The gorillas you see in zoos are lowland gorillas. A recent
survey out of Gabon suggests there are as many as thirty
thousand surviving lowland gorillas. A bridge group, the
eastern lowland gorilla resembles the mountain gorilla but
is actually a separate race. The mountain gorilla—with only
a few hundred individuals surviving—would be a prize animal for any zoo in the world. Some zoos—a very few—are
unscrupulous.

To obtain a baby mountain gorilla, poachers would have
to kill the silverback and the mother. In November 1982,
this is precisely what happened. A wave of poaching struck
the Virungas. In widely separate incidents, ten gorillas
were killed. No hands or heads were taken. Officials at
AWF feared that a contract had been put out for a baby
gorilla. Suspicion centered on private collectors from the
Mideast. Shortly thereafter, it was discovered that a European zoo had purchased a baby mountain gorilla. (In fact,
the animal turned out to be an eastern lowland gorilla.)

The zoo denied any complicity in the otherwise inexplicable wave of poaching. The gorilla hadn't come from
Rwanda or Zaire, the zoo pointed out, but from a neighbor-

ing country. It seems that a kindly traveling missionary had found an orphaned baby gorilla. Well, of course the missionary had his good work to do and couldn't spend his life caring for a gorilla, but he did want it to have a good home. This religious individual had simply given the gorilla to the zoo, a gift that would benefit everyone. And since the animal was given as a gift, there was no paper trail to follow and no way to check the story out.

Many people involved in gorilla conservation found the tale of the kindly missionary tough to swallow.

The most dangerous poaching activity in the Virungas, however, involves the trapping of duiker, a small antelope about the size and color of an Irish setter. Wire snares are positioned along game trails, and gorillas often blunder into the antelope traps, catching a hand or foot in the wire. They are generally able to extricate themselves, but the wounds fester in the dampness of the jungle, they become infected, gangrene sets in, animals die. Some lose limbs. Ndume, my favorite silverback—the gorilla with a Gore-Tex fetish— lost a hand in a duiker trap.

Over the years, Dian and her trackers removed literally thousands of wire snares from the park and specifically from the area around Karisoke. In 1980, park guards, working under Mountain Gorilla Project coordinator Jean Pierre van der Becke, were working to remove snares from the more remote areas of the park.

Poaching is a well-publicized and emotional issue, but the clearest danger to the mountain gorilla is the destruction of its habitat. In 1979, a Mountain Gorilla Project worker named Bill Weber took a survey of the people living on farms below the park. The majority seemed to see Volcano Park as a white man's playground. They thought the land should be turned over to more farms.

To understand Rwandans' hunger for land it is necessary to know a bit about the history of the country. The aboriginal people were the Twa, a pygmy people who lived as hunters and gatherers in the great expanse of forest that Rwanda once was. Then came the Tutsi, a race of giants, the tallest people on the face of the earth, who cleared some land for grazing purposes. Finally, the Hutu came out of the north. An agricultural people, the Hutu set about feverishly clearing the land.

Today, the Hutu farming ethic informs the fabric of Rwandan society. When I flew into Rwanda, my seatmate seemed staggered at the contrast between the jungle of Zaire and the bare, rolling hills of Rwanda. "These people hate trees," he said. More to the point, these people need to eat. Rwanda is the poorest sub-Sahara country in Africa. About the size of Delaware, Rwanda has a population of 4.7 million people; 95 percent of those people are subsistence farmers who eke out a living on farms that average a mere two acres apiece.

Worse, the population is growing at a rate that exceeds 4 percent a year, which puts another 23,000 families on the land each year. And there is no more land. None. The tiny farms are simply subdivided. Famine is a very real possibility.

No wonder Rwandans look to the park's forty square miles for desperately needed farmland: the volcanic soil is some of the richest land in all Rwanda. It is there, people feel, for the purpose of putting food into the mouths of children. And there is precedent for turning the land over to farming.

In 1968, 40 percent of the park was cleared, and pyrethrum, a natural insecticide, was planted. It would be a cash crop that would provide jobs and bring money into the country. In that year, there were an estimated 480 mountain gorillas in the park. Now there are about 260. The destruction of 40 percent of the gorillas' habitat was followed by the loss of almost 50 percent of the population.

It is a commonplace observation that the quickest way to destroy an animal is to destroy its habitat. The Rwandan government, for its part, had a clear duty: its people must not be allowed to starve. One proposal under consideration in the capital city of Kigali involved turning over a major section of the park to cattle ranching.

The Mountain Gorilla Project tourist program was a strategy for saving the gorillas' habitat. Tourists would bring money into Rwanda, they would provide jobs for local people, they would spend for ancillary services, for hotels and food and transportation. A healthy tourism industry would help feed Rwanda, and a healthy tourism industry required a healthy population of gorillas secure in their traditional habitat.

uring my visit to the park in 1981, Dian's highly trained trackers were still patroling the area around Karisoke. Jean Pierre van der Becke, of the MGP, was leading antipoaching patrols into the remote areas of the park. Mark Condiotti, an American working for MGP, was habituating two new groups for the purpose of tourism. The program was two years old.

The park had always operated at a loss—salaries for guards and administrators and the cost of maintaining facilities were a drain on the already strained economy—but fees paid by tourists had increased by two and a half times in the two years MGP had been operating. In 1981 the park managed to pay for itself for the first time in its history.

In only two years, some real progress had been made. Aside from the tourism program and the antipoaching patrols, the MGP was working with the people who lived on the farms—called *shambas*—that roll, bare and treeless, to the very borders of the park. An estimated 780 people occupy each square mile in the land below the park. Conrad and Rosalind Aveling, working for the MGP, were charged with convincing these people that the fertile land above them was best left uncleared, uncultivated, unspoiled.

One evening, about twilight, the Avelings went down to the first village below the park to get their tiny pickup truck. It was time to take the traveling MGP show a few miles down the muddy, rock-strewn joke of a road to a village called Karindagi. There were perhaps fifteen huts in the village—one- or two-room affairs with dirt floors—and Conrad parked just outside town in a large, fallow potato field. He set up a loudspeaker on the top of the truck, dropped a cassette into the tape machine, and cranked the sound up, loud. It was a song with a disco beat about "Rasputin, rasputeen, lover of the Russian queen," who, the singers declared earnestly, was "Russia's greatest sex machine." To the west—by way of a light show—a florid equatorial sunset backlit the line of volcanoes above.

People gathered around the truck. There were more of them than could possibly have lived in those few poor huts. Farmers seemed to rise up out of the ground itself. By the time it was dark, there were hundreds of people surrounding the truck. Some were dancing to the song about Russia's greatest sex machine, others were watching Rosalind work the clever panels on the pickup, which folded out to form a large movie screen. When Conrad snapped on the projector, the people of Karindagi sat rapt before a film about gorillas.

There was much laughter, as there is anywhere in the world when gorilla films are shown. I suppose it has something to do with the obvious intelligence in the animals' eyes, the human quality of the facial expressions. There is a shock of recognition. The people of Karindagi, who do not go into the park, who do not have televisions and never see specials about mountain gorillas, who do not subscribe to *National Geographic*, were beginning to learn what Dian Fossey had taught many in the outside world: the gorillas who ranged above, who could be heard roaring at the edges of the park, were not savage beasts after all. The animals in the film were gentle with humans, inquisitive, trusting. It seemed a revelation to the people of Karindagi.

Afterward, Conrad showed some slides intended to demonstrate that clearing any more of the slopes above would destroy the watershed and that the rivers would die in the dry season, just as the rivers below the pyrethrum project had. There was a discussion of the economic benefits of a tourism program.

On the way back to the park, I told Conrad that the

program had certainly worked as entertainment. The question was: did the message sink in? Conrad thought it was too early to tell.

Back in the States, Dian was working on her book *Gorillas in the Mist* and—in letters and conversations—railing against "comic book conservationists," and "the hordes that have climbed onto the 'Save the gorilla bandwagon.'" She had grave doubts about the MGP tourist program and how it would affect the gorillas' health, but an incident with a pair of MGP workers probably closed off any avenue of compromise.

I don't know the gist of that conversation. I suspect it was a discussion that turned into an argument, and that spur of the moment anger triggered the final fatal comment. Perhaps the MGP workers were talking about the education program, suggesting that farmers who saw an economic advantage in a healthy gorilla population would not tolerate poachers. It wasn't like the old days anymore. You couldn't keep the people below ignorant of the forest, fearful of the conservationists. It couldn't be done single-handedly, not anymore. Some benefits had to accrue to the native people, and the fight couldn't be personalized, so that it seemed as if there was only one person in the world who cared for the gorillas. Perhaps voices were raised at this point. And then the MGP workers said something that others had suggested, but never to Dian Fossey: they said it was possible that some of the gorillas had been killed for no other reason than revenge. They had died not in spite of her work, but because of it.

Ann Pierce, who became friendly with Dian toward the last, asked me if I had any idea how badly that comment had hurt Dian. "All those years up there," Ann said, "can you imagine, can you even begin to imagine, how badly Dian was hurt."

I said I thought I could. In 1981 I had seen something in Dian's cabin at Karisoke that gave me an idea of her pain.

Nick and I had been given to understand that Dian would not be back, and her cabin was opened to us. The house may have been cozy with a fire blazing away, but on this gray afternoon it seemed cold and barren. Outside, a steady chilling rain fell, and I could hear it on the roof. Papering one wall was a series of black-and-white pictures, full-face shots of gorillas. In the constant damp of Karisoke, the photos had begun to curl at the edges.

Did Dian Fossey need photos to keep the animals straight? Gorillas are eminently recognizable when you've lived with them for a while, and Dian certainly did not need to memorize photos. I knew that scientists usually sketch nose prints as an identifying technique. The positioning of the nostrils, the horizontal ridges above, are all distinctive. Maybe these photos were for the purpose of redrawing nose prints taken in field notes. Or for students who might study with Dian.

Nick and I stood side by side, looking at the photos. What was their purpose?

I thought of Rosalind Aveling, her refusal to hold the baby gorilla, and wondered if she wanted to avoid the kind of intense relationship with individual animals that typified Dian's best work. It is very difficult to do field work with primates of any kind and not be drawn, emotionally, into that world. There was, I imagined, a danger beyond science in loving not wisely but too well.

The photos on the wall were head shots, nothing artsy, just gorillas in different moods, but mostly smiling. I thought of actors and their eight-by-ten glossies. Strange, though. We had been in Rwanda more than a month, Nick and I, we had met most of the habituated groups and a good number of wild groups. We knew the local actors, and these were strangers.

I looked over at Nick. He turned away, but not before I saw a sad, stricken expression on his face. A prickling sensation ran up my back and along the tops of my arms. "Sweet Jesus," I said, "these are the dead ones."

1985 was a banner year for the Mountain Gorilla Project. Tourist fees, paid to the park, had become the third largest source of revenue for the nation. The tourists spent even more money on transportation, hotels, food, and local services.

Dian's suspicion that tourist visits might upset the gorillas' reproductive cycles did not prove out. Kelly Stewart and Sandy Harcourt could show that there was no difference in fertility between the research groups and the tourist groups. Perhaps this is because tourism is strictly controlled. There is no touching allowed, and tourists are kept a respectful distance from the animals. Mark Condiotti was actually able to habituate two groups to accept humans, but only from a distance. Additionally, tourists are limited to six individuals, and visits may last no more than an hour and a half once a day.

Both the tourist groups and the research groups were found to be more stable than the wild groups. The animals in the tourist groups were as healthy as those in the research groups, and both were healthier than the animals in wild groups.

There had been no gorillas killed since 1983, probably because the groups most accessible to poachers, those closest to the edge of the park, have been turned over to tourism and are closely monitored; because the trackers take time to destroy traps even with tourists in tow; because the MGP and Karisoke both ran continuing antipoaching patrols.

The combined thrust of tourist dollars and the MGP education program had changed some minds. Bill Weber found that almost all the people living under the park wanted it turned over to farms in 1979. Six years later, another Weber poll showed a majority of farmers in favor of the park.

The government abandoned its plan for cattle ranching in the Virungas, and, in a stunning reversal of policy, actually put forty-five acres back into the park. The Kato Forest, a partially cleared stand of bamboo, was reclaimed. Group thirteen, a tourist-habituated group, ranged close to those acres, but it often passed over into Zaire. The proximity of good feed, it was thought, might keep them in Rwanda. That has been the case, and recently one of group thirteen's females gave birth in the Kato Forest.

Conrad and Rosalind Aveling were at work in Zaire, setting up that country's version of the MGP.

Russ Mittermeier, director of the World Wildlife Fund's Primate Program, calls the MGP "one of the most successful, if not the most successful, conservation program on the continent." It is, in fact, a model project, and its three-pronged approach—controlled tourism to provide revenue, education, and antipoaching work—is being copied by the WWF in their efforts to save the golden lion tamarin and the muriqui in South America. "Of all the endangered primates," Mittermeier said, "and I'm talking about the ones who are down to a few hundred individuals, the outlook for the mountain gorilla looks best. The Mountain Gorilla Project is a proven program that works."

And while the MGP prospered, funding was becoming a problem for Dian. She felt that many people were giving money to the African Wildlife Foundation (which had emerged as the principal MGP funding organization) in the mistaken belief that it was going to her. She felt AWF was siphoning off "Digit's blood money." An organization that had funded much of the research work at Karisoke pulled out.

Back at Karisoke in December 1984 for one of her visits, Dian wrote, "My lifework is now being deprived of funding it badly needs. Then, one evening, earlier this year, while I was sitting on the living room floor with my African tracker and patrol workers counting the traps and snares they had brought to camp that day, I realized fully that this was what active conservation was all about and if others want to emulate our efforts, lots of luck to them, the gorillas will ultimately profit by it. In the meantime, the African staff and myself wake up each morning with our integrity intact knowing that our day will be fully utilized for the benefit of the gorillas. Integrity is the name of the game."

Dian was also having trouble with the Rwandan government. The Office of National Parks and Tourism took the position that it would deal with only one extranational conservation organization. Predictably, they chose to do business through the MGP rather than the Digit Fund and Dian Fossey, who was intimidating and notoriously "difficult." To get visas for her research staff at Karisoke, Dian was forced to go through Jean Pierre van der Becke, who had been made director of the MGP. The Rwanda government would only grant Dian herself a three-month visa.

Dian was fifty-one years old and her health was failing. Emphysema kept her out of the field, away from the animals she loved, and it was so difficult for her to breathe at Karisoke's altitude of ten thousand feet that she had a small "oxygen machine" in her cabin. In November 1985, back in Karisoke on one of her visits, Dian wrote a sad letter to her friend Dr. Shirley McGreal. "There is no way I can be optimistic about the species' survival, albeit the poachers don't roam like buffalo anymore, nor are traps easy to find. It is the human presence that is certainly interfering with their privacy and preservation."

A month later, during the late evening hours of December twenty-sixth, someone hacked through the wall of the cabin at Karisoke with a long knife, and Dian Fossey was brutally murdered.

any people have theories about who killed Dian Fossey. When I heard the news I thought immediately of those stories I had heard drinking *pombe* under the park. Some men have been jailed in Rwanda, but no one really knows who killed Dian, or why.

The press reports and obituaries were appropriately respectful, though, slowly, some negative information began creeping into the reports. The *Philadelphia Daily News* ran an opinion piece titled (incredibly) "Dian Fossey Asked for

It." Insisting that "arrogance gets conservationists no-where," the article claimed that Dian had alienated the local people and that she showed "a contempt for their exis-tence."

Shortly after that article appeared, I received a note from Dr. Shirley McGreal, chairwoman of the International Pri-mate Protection League. "Dian is being murdered twice," she wrote. "First her body, now her reputation."

McGreal enclosed a copy of an *International Primate Pro-tection League Newsletter* devoted entirely to the memory of Dian Fossey. Inside was a tribute from the government of Rwanda, a refutation of various attacks, and copies of letters from Dian that showed real affection for her African track-ers and patrol workers. There was a funny story—bitter-sweet now—about Dian's five-month-long quest to get one of her patrol men a decent pair of boots that fit. The man was a Tutsi, six feet seven inches tall with size fourteen feet that Dian called "gunboats."

Dr. McGreal has emerged as one of Dian's most ardent and eloquent defenders. Yes, she told me, her friend could be arrogant at times. "But you have to understand," she said, "Dian lived up there, all those years, alone. Her friends were being killed." There was emotion in Dr. McGreal's voice. "She was a martyr."

The graveyard lies beside the cabin at Karisoke. It is sheltered by great gnarled trees. Yellow-green moss hangs from the branches that shade the graves where Dian buried Uncle Bert, and Macho, and Digit. Now Dian is buried there, next to Digit.

There has been some talk of turning the cabin into a museum, the graveyard into a memorial. Perhaps, in another century, there will still be gorillas in Rwanda and people who will come to see them. The tourists—the hated tourists—will stand by the grave of Dian Fossey and a guide—speaking in English, or Japanese or Swahili—will tell them of the accomplishments of the woman who is buried there. And the tourists will know that they are looking at the final resting place of a great hero. Not a saint. A hero.

Postscript: The Karisoke Research Center is now funded by the Morris Animal Fund, which also administers the Digit Fund. The center is thriving.

As are the gorillas. In 1980, a census indicated that there were 254 gorillas in the Virungas. Today, that number is 290. There are, according to scientists in the field, "significant numbers of immatures," indicating "a healthy population." The biggest population increase has occurred in tourist groups. Dian's fears that tourism would disrupt the animals' breeding cycles appear to be unfounded.

The Mountain Gorilla Project's approach to the problem is being emulated worldwide. It is a hopeful story.

TRUE BELIEVERS
AND THE
GUISES
OF THE
WEASEL

Saugus, Calif.—Just up and over Soledad Pass, Sierra Highway drops into the Mojave: a spare, unyielding, unspectacular desert. And just over these bare hills, in Newhall, California, Charles Manson and his Family planned their frenzied armored dune buggy attack on all that was evil in our world.

Here in Saugus, a few miles to the north, there is another army of young hyperthyroid-eyed true believers. They belong to the Tony and Susan Alamo Christian Foundation and believe that Christ is coming soon—within ten to twenty years is a fair estimate. He will be a Christ of Wrath, and there will be the weeping and the gnashing of teeth. The Lord, in his Celestial Anger, will take the unsaved by the collar, jerk them heavenward until the whole of earth is a sphere in their eyes. And then Jesus Christ will have his Mighty Vengeance. He will hurl the unclean earthward as God once hurled Lucifer from his Heaven. Our planet will open and swallow its sinners into the fiery bowels where the Bible tells us hell is located. The saved, those of the Foundation, will be raised to the right hand of the Heavenly Father, who will direct them to actual physical mansions he has prepared for them: mansions perhaps not unlike the one in which Tony and Susan Alamo live right here on earth.

We—writer Bill Cardoso and photographer Tim Page and myself—were driving up to Saugus, fifty miles north of the sprawling Los Angeles Basin, to plan an escape. I was going to infiltrate the Foundation to investigate the charges of a loose-knit group of broken-hearted parents organized under the unfortunate acronym of FOC, which stands for Free Our Children. The focus of FOC is a forty-three-year-old black man named Ted Patrick. Formerly a San Diego community relations consultant for California Governor Ronald Reagan and currently unemployed, Patrick is the tough, tireless "deprogrammer" of Jesus Freaks. He has been spectacularly successful in convincing young Christians that they have been duped by their leaders, that they are possessed by demons, that they have been involved in voodoo, not Christianity. He does this by having parents bring their children—sometimes, it is alleged, by force—to one of several designated motel rooms across the country called deprogramming centers, where the devout young are confronted by teams of parents, friends, and former sect members who counter their chanted prayers with reason: high-volume, high-pressure reason under conditions that would be called third degree if practiced in any police station in the country. The prayerful children are not allowed to "run away," though the vast majority of them have been over the legal age of consent. Patrick claims 125 successful deprogrammings.

Tony and Susan Alamo, and the Christians of their Foundation, pray to Jesus that this Devil coming against the House of God will be stopped. Mike Pancer, a San Diego attorney and an unpaid panel member of the American Civil Liberties Union is, involuntarily, in the Lord's Service in this matter. He is the answer to the Alamos' prayers. Pancer saw in the papers that adults, the Jesus Freaks, in the process of being deprogrammed, were subjected to what looked like kidnap, assault, and false imprisonment. He contacted the Alamos and began an investigation. While eternal Vengeance belongs to the Lord—and isn't long in coming—earthly justice, apparently, was in the hands of the ACLU.

Patrick was in good spirits Thursday of Holy Week when I visited him in his suburban tract house just south of San Diego.

"If we bust one of these groups, we've got them all," he said. According to Patrick there was little difference among any of the sixty-one different groups he knows about. They all are guilty, he says, of "psychological kidnapping."

"All these groups have the technique of hypnotizing a person on the street or anywhere. And they can do this within five or ten minutes. And they can talk about anything. If they know you are a reporter, they can talk about the news. But the key is to get a person to look you straight in the eyes. And if they can look you straight in the eyes for five or ten minutes, you'll find yourself unable to take your eyes off of theirs. You remember Susan Atkins? She said when she first saw Manson and looked into his eyes, she couldn't take her eyes off of his. All of the kids say the same thing. And I've heard them, heard kids give testimony, give testament of these various groups and they say, 'Well, I was on my way home and I met this person on the street and I looked into his eyes and I couldn't take my eyes off of theirs. . . . I left everything and went with them.'

"Of course these kids are programmed to use this technique, but they are not conscious of being able to use it. They are instructed by their leaders always to look a person straight in the eye. And they use certain Bible verses, and then they talk to a person, and after looking them in the eye for so long a time their subject will leave and go with them. And that is what we call psychological kidnapping.

"The person is taken to a bus, a van—most of these groups operate from a bus—and the first thing they do is give the kids either coffee, tea, or punch; cookies or sandwiches. And we have reason to believe that they have some type of mind-controlling drugs or herbs in this food or drink."

Patrick was vague on the types of drugs used, though he mentioned that the police found "speed" in cookies given by a militant Christian organization in Bellevue, Washington. After being drugged and hypnotized, according to Patrick, the recruit goes through "an intensive questioning."

"They ask them all about their family condition: 'Do you have a car; is it paid for; is it in your name; do you have a bank account; do you own furniture . . . do your people have money; do they own a business?' After getting all this information, they sign their whole life away. Everything they own; everything that they ever owned will belong to the leaders of this organization."

Then, according to Patrick, there are the "brainwashing" sessions, lasting up to thirty hours apiece. "Two people work on [the new subject] at all times without food and maybe a little water and maybe a little rest. Somebody is constantly in there working and telling you we are the Leader, we are God, and all this jazz. And when they get through with them, they are zombies. That's all they are, complete zombies. They destroy their minds. They take their minds completely away. They have no will to think whatsoever. And all the things they are eager to do are what they are programmed by their leaders to do."

I asked Patrick if he felt he was engaged in a Holy War with the Jesus Freak groups. "I have nothing to do with religion," he said. "These are not religious groups. These are more Satan groups than anything else. And I will stand behind this 100 percent. There is nothing religious about any of these groups. They . . . they're more Satan and they know they are Satan. Because God does not lie and cheat and steal and even kill. . . ."

"These are strong allegations," I said.

"You haven't forgotten Manson," Patrick countered sharply.

"No, I haven't forgotten Manson."

"These groups are the same. The Family looked on Manson. They thought he was God. All of these groups are *exactly* the same as Manson. Tony and Susan and all the rest of them are exactly like the Manson Family. Only thing is: they're worse. They're more dangerous than Manson. He had a small Family. But these groups—Tony and Susan—have five hundred or six hundred people, and they're better organized. They're more dangerous than Manson. These groups would do anything. Believe us. . . ."

Patrick's charges strained my credulity, and I wasn't about to believe much of what he said without documentation. He said he could prove his allegations, but—and here he gave me a squinty-eyed suspicious look, as if I might be a devious Christian spy—he wasn't going to release the information to me.

I told him of my plans to infiltrate the Foundation and suggested that we talk at a later date. Patrick agreed but expressed grave concern for my safety. William Rambur, father of Kay "Comfort" Rambur, presently living in parts unknown with the Children of God, a militant Christian organization, told me that I was dealing with perhaps "the most vicious of the California sects."

"Watch out for your mind," he cautioned, adding that the brainwashing techniques used by the Alamos could be as fearsomely effective as those used against American POWs by the Chinese Communists during the Korean War.

"We've lost contact with many of the people who have gone up there," he said softly.

"Are you suggesting murder," I asked.

"We've lost contact with them. They haven't called us. We can't reach them. All I'm saying is that we've lost contact."

So, during the Holy Hours of Good Friday, when Christians commemorate the agony and death of Christ on the cross—when the sky darkened above Golgotha and the earth shook—a Volkswagen containing three journalists was moving east out of Saugus, toward the Tony and Susan Alamo Christian Foundation. The town itself is not more than a few stores and a classic *High Noon* railway station. The Foundation is another ten miles up into the rocky hills, past the beer and burger roadhouses, past the tough-looking country music bars, past the auto graveyards.

It was *Grapes of Wrath* country, home of the thirties migration that didn't make it to the Promised Land. It is a hot and tired land on the fringes of the Mojave, and it attracts failed cars: Corvairs and Edsels and Falcons haunt these holy roads. People in trailers own their own land, which they share with rattlesnakes and scorpions. Great steel pylons carrying high-tension wires march two by two across the arid hills.

I experienced a definite tightening of the sphincters as we neared the Foundation. As the highway rose, the homes and trailers dropped away, leaving only a few widely spaced roadhouses. If there was a fence around the place, I meant to find a weak spot. I assumed that I could escape overland, avoid the snakes, and come out at a designated point somewhere below.

But there was no fence, and the Foundation looked exactly like what it was, a converted bar and nightclub once called the Wilson Cafe. The large parking lot held several buses, vans, and cars all painted red, white, and blue and clearly marked as belonging to the Tony and Susan Alamo Christian Foundation. One sign admonished readers to REPENT OR PERISH. There was a fire station nearby, and we pulled into the parking lot.

Cardoso and I worked out a telephone code. If I called and said I was feeling "swell" somewhere in the conversation, I was in no danger. If I said I was "enjoying myself," I wanted him up there immediately. If I didn't call within three days, I wanted an all-out assault on the place by local sheriff's deputies.

We pulled out of the firehouse and coasted slowly by the Foundation. The hills were green this spring after a wet winter, but in a month they would be brown and bare and choking with dust. They were hills, Susan Alamo was to say later, very like the hills of Galilee, upon which Christ walked. And though she didn't say—and surely didn't think it—they were the very hills upon which Charles Manson had walked.

Four-thirty, Good Friday afternoon. Hollywood Boulevard, two blocks up from Grauman's Chinese Theater. I'm lounging in the entrance to a toy store, unshaven and looking, I hope, profoundly confused. Page is across the street in the VW, camera at the ready. Two brisk but seedy-looking Alamo-ites are coming my way, tracts in hand.

My witness was an exceedingly short Christian named Chris who stared up at me with a pair of smarmy eyes that rippled and glittered wetly behind a pair of thick glasses. Did I know that Christ was coming again, that the world was about to end, and that vengeance belonged to the Lord, he said all in a rush.

I considered the question in silence.

Apparently encouraged, Chris explained that he wasn't exactly sure when Christ would make an appearance here on the boulevard, but that it was the "Season of His Coming."

"I know that when the trees bloom summer can't be far behind. Right?"

"Right," I said.

"Well, the Bible gives us certain signs that indicate when Christ will come again." According to the Bible and Chris, the end would be at hand when the armies of the world were massed around Jerusalem. I nodded. "The waters shall become bitter as wormwood," Chris intoned, then added reasonably, "that's pollution." He paused to let this sink in, then hit me with what I suspect he felt was a boggler. "The Bible tells us that the Second Coming is near when the Jews preach the gospel and . . . *the Alamos are Jewish.*"

The evidence, I had to admit, was certainly piling up.

I saw a pattern developing: fire a series of soul-rockers, then hit them where they live with a Clincher.

"The Bible says that Christ is at hand when the cities are enclosed in a smoking haze." Chris directed my attention to the whisky brown skies of Los Angeles. From the rapt and worshipful attention on his face, I think he half-expected Christ to descend from heaven, then and there, right through the smog in a blaze of glory, to smite the shit out of all the hustlers and the winos and the Godless shoppers of this choking Babylon.

We talked about the greatest war the earth has known, a war that raged on even as we stood there, in which the Devil battled Christ for the possession of men's souls. I stared into Chris's eyes for fully thirty seconds in an effort to determine if he was trying, consciously or unconsciously, to hypnotize me. I think he felt menaced because he took a backward step and stared at the tracts in his hand for several uncomfortable seconds. Hypnotism was definitely not Chris's forte. He collected his thoughts and came back with a strong verbal blast of fire and brimstone.

"Ah, come on," I said, "why would a loving God make someone with the express purpose of sending him to hell."

"You think God is Love," Chris accused. His voice took on a sneering singsong quality. "You believe in a forgiving God. You only see what you want to see." His voice dropped an octave. "Well, He is a God of Wrath. He is not a . . . permissive . . . God." I further learned there was no hope for me, that I was surely hellbound, but that God had taken pity on me because I was talking to Chris, and that I could save my soul by catching the Alamo bus at six.

"I put before you this day," Chris said, "both a blessing and a curse."

"Here's the good news and here's the bad news," I said, smiling.

Chris did not smile. He apparently disapproved of jokes. His face became pinched and severe. The blessing was eternity in heaven praising God for Christ's sake and the curse was a burning eternity of hellfire.

We had been standing in front of the toy store, talking for nearly twenty minutes. I would have stayed longer but Chris had better things to do.

"Read the tract," he commanded, "then come get on the

bus. Remember, the Devil is going to try his best to stop you from getting to the Foundation."

"I'm going to go drink a beer or two and think it over," I said. Chris folded his face into an ugly mask of contempt. "That's the devil talking," he stated flatly and stalked off down the boulevard to win another soul for Christ.

There are, of course, multiple unknowns in the world, and it could very well have been the Devil himself who caused me to almost miss the Alamo bus, but if it was, his agent was photographer Tim Page, who was waiting around the corner for me. Page, a British citizen, was wounded five times in four years as a combat photographer in Vietnam. His brushes with death left him with an insatiable appetite for "scummy bars," places with what he calls, in GI parlance, a "numbah ten clientele."

The bar we found pleased Page immensely. At five in the afternoon of Good Friday, it was filled with cheap hustlers and even cheaper hookers. We ordered a couple of drafts and studied the tract, which informed us that Tony and Susan Alamo were the first two to take the gospel to the streets. This was about 1967, when the young people were declaring war on the Establishment, taking drugs, and talking about burning down the churches. So it said. Tony and Susan stopped this nonsense in its tracks and turned the dregs of the drug society to Jesus. The tract hit heavily on the theme of drug temperance and rejoiced that these former stoned revolutionaries now go about "appealing to the Establishment to turn away from their sins."

Tony, born Bernie Lazar Hoffman, confessed that he was a vocalist, a record company owner, a fast-stepping PR man, and the owner of a chain of health spas. "All highly successful ventures," it said, but neglected to mention that in 1967 Tony was "broke," by his own admission. His life "was filled with sin, filth, despair, torture, and torment." Now, six years later, after committing his life to the Lord,

Tony Alamo drives a black Cadillac Fleetwood with personalized license plates and lives in an elegant hilltop mansion in Saugus.

A bulletproof waitress in a miniskirt arrived with our third beer, and I asked her to look at the picture of Tony and Susan on the tract.

"He looks sneaky and she's got a face like an elbow," she said.

"Ah, Sister, that's the Devil talking," I said mildly.

She gave me a quick sideways glance and left, I suspect, to tell the bartender to keep an eye on us.

So much for the testimony of sinners.

T he red, white, and blue bus—with a destination sign reading HEAVEN—was right there on the corner of Highland Avenue and Hollywood Boulevard as it is every day at six o'clock. On the way a fresh set of Alamo-ites tried to hand me another tract, but I told them I was getting on the bus anyway.

"Don't let the Weasel talk you out of it," another very short Christian told me.

"The Weasel?"

"The Devil, the Weasel, the Old Boy. He's going to sit on your shoulder and tell you to go have some dope instead."

"He is?"

The diminutive evangelist thought it best to walk me the last thirty yards to the bus.

"Thank you, Jesus," he said to no one in particular as I stepped aboard. It looked like a school bus, and a capacity crowd of about sixty was aboard. Perhaps fifty were reading Bibles. The other ten were lost sinners, like myself, on their way to the Foundation for the first time. I sat next to one of the few clean-cut Bible readers, a man of about twenty named Hal, who immediately noticed the beer on my breath. "The services aren't like any you've ever seen," he told me through an obviously forced smile. "*You . . . will . . . like them.*" He opened his Bible and said no more. If

Hal was a hypnotist, he had a serious problem with technique.

A Christian cheerleader of sorts made his way down the aisle, stopping every five rows or so to break into song.

> *My Savior leads the way*
> *My Savior leads the way*
> *My burdens all seem light now*
> *Since Jesus came to stay.*

The bus, I surmised, was a purchase from the Mexican government. All the exit signs were in Spanish. Someone was reading the Bible verses to the driver and he had to shout them out as the engine labored and the gears rasped on the steep hills of the Golden State Freeway. I caught a startling verse about the "loathsome diseases of the loins," and simultaneously wished that I had taken the time to relieve myself in the bar. Here I was, I thought, on a Mexican bus, on my way to Heaven, and I had to take a piss.

I began to chuckle softly, and Hal looked up from his Bible and gave me a severe look, a look that seemed to say, "laughter is the Devil's tool and no Good can come from it."

"Excuse me," I offered, and Hal, sorry hypnotist that he was, went back to his Bible. I sat with my legs tightly crossed and bit my lip for the next twenty miles.

The Foundation is a single-story building quartered by a kitchen and a boothed-off dining area where much of the Bible study takes place. The other half of the building might once have been the dance floor and bandstand. It was now a church, set up with a combination of lecture-seat rejects and folding chairs. A crowd of about four hundred were waiting for services to begin and engaging themselves in exalted conversation.

"Christ is so close to coming. I feel it in every pore."

"Amen."

"It says so in the Bible."

"It's the Word of God, Brother."

"Thank you, Jesus."

No one seemed interested in hypnotizing, brainwashing, or even talking to me at this point, so I circulated aimlessly through the well-integrated crowd. Males outnumbered females vastly, and the typical resident might be described as a male longhair, between the ages of twenty and thirty and dressed pretty much like street folk the country over.

I found myself near a door to the left of the pulpit that said PRAYER ROOM. Inside I could hear people shouting in undifferentiated syllables, without cadence. An occasional man's voice leather-lunged, "Oh, God, I wanna be ready." A hand-lettered sign on the door listed three things to pray for: Susie's health, someone's sister, who had "a cancer," and "that God will stop Ted Patrick and all other Devils coming against the Foundation."

A young black resident took the pulpit and said, "Let's hear a mighty Amen!"

"Ahhhhhhhhhhhhhhhhhhhhhhhh-men!" the four hundred shouted.

This was followed by a prayer, and then the band—a disparate collection of about sixty tubas, trombones, saxophones, flutes, and clarinets dominated by an electric bass, an electric organ, and three sets of drums—was off and running, slicing into standards like "The Old Rugged Cross" and country devotions like "My Savior Leads the Way." People stood and clapped and expressed thanks to God for the music. The orchestra sounded like a tank town high school band.

After "King of Kings," the big finish, various of the Saved stepped up to the pulpit to give testimony. "I know there's a burning Hell," one crisp sister in gingham non sequitured, "because I experienced a little bit of it out in the World." Hell, in fact, seemed to be the big selling point for salvation and it beat out heaven in terms of mention about ten to one.

The words "born again" and "born again in the blood" were mentioned often. Very big was the phrase *I know beyond the shadow of a doubt.* The theme was drugs, rotten lives, torture, torment, filth, and despair in "the World" as opposed to "Peace" at the Foundation while "Serving the

Lord." Most testimonies ended "so come on up and get saved."

"You may think you came here for a free meal," the leader said, "but God drew you here for a very special purpose." He hit briefly on the soul rockers: hellfire, the end of the world, judgment before the Lord, and the Prophecy of the Second Coming before revealing to sinners in the crowd that the Biblical promise of eternal life was within our grasps that very evening. All we had to do, it turned out, was to humble ourselves before God—and, of course, everyone else at the service—by kneeling in the little area between the first folding chairs and the pulpit. There we would publicly confess that we led sinful lives in the manner of American POWs taping war crimes confessions before international cameras.

"I put before you this day both a blessing and a curse," he said.

The organist began a churchy solo, and elect Christians threaded through the crowd, looking for obvious sinners. Another short, rather pleasant-looking man in his midtwenties stood by my chair.

"Why don't you come up and get saved," he stage-whispered.

I shrugged stupidly.

"It's easy," he said. "I'll come with you."

A few sinners and their Christians were moving toward the saving block. The organ finished, stopped momentarily, but at a signal from the man at my side, it started again. The same song, from the top.

"I couldn't say that prayer and mean it," I pointed out.

"It doesn't matter. If you kneel and say it with your lips, God will come into your heart in a very special way. Why do you think God brought you here?"

It was difficult to argue the point with every person in the place watching us, so I let myself be led forward to kneel on the hard linoleum floor, under a long fluorescent light. I said the prayer word for word and at no time did I feel God come into my heart, which, I suppose, is as it should be.

"Ahhhhhhhhhhhhhhhh-men," everyone shouted.

A brief announcement before dinner. Baby Christians—the newly saved—had another gift in store for them, "the baptism of the Holy Spirit." Our older Christians would tell us about it.

"God promised that the saved would speak in tongues," I was told by the man who was to become my teacher. "Don't be denied. Seek for the gift with all your heart. Just keep saying, 'God, you promised.' " The process, as it was explained to me, was that one started by "just praising and thanking Jesus." At a certain point, he will begin to stutter, a signal that he is about to begin speaking in tongues. My older Christian invited me into the prayer room to give it a whirl, and since it seemed to be the thing to do after being saved, I followed him through the wooden door.

Given a generally tense state of mind, the prayer room is no place to be reassured about the sanity of the Foundation's saved. The room was a windowless expanded closet, perhaps four steps wide and ten long. There was a muted light in one corner, and as my eyes became accustomed to the darkness, I saw that there were wooden bench seats along three walls and an ancient, puffy sofa along the fourth. The linoleum had been torn up to reveal a wooden floor. The walls were rough-hewn wood, like a rustic sauna.

After the first few seconds of ripping claustrophobia, one became aware of a milling crowd and the monotonic sound of spoken gibberish. People were tromping back and forth lengthwise, and their footsteps produced a constant low rumble, a counterpoint to the words "thank you Jesus, praise you Jesus." Christians stood in various corners and trilled out nonsense syllables: "Ah na na na" and the like at a rapid rate. Talking in Tongues.

I was later to happen upon a few verses in Chapter Two of Acts concerning this phenomenon. Forty days after the death of Christ, the Apostles gathered, "And they were all filled with the Holy Ghost, and began to speak with other tongues, as the Spirit gave them utterance." Bystanders were amazed that the Apostles were speaking in their own languages, while, "Others mocking said, These men are full of new wine."

My older Christian sat me on the bench and took up a position on my right. Someone else sat close by on my left. Both men began rocking back and forth, chanting, "Praise to you Jesus, thank you Jesus."

I have been at Catholic services, where everyone suddenly kneels at some signal, and willy-nilly, I found myself on my knees. It was impossible to remain seated. In the same way, it was difficult to sit in that room and not rock and chant.

"Thank you Jesus, praise you Jesus," I said for a little over an hour.

Presently the three of us began rocking faster, chanting locomotive-style, "Thank you Jesus, thank you Jesus, thank you Jesus . . ." I assumed—half-believed—that there was some sort of self-hypnotic process in the works, and I intended to get thoroughly stoned. Several people seemed to be in a state of trance. I thought there might be some psycho-physiological process in which the tongue spewed out syllables of its own volition after a long chant. For me this was not the case.

"Thank you Jesus," my older Christian said, then began stuttering slightly. "Thank you Jesisisis, thank you jisisisis, dank eh jsiis, dada a jisisisis." I found myself stuttering along. The pace increased and the man on my left broke into tongues. "Ah yab dadaba doedoedoe," he stated. "Ah ra da da da da," the man to my right replied. "Thank ooo jeejeejee," I ventured. Apparently it wasn't enough, and we started the whole process again.

I could not, try as I might, get from the stutter to the tongues organically. I sneaked a look at my watch and realized that I had been rocking and chanting for almost two and a half hours. I was developing an unpleasant prayer sore at the base of my spine, and it was becoming painfully obvious that I wasn't going to get out of there until I began speaking in tongues.

We were working toward another crescendo. "Dank oo jejeje," I said and burst into a tense, conservative burst of tongues. "Er rit ta tit a tit a rit," I said, taking care to roll my *r*'s. "Ah yab a daba daba daba raba," the man on my right shouted. "A nanananan nana nah," the other Christian said.

I opened my eyes slightly on the down rock, saw feet gathering around me and experienced a mainline shot of mortal dread. They knew I wasn't speaking in tongues. They were going to stomp on me like a rat caught in the cheese box. "Er rit a tit tit tita," I babbled, heavy on the rolling *r*'s. "Rit ti tit tit."

There were more feet. Several people stopped chanting and were standing in a semicircle, speaking in loud and extravagant tongues. Someone shouted, "Oh, thank you Jesus, thank you for the victory." The victory, I realized with relief that approached joy, was that I had said, "Rit ti tit tit." I was in. I belonged. Everyone was with me. "Rit ta tit tit, diddla dit dit," I said, introducing a pleasing variant on my basic tongues. This was well received. "Rit a little did a dit diddle dit dit."

Beside me, my older Christian ran through a few change-ups, interspersing his standard "Yab ba da ba da ba" with nice syllables that sounded like the names of Biblical towns. "Ah Shal-la-dah, ah shal-ah-dah-dah."

I began to realize that whatever nonsense syllables you said were all right as long as you said them rapidly, in a loud trancelike monotone. It was best if your tongue bounced rapidly off the roof of your mouth. I tried to come up with some good Old Testament sounds, but the only nonsense that came to mind belonged in old rock and roll songs.

"Ah Sha nana nana nana nana nah," worked excellently. I was confident enough to vary my rhythms. My tongue was very loose. My friends and I took short, increasingly more rapid solos: dueling tongues.

After about twenty minutes, we tapered back down to a half an hour of "praise you Jesus, thank you Jesus." It was past midnight when we left the rat box, and the man who accompanied me to the saving block marked down three and a half hours on a sheet of paper on the outside of the door.

We stood outside the door and finally introduced ourselves. My Christian's name was Frank, and he wanted to
know if I would like to stay at the Foundation and serve the
Lord. The bus was about to leave.

"Any guests want to go back to Los Angeles?" the driver
called.

Frank gave me to believe that my rebirth might not take
if I returned to "the World" with its manifold temptations.
He said I could backslide into "filth," which he defined as
dope, pornography, and possible homosexuality. Women,
he said, were often agents of the Devil. I told him I would
stay a few days because I was curious about what was involved in "serving the Lord."

Frank shook my hand, said praise the Lord and introduced me to several other Christians who greeted my decision with "praise the Lord," uttered in the same vague tone
other people say "far out." I was given a dog-eared Bible,
and the two of us moved to the far section of the church and
sat in a booth. I should, I learned, read only the sections
Frank recommended. "See," he said, "if you just opened it
up, you might get into some of the heavy prophets and it
could blow your mind."

We were to read the Book aloud. Frank asked me to begin
with Matthew, Chapter Nine. Before I could start, he closed
his eyes and rotated his head from side to side in a painful
manner, as if he had a chiropractic problem with his neck.
He muttered something about "burning the words upon
our hearts" and looked up crossly while I stared at him. I
realized he was blessing the reading and obligingly rotated
my head and muttered along. I got through the first fifty-
seven verses without incident, but when I came to fifty-nine
through sixty-two, Frank stopped me momentarily to say
that I was coming to "heavy scripture."

In these verses, Jesus is preaching to the multitudes, and
a man tells him he will follow him after he buries his father.
"Jesus said unto him, 'Let the dead bury the dead.'"

"Thank you Jesus," Frank said.

I continued. "'And another also said, Lord, I will follow
thee; but let me first go bid them farewell which are at home

at my house. And Jesus said unto him, "No man having put his hand to the plow and looking back is fit for the Kingdom of Heaven." ' "

I asked Frank to "interpret" that last verse, and he bristled. The Alamos do not interpret the Bible, he said. They tell you what the words mean, and in this case the words were plain enough. If I took my hand from the plow, that is, if I left the Foundation and scorned the work of the Lord, I wouldn't be fit to enter heaven. He pointed out that there were only two places to go after one dies.

"Hell is so terrible you can't even conceive of it," he said, and as he spoke, I felt his genuine Fear. The Alamos had a friend, he said, a woman who was a born-again Christian but who had fallen in with backsliders and found herself surrounded by Devils in some sleazy gin mill. One of the Alamos told the story over the pulpit: how the woman had passed out behind the jukebox only to have a horrifying vision of eternal torment. The lost souls were confined in a blast furnace with sloping sides. Some tried to scramble upward, toward heaven, but they fell back into the pit. The others stood stiffly, like mannequins, and cried out to God like dumb beasts.

"Mercy, Lord, mercy." Frank imitated the hoarse, hopeless croak of the damned, and a shiver ran through his body. "The woman said that if her own mother tried to stop her from serving the Lord, she would gouge her eyes out with her high heels."

This all made it difficult for me to tell Frank that I wanted to call my friends and tell them I wouldn't be home. Still, I insisted, and he agreed on the condition that I "witness to" my friend. "Remember, he hasn't been saved, so the Devil will be working through him. He'll mock you, and you're going to have to be strong." He stood at my elbow while I dialed Cardoso. "Don't forget to tell him you've been born again in the blood," Frank whispered.

"Hello?" Cardoso sounded sleepy or fuddled in some other way.

"Bill, it's me," I said, while Frank hung on every word. "Say listen, I've been born again in the blood and I'm going

to stay in Saugus and serve the Lord. Everything is . . .
swell."

"Swell?" Plainly Cardoso couldn't remember what that
was supposed to mean. "You sure it's swell? Are you all
right?"

"I'm . . . swell," I gritted.

"What's the matter, can't you talk?"

"Praise the Lord."

"Need help?"

"No."

"Call tomorrow."

We hung up.

"You have to witness to them stronger than that," Frank
said. "Pretty soon they say to themselves: that guy must
really have something up there."

"Yeah, well, I'll call him tomorrow night when I know
a little more," I said.

"Well . . ." Frank didn't seem to think that was such a
good idea. We moved back to a booth and called for some
food. While we waited, I learned that as a Baby Christian
I was forbidden to speak to other Baby Christians and that
I would have an older Christian assigned to me who would
be my instructor and guide. As I learned later, you could
literally not even go into the bathroom without your older
Christian.

The food consisted of a pile of noodles, some vegetables,
and a tomato stuffed with beans. I shared five meals at the
Foundation and never did I eat anything that contained
either mind-controlling drugs or enough protein to propel
a mouse. We spent another hour in Bible study, Alamo-
style, before Frank finally took me to the bathroom. It contained a row of dirty sinks, two urinal troughs, two
sit-down toilets, and a shower filled to the ceiling with
sleeping gear. I was given two mothy blankets. Frank had
an old sleeping bag made out of some miracle fiber; the kind
of thing you find at J.C. Penney's with pictures of the characters from "Bonanza" on the inside.

The folding chairs in the church section had been taken
up, and the two of us found a spot to sleep right there on

the holy linoleum. We formed a small part of a wall-to-wall human carpet consisting of perhaps as many as 125 sleeping men.

"When we get up," Frank said, "we wake up just praising and thanking Jesus." I agreed to wake up praising and thanking and said good night.

"Amen," Frank yawned.

Belly down in the sibilant, snoring silence, I reviewed Patrick's charges. I had not been hypnotized, drugged, nor asked to sign away my worldly possessions. And if I were to discover that the brainwashing charges were not altogether groundless, the plain fact was that it was being done with the complete and devoted cooperation of the saved. There were, in fact, five separate occasions when I could have refused the Foundation without substantial rebuke: when my first witness left me on the boulevard; when I got on the bus; when I moved up to be saved; when I entered the rat box; and when I chose not to take the bus back to Los Angeles. At no time was there anything that resembled a physical threat, and what mental coercion there was fell far short of being irresistible.

No, the people at the Alamo Foundation were there because they *wanted* to be there, a fact that strained my perspective immeasurably considering they lived what struck me as a joyless life vibrating with a strong undercurrent of psychic terror.

A week later, in search of a historical context, I visited the San Francisco offices of psychotherapist Dr. Nathan Adler. I mentioned that in my stay at the Foundation, I was surprised to discover that many of the saved had been jailed at one time or another—in two cases on the chickenshit charge of loitering. In general, the people I met were not the familiar middle- and upper-middle-class dropouts of the mid-sixties. My impression was that the majority of them were stone down and outers, kids with a lower-middle-class background suddenly on their own and riding the ragged edge of poverty. Few of the saved I talked to had steady jobs before being born again.

"Youth is underemployed in our country," Adler said.

"There are simply no jobs for young people. They used to be apprentices or errand boys, but today our society seems to have no place for people under twenty-five. They are treated like old people in this respect."

We discussed the sociological statistic that there are presently some one million people under the age of twenty-five on the road and in the streets: the largest body of unemployed nomads since the Depression years. They can't get case work services, food stamps, or welfare because they have no permanent address. A goodly number, of course, could give a shit because they are stoned on whatever's cheap and available on the street.

Adler thinks a parallel can be drawn between our time and the years between 1825 and 1837—the Great Awakening—in upstate New York. Young people were moving en masse out of Boston and New York as society stratified. There were jobs to be had digging the Erie Canal. Towns like Buffalo and Binghamton experienced exponential growth, and 60 percent of the population was under twenty. Those who couldn't find work, drank. The American Temperance Union sprang up, and the term "nation of drunkards" was coined.

Besides the Union there were rural communities, utopian communities, and—more to the point—a huge Christian revival movement. It was characterized by a rejection of traditional work roles, a contempt for the false values of "the World," a conviction that the Devil was hard at work battling for the souls of men, and by ecstatic behavior, such as speaking in tongues. Above all there was the Apocalyptic vision: the sure knowledge—knowledge beyond the shadow of a doubt—that the world would end soon. The event was flat-out scheduled for 1837.

While the situations are not strictly analogous, certain similarities between the people of the Great Awakening and today's Jesus people suggest themselves. We are experiencing a youth population explosion as a result of the postwar baby boom. There is widespread joblessness and an accompanying heavy drug use. "In 1825 it was alcohol, today it's speed or heroin or downers," says Adler, who believes the specific drug is "an accident of the market."

Further, according to Adler, we are in the midst of a vast social upheaval. Corporate clerical workers are no longer treated like professionals, and small shopkeepers are going out of business at an unusually high rate. A country that buys its clothes from ready-to-wear manufacturers doesn't need tailors; one that buys its furniture from automated factories doesn't need woodworkers. The craftsman class is sinking into the muck of history.

The threat of nuclear holocaust and/or ecological disaster is seized upon by people like Susan Alamo who see doom in Biblical verses. And war, Adler points out, has always generated a conviction that humans are so hopelessly cretinated that they must soon perish. In the seventies we will have to contend with the stale carcass of Vietnam. In the 1820s Americans were recovering from the War of 1812, while Napoleon raged in Europe. The landed gentry in upstate New York suffered status-death as a basically rural economy shifted over into an urban waterpower society virtually overnight. Everyone, it seemed, was either waiting for the end or smashed out of their senses on demon rum.

The end of the world, however, failed to roll around in 1837, and a lot of people got splendidly drunk on New Year's Eve. "By the 1840s," Adler said, "all these groups had become lost little islands of impotence and incompetence."

But for me, a week earlier, lying sleepless on the floor of the Alamo Foundation in the blackest hours of the morning on Holy Saturday, there were no convenient sociological communalities. I found myself seriously disoriented; thinking, on the one hand, like an FOC parent, that these gentle Jesus folk were wasting their lives babbling inane gibberish and living in some of the most squalid and humiliating poverty in America. On the other, like ACLU lawyer Mike Pancer, who has been battling Patrick, I felt that since they had freely chosen this life, they should be free to live it. Even if they were being sorely victimized.

I dropped into a fitful sleep, full of nightmarish disasters, and started awake shortly thereafter overwhelmed with the conviction that something weird was going on. Frank was sitting near my head, a human alarm clock, demonstrating the proper way to wake up when you've just been saved.

"Praise you Jesus thank you Jesus praise you Jesus thank you Jesus praise you Jesus thank you Jesus praise you Jesus thank you Jesus praise you Jesus thank you Jesus . . ."

My Thank you Jesuses were as cold and hard and artificial as the linoleum floor I had slept on.

"The Lord loves a broken spirit," Frank told me. My soul, apparently, was in danger, and the signs could be read in the sleepy sullenness on my face. We had rolled up our gear and were stepping over some still-sleeping bodies, moving into the bathroom, which was pervaded with an unpleasant diarrhealike odor. The two sit-down toilets were in constant use, and I made an immediate vow of voluntary constipation for the duration of my stay. Showers were out of the question because the stall was already half full of blankets and sleeping bags. A speaker above the last sink spewed out scratchy Bible verses: Leviticus it was, information on how to offer sacrifices, what to do when the smoke doesn't rise, how to tell the difference between what is holy and unholy, what is clean and what is unclean.

"Hallelujah," the brothers said, standing before the filthy sinks. There was no hot water, and my sink filled to the top and overflowed because the drain didn't work. It had to be emptied with a cup into a floor waste-pipe. It occurred to me that it was best to keep the mind firmly focused on Jesus in a crowded stink-hole like this: Satan was ever-present, trying to pump the brothers full of pride.

"The Weasel wants you to think bad things about the Foundation," Frank said. "Just say 'The blood of Christ is upon you Satan' or 'Get thee behind me Satan' until he goes away."

Like everyone else, I had slept in my clothes. I was itchy and distinctly showerless. My mouth tasted like the foulest depths of the Pit, and I wanted a cigarette.

"We smoke in the back," Frank said. He didn't smoke,

but stood about five feet away, an inspiration of self-denial while I indulged my vice. "The Bible doesn't say anything about smoking, so that's up to you," Frank said, but he had a shivery tale to tell about tobacco. "Tony used to smoke a lot and then one day after he was saved, he was about to light up and Jesus came down and stood right in front of him." Frank stepped over and stood in front of me. "He put his hands on Tony's arms"—Frank put his two hands on my biceps—"looked Tony straight in the eyes"—Frank looked straight in my eyes—"and did this." Frank shook his head no, slowly, sadly. Instantly he brightened, laughing with the cosmic logic of it all.

"If Jesus did that to you, wouldn't you quit smoking?"

I admitted that it would be a powerful incentive.

Later, we stopped into the prayer room for a quick half-hour chant, then spent a few excruciating hours while Frank read aloud, stumbling over the big words in Matthew, chapters one through six. I felt surly and argumentative. We came onto a verse in which Jesus instructs the multitudes not to pray using "vain repetitions, as the heathens do. . . ."

"Wait a minute," I said, "we just spent half an hour saying 'praise Jesus' in there."

Frank considered the problem in a sincere, furrow-browed silence. Three older brothers were summoned for a boothside conference, out of my range of hearing. After several minutes, one of the strange brothers approached with the answer.

"The repetitions," he said severely, "are not vain."

"Of course." I slapped my forehead, Dumbo-style. "I should have known."

"After you've been here for a while and are older in the Lord you'll be able to think better."

"Thank you Jesus."

"Praise the Lord."

"Hallelujah."

"Thank you Jesus."

"Praise the Lord."

Frank told me there were rules I had to live by if I wanted to serve the Lord. I couldn't go anywhere without my permanent older Christian. If I wanted to leave the Foundation for any reason, I had to put the request on a list on the bulletin board entitled "Ask Tony."

"We ask Tony everything: if a guy wants to work on the ranch or drive the bus, he asks Tony. Tony is so smart. Sometimes he'll just write, 'You're not ready,' and a guy'll think about it for a while and realize that Tony was right."

Another strict rule was "no pairing off." This meant that I was not supposed to associate with the Christian women or even to read the Bible with them. Frank read some verses in Proverbs to reinforce the rule: " 'For the lips of a strange woman drip as a honeycomb, and her mouth is smoother than oil: But her end is bitter as wormwood, sharp as a two-edged sword. Her feet go down to death; her steps take hold on hell.' Heavy scripture," Frank muttered.

I was curious. Frank has been at the Foundation for three years. Had he never had a date? He was a handsome man.

He tried to smile—a quick man-to-man glance—but his eyes were full of bitter experience, dark with wormwood. "Most women," he sneered, "are tramps. They're evil."

Later I spoke to Richard, a gangling former songwriter and reader of poetry. Now that he has been saved, the works of his favorites, people like Dylan Thomas, strike him as "trash." "Anything outside the Word of God is a lie and it's a waste of time to listen to lies," he said.

Jim, a frail, watery-eyed Christian, had come to California "to take a lot of acid in the mountains" because—here he laughed at his own stupidity—he thought he would find God there. Somehow he ended up in the city, where he was arrested for fuddled loitering. Shortly thereafter, he was born again.

Syll, a big, handsome black man, is a star at testimony time. He hated whites, thought black was beautiful, and, says he, ran guns for "the Black Nationalists." Now he works for his people by "bringing the Gospel of the Lord Jesus Christ to them." His testimony stuck with me, and when I saw the Alamo house, the word *plantation* occurred to me. Much of the money used to build that house came from outside donations: gifts, presumably, from the kind of people who rejoiced that men like Syll had broken their spirit before the Lord.

Even more lucrative, perhaps, were the former addicts who cold-turkeyed with Jesus. And while I was to meet a few out-and-out addicts, the majority of the people I met seemed not to have or have had serious drug problems. Every man or woman who had ever dropped a pill or toked a joint seemed anxious to represent himself as a former junkie.

A man I'll call Allen made much of his drug habit. He was a slight, nervous man of twenty-two who bit his fingernails as close to the quick as possible but still managed to get dirt under them. His face was literally corrugated with a case of acne that could only have been the result of diligent neglect.

"Before I was saved . . . I took a lot of dope all the time and . . . got arrested a lot . . . mostly for drinking and taking dope and fighting. . . ." Allen told me that his mother had been saved and that she loved the Foundation.

A week later, out of curiosity, I visited Allen's mother in the low-rent flatlands of Los Angeles. Like her son, she was slight and nervous. There was a Bible on the coffee table, and in the back hall, pinned to the wall, there was a blowup-sized poster of Allen in his army uniform looking clear-skinned and patriotic.

We talked about the Foundation and the work of the Alamos for a few minutes, and I asked her how long Allen had been at the church.

"About a year and a half," she said, and her voice quavered strangely. "He . . . he went up there a few days before Christmas, and he called. . . ." Here, to my intense and sympathetic discomfort, the woman burst into tears. "He called and said he wouldn't be ho . . . ho . . . home. . . ." She took a tissue from her purse, wiped her eyes, and put the spent Kleenex beside her on the sofa.

I changed the subject. "In Allen's testimony, he said he did a lot of dope."

"Yes, it was dope. It had to be dope. He came home one night and he had a gadget with a feather on it . . . you take it and hold cigarettes with it? I can't remember what he called it."

"A roach clip?"

"That's it! A roach clip. Stupid thing. He was real gay and happy and he told me that he had been drinking wine. Sally, his girlfriend, told me he had been smoking marijuana, too."

Shortly after this confrontation, Allen turned away from his drug-crazed life on Sunset Strip and was saved. Sally joined the Foundation some time later, by her own admission to be near Allen. "A few weeks later I drove up to see them. I asked Allen, 'Where's Sally?' He said, 'She split. I don't want to talk about it. I'm all through with her. Don't ever mention her to me again. She was saved and she walked out on God. It's just like . . . *nailing Christ to the cross again!*'

"I said," Allen's mother continued, " 'Oh, Allen, you're sick. She didn't want to stay up here and sleep in a sleeping bag on the floor and you think she's nailing Christ to the cross. My God, you're mad.' "

In a later conversation, Sally told Allen's mother: "I went up there to see if I could be near Allen, but they wouldn't let me near him. We had to sit on opposite sides of the church. I couldn't stand it anymore, so I left." Allen's mother was crying again. She blew her nose and dropped the Kleenex beside the others on the sofa. "Sally said, 'I love Allen and I always will but I know he'll never speak to me again.' "

Not too long ago a well-dressed black man appeared at the door and told Allen's mother he was doing a survey about the Alamo Foundation. He expressed great surprise that he was speaking to a woman whose son was actually there.

"Was this man Ted Patrick?"

"No. I saw him in the papers. It wasn't him. I don't want to be involved. All these kidnappings."

The black man, who was not Ted Patrick, asked her, "How do they run that Foundation? Do you mean to tell me that they can have that home and buy all that property from that little thrift shop they run on Hollywood and Vine? You're a brilliant woman, you know as sure as we're both standing on this porch that they couldn't possibly make any money in that little store. The rent would be enormous."

"He was a very smart man," Allen's mother said. "And he was dead against the Foundation. He said: 'I've got so many many mothers and fathers and—' "

But Allen's mother cut him off. "My son wouldn't appreciate it for me to join anything like that," she said. The tears were flowing again, and she took a moment to wipe her eyes.

"I love my son very much and I give Tony and Susan credit for being, for being able . . ." She found herself choking on the words and had to start over. "For being able to go to Hollywood and walk out and preach Jesus to these children, drug addicts. . . ." There was an uncomfortable silence. Finally: "It's just so sad. Even Jesus, when he was dying on the cross, he told one of the Apostles, 'Take care of my mother.' Even when he was dying. Oh . . . oh my God, I must have done something wrong."

I tried to assure her that that wasn't the case and left her sitting on the sofa in a sad little nest of moist tissues.

Whether the black man at the door was Ted Patrick or not—and Patrick maintains that he has so many parental requests for deprogrammings that he has no need to recruit additional work— the fact is that the people who pay his expenses are broken-hearted parents who feel, with some justification, that they have been trespassed upon. Their children will not come home from most of the new cults— from places like the Alamo Foundation, from the Children of God Colonies, from Love Israel's Commune in Seattle, or from their own apartments once they have joined Hannah Lowe's New Testament Missionary Fellowship in New York.

After years of love and mistakes, of dental bills and tears, the sons and daughters of FOC parents will not, in many cases, so much as have dinner with their fathers and mothers. If they do, they bring a scowling older Christian with them. Some parents have been told to drop to their knees and repent before the children will embrace them. William Rambur's daughter Kay told him, he says, that she would murder him if her leaders told her it was necessary.

So the parents come to Patrick and to deprogrammers Mrs. George Meese, a San Diego grocer's wife, and William Rambur, Lt. Commander USN (ret.), now an industrial arts teacher in a high school near San Diego. When the loose-knit organization formed, about two years ago, it was focused on the activities of a mysterious Apocalyptic Christian organization called the Children of God, which was scooping up San Diego young with such terrifying frequency that, the deprogrammers felt, it could only have been the result of hypnotism. A Los Angeles television show and a later network show about the group garnered new recruits nationwide.

Mrs. Meese's daughter joined the Children for one evening until her mother marched in and "rescued" her. Mr. Rambur's daughter now lives in a Children commune and does not communicate with her father. Ted Patrick's fourteen-year-old son was approached by the evangelical Children on a San Diego beach.

In 1971, Patrick helped to organize a Committee to Free Our Sons and Daughters from the Children of God (FREE-COG). He drew up a legal complaint and submitted it to State Attorney General Evelle Younger, who refused to act. In search of proof of his accusations of hypnotism, brainwashing, and financial fraud, he and the parents of a young Children of God man swept down on a southwestern colony for a rescue. The deprogramming took only a few hours. Other rescues followed. Authorities on both coasts refused to take legal action against what the Children called kidnapping. Because parents were involved, police tended to look on the events as family squabbles not worth prosecuting—from either side.

Working out of San Diego, Patrick and Mrs. Meese collected data from all over the country on the Children of God. The majority of the claimed successful deprogramming subjects are former Children, and Patrick earned his nickname, "Black Lightning," from the sect. Largely because of FREE-COG pressure, the Children of God virtually moved out of California and Texas, two of their most fruitful recruiting grounds. They adopted a low profile and swept across the Midwest, establishing nomadic colonies, and eventually reached into England, Ireland, and West Germany.

Emboldened by success—which Patrick cites as proof of the righteousness of his cause—FREE-COG, for all intents and purposes, became FOC: Free our Children—from *all* religious cults practicing what Patrick calls "mind control." In addition to the Christian groups, he has also moved against disciples of Eastern mystics, notably the Hare Krishna people.

A typical deprogramming, reproduced from the statements of Patrick, Meese, and Rambur, as well as newspaper accounts, may last anywhere from several hours to fourteen days. Patrick claims—and the sects refute this—that he is not involved in the "kidnapping." The parents ask their children out to dinner and try to talk about pleasant subjects. Afterward, instead of driving back to the commune or apartment, the young people are taken to a motel room—Patrick likes the Royal Inn Motel in Chula Vista, though at least two other motels have been frequently used, notably one near Masontown, Pennsylvania.

"The only thing that might seem a little harsh," William Rambur says, "is that we don't allow them to run away. If we did that, there would be no point in getting them there in the first place." The parents may talk to the children first, then Mrs. Meese or Mr. Patrick. Generally the deprogrammers hear "programmed" replies: "You are devils; I want to go back and serve the Lord with Tony and Sue." Patrick gets rough, verbally. He tells the devout young that they are mentally incompetent, that they are being duped and defrauded, that they are possessed by devils and that they hate their parents. He will sling insults about the sect's leaders. An emotional scene develops.

The young person may then be asked to pray with the deprogrammers. Certain Bible passages will be discussed and evidence of twisted interpretation will be pointed out. A taped message from a deprogrammed sect member may be played. More insults and accusations may be hurled until an excruciating emotional peak is reached.

At this point someone—a calming, loving influence— may read a selected Bible verse: something perhaps from Corinthians about love and kindness and compassion. The subject "breaks," and may burst into tears or rush to embrace his parents. In Patrick's terms, the spell has been broken.

"That 'break' is a harsh word," William Rambur says. "I would prefer to think of it as an awakening."

The religious sects charge that Patrick is guilty of his own accusation: brainwashing. The impossibly complicated thing about this word is that no one seems to know exactly what it means. It was originally a term invented by a Western journalist to describe what happened to American POWs during the Korean War. The Chinese communists called it "thought re-education." The processes involved, according to psychologist Nathan Adler, are similar, if not identical, to those in religious conversion and the kind of personality reorganization that takes place in such organizations as Synanon or Alcoholics Anonymous. Or army basic training, for that matter.

There is always the theme of death and rebirth. Alamoites, of course, are "born-again Christians." In deprogramming, the devout young are made to feel that they are social nullities unable to live normal lives in "the World," and that, in reference to actual human beings, they are nonpersons: walking dead.

Biff Alexander, twenty-four, a former Alamo-ite, deprogrammed in three days during October 1972, describes his breaking sensation this way: "It's as though my whole life passed before me . . . I began to try to recount the events of my two and a half years at the Foundation and at one point I just . . . it's as though a miracle happened and I felt so free. Because I realized that I had been deceived, and I reached out my arms to the side, just like wings, and I flapped my arms. I said 'I feel so free, I could fly away.' "

A second important part of the brainwashing/conversion process is the dynamics of the group involved. Humiliation and degradation are common devices. The deprogrammers apply it mentally and emotionally; the Alamos physically: that is, born-again Christians must sleep on the floor, shit in a disgusting stink-hole of a bathroom, and eat what is often literal garbage salvaged from the back of grocery stores. The group then provides models for emulation, i.e., Tony and Susan Alamo. And Ted Patrick. Biff Alexander is now heavily involved in deprogramming activities.

Indeed, out of the contexts of faith and fraud, there is little difference between the activities of the Alamos and Ted Patrick. An important exception: deprogramming subjects are sometimes, it is alleged, brought to the motels and are admittedly not allowed to leave.

There have reportedly been six Patrick raids on the Alamo Foundation. Not all have been as successful as the Biff Alexander affair. Patty Thorpe, a woman of twenty-three, was holding her three-year-old daughter, Britt, and talking to her parents in the Alamo Foundation parking lot one crisp Sunday in October 1972. She heard her mother say, "Okay, now grab her." Her brother and a family friend shoved her into the backseat of the car, ripping her dress. They sped to a Saugus parking lot where they met another car. Britt was transferred to the second car. About nine that night, the new model Cadillac arrived at the Royal Inn in Chula Vista.

In a report she wrote some time later, Patty claimed that Mrs. Meese and her daughter told her that she had been deceived, that the Alamos were only using her for her money, and that she was incapable of making her own decisions. Her parents said they were worried about her. She was not allowed to use the phone or leave.

The next day Ted Patrick arrived, introducing himself as a man of God. He started quietly but soon became abrasive, once allegedly telling Patty that she ought to "check into Camarillo [a mental hospital] and weave baskets and string beads for a while." He called Susan Alamo a witch and claimed that she had called Patty a "no-good." The Alamos, he said, taught hate and were only in it for the money. When Patty went to the bathroom, she could hear the deprogrammers discussing tactics.

Patrick had a tape recorder and tried to make her say "slanderous things about the Alamos." At night people slept on a mattress by the door so she could not escape. Despite constant pleas, she was not allowed to see her daughter. The "torture sessions," as Patty called them, lasted up to fourteen hours a day. Patrick continued to insist, she said, "that the Alamos were starving us, that we were forced to live like pigs in deplorable conditions, that we lived in filth, never bathed, never washed our hair; but I knew none of these things were true.

"Things became really intense. They kept hurling accusations at me, degrading me, six to twelve at a time, standing over me, always telling me that I was possessed by the devil. . . ."

Mrs. Meese maintains that the conversations were milder, the sessions shorter, and that there were only a few people in the room at any one time.

After ten and a half days, Patty was allowed to go to her brother's house, where she was reunited with her baby. She was under strict supervision, but, two days later, in a lax moment, she escaped, hailed a cab, and went straight back to Saugus. "I believe," she wrote, "that Ted Patrick actually thinks he has been appointed by God to force his religious and political beliefs on all people of every faith, even if it means violence or even murder."

"**G**od," Ted Patrick told me evenly, "is on our side." We were sitting in the kitchen of his modest tract home just south of San Diego. On Holy Thursday, a school holiday, the house was filled with children, both Patrick's and others who had spent the night. Plastic runners protected the carpets in heavy-traffic areas. A large Bible filled with paper markers sat on a sofa-side table, and, in Patrick's study, in the place of honor above the desk, an official portrait of Ronald Reagan blessed the room.

Until last year, Patrick had worked as a social services consultant for the governor. It was a $105-a-month job he got in part because of his 1965 efforts to see that the Watts riots didn't spread to San Diego. He is a forceful man, and if he is not so short and stout as some young Christians have described, neither is he the image of the black savior some parents have talked about. The strongest impression I got from him was that of a physical certitude.

Virtually all of the deprogrammings Patrick has dealt with have involved white parents and children, a fact Susan Alamo makes use of in her characterization of him as an "Uncle Tom." It is true that parents of "rescued" children have referred to him as "wonderful" and "a savior." He is quick-witted. He is tough. And, as some would have it, he is a "hit man for the PTA."

It has been charged that Patrick makes use of his former position to impress parents and convince them the government is behind him. In our conversation on Holy Thursday, however, he seemed to have little use for politicians. "The parents send letters to the U.S. Attorney, to senators, to congressmen, but everyone is afraid of it. They're afraid to stand up for what is right. And this is your problem. Our leaders are your problem. Your government is your problem."

Aside from the foreboding dangers of the new cults, Patrick also sees a strong political reason to stop them as

quickly and as coldly and as decisively as possible. It is a
reason perhaps more rapidly perceived in this conservative
area of California. "We're fighting against a movement that
is sweeping the nation. It's sweeping the world. It makes
you sick. You learn about a new group every day. If you
knew half as much—one-eighth as much—as we know
about this, you'd be frightened for the nation. We got books;
we got everything. I mean these were written two thousand
years ago by Plato. Ah, he talked about being able to live in
a nation without police, without guns, it's . . . it can be done
. . . it's *mind control*. We *know* about Russia, we know about
their ESP program. They're so far ahead of us it isn't even
funny. As an example, when the space program first started,
Russia was ahead of the United States, and then, all of a
sudden, it ceased to be."

Patrick thinks that the Russians have taken their money
out of space and poured it into psycho-political experimen-
tation. "Their ESP program: They have the largest budget
in the world. It's already been tested. *You can control a man's
mind one thousand miles away.* . . . "

As I understood Patrick, he was telling me that the Jesus
sects were the first tentacles of a new strategy devised by the
international communist conspiracy. And because so few
see the danger, because our leaders are so weak, the responsibility of saving America from Jesus-tainted communist
mind control has fallen on Ted Patrick's willing and patriotic shoulders. He has been working—often seven days a
week, sometimes around the clock, accepting only expense
money, logging over three hundred thousand air miles in
the last six months—to keep America free.

There is a tendency to regard the increasingly bizarre
events of the holy conflict as an amusing diversion, something like toting up the bodies in a Mafia war. But the
people primarily involved, the parents and children, are not
criminals, and with the mounting number of confronta-
tions, there is the distinct and bloody possibility of a disaster neither side wants. Both groups feel that they have God
on their side. Both know the others are possessed of devils.
Chances are great that a member of either group, cornered

or trapped by people whom he feels are capable of murder, may react with mortal violence.

The Jesus People have launched an unorganized legal campaign to stop Patrick. Daniel Voll, twenty-two, a member of the East Coast's New Testament Missionary Fellowship, filed assault charges against Patrick on February twenty-fifth. He alleges that his father, aided and encouraged by Patrick, grabbed him on a New York street and tried to force him into a car, dislocating his finger in the process. The Children of God have filed a $1.1 million libel suit against Patrick. Joel Mandelkorn, twenty-two, of the Children of God, filed a $200,000 damage suit against various deprogrammers after he was "rescued" and put through several vigorous sessions.

Mike Pancer, the American Civil Liberties Union lawyer working on the Patty Thorpe case for the Alamos, generally handles criminal law in his private practice. He is an efficient, precisely spoken young attorney of no conspicuous religious bent. There is very little, in fact, that Pancer seems sure of beyond the shadow of a doubt. But he is deeply committed to a certain principle: "Whenever people start to enforce their ideas on others, when one person's tactics are illegal, in violation of the civil liberties of the others involved, you have to take a stand against them. You have to protect the free choice of the individual involved.

"People may pick a very stupid way of life to lead, or believe in a stupid set of ideals—I'm sure Republicans think Democrats are stupid—but they have their rights. It's really important to identify the principle that's involved, which is coercive activity—the use of force—by one of the parties involved."

On May 5, 1973, Esther Diquattro, thirty-one, a Columbia Teacher's College secretary and member of the New Testament Missionary Fellowship, was abducted during a prayer meeting near the Columbia campus. Two days later, her husband and Ted Patrick were arrested by Briston, Pennsylvania, township police and charged with second-degree kidnapping, conspiracy to kidnap, unlawful imprisonment, and assault. Patrick pleaded not guilty and is currently free on a $5,000 bond.

After a lunch of bread and soup, Frank and I stopped off into the prayer room for a few hours. I asked about the sign on the door: Why should we pray for Susie's health? In sepulchral tones Frank told me that she had "terminal cancer." We babbled in tongues for an hour or so with about ten other Christians. Someone began shouting, "Heal Susie, oh God, heal her." Others shouted along.

Suddenly the prayer room seemed to erupt with emotion. It started as a plea, "heal Susie," and ended as a demand, "heal her God." A man on my right held his face in his hands and sobbed. I felt a lump growing in my throat as I chanted along. Somewhere, back in an objective corner of my mind, I remembered aged friends of my grandparents: folks who knew the end was near. Minds fixed on the glories of heaven, they withered and died.

Psychologists are familiar with this tendency on the part of the ill to confuse their bodies with the cosmos and their own death with the end of the world. Susan Alamo, I was to learn later, had little use for this kind of worldly and irreligious blather.

Later Frank and I sat in a booth and read another tract by Tony Alamo. I was surprised to see my teacher close his eyes and ask God to "burn the words upon our hearts"—the same blessing he had lavished on the Bible. But as Richard had told me in an answer to a question, there has never been a time when Tony or Susan were wrong, "because, their judgment is the Word of God and God is not wrong."

Frank read aloud. Some highlights from the tract: "I had no respect for women at all. Every one I encountered was worse than the one before. I actually hated them and decided for some reason that I had been put here to punish them because they were so evil. All my former friends break up now when they see little five-foot-two Susan bossing me around, and believe me, I love it."

Tony's routine, in the old days, was to take "complete unknowns" and "promote them into big stars." He liked limousines and enjoyed having an entourage of "yes men," people, apparently, who treated his orders as if they were the word of God. It was during one of his most outrageous "promotional extravaganzas" that he met Jesus of Nazareth. In the midst of an important business meeting, in which Tony was going to have to borrow money, his ears went completely deaf. People were speaking but Tony only saw their mouths moving. "Suddenly I heard a voice: a voice that came from every direction." It told Tony, "I am the Lord thy God. Stand up on your feet and tell the people in this room Jesus Christ is coming back to earth, or thou shalt surely die."

Tony struggled against the voice. He tried to excuse himself, claiming sudden illness. But God would not allow this and began playing with Tony's soul "like a yo-yo." He yanked it half out of the body, then put it back. "No, God, no," Tony screamed. "Please don't kill me. . . . I'll tell them, I'll tell them.

"I know you won't believe me," he said, "but Jesus Christ is coming back to earth again." No one said anything. It was a weak effort, and once again God yanked Tony's soul.

"Repent," he screamed. "Jesus is coming." He lurched about the room, knocking spindles from desks and backing people against the walls. The attorney Tony had come to see yelled, "Get him out of here, he's nuts."

Tony could no longer work because he was "afraid that God would come down on me in front of people." He was broke, at the nadir of his career. His former friends thought he had cracked up, and the God of Wrath gave him visions of a burning hell. One day, alone in the rain, he walked into a restaurant where Susan was sitting. Though they had met one another casually, Susan had generally refused to speak to him. "I always knew there was something different about her." He sat at her table, and her first words were, "Tony, do you know that the Lord Jesus Christ is coming back to earth again?" Tony jumped up and knocked all the silverware off the table.

"How do you know?" he demanded. "Did God come and tell you too?"

Tony subsequently joined one of Susan's small Bible classes, and presently "God spoke to Susie's heart in a very supernatural way," and they were married. God let Tony do one more big promotion so nobody would think that he was crazy, but Susan prayed for him to go broke and God obliged. "She wanted to go out into the street and bring the Bible to the hippies." Against Tony's better judgment.

The Jesus Movement, Tony averred, began one Saturday night in Hollywood when he and Susan started handing out tracts. It was not the product of "some youth with psychedelic lights flashing in his head." In the penultimate and most powerful paragraph, Tony says, "the price has been high. Oh my God, so high. Higher than human flesh wants to pay. . . . I am glad that the Lion of the Tribe of Juda, the eternal keeper of the Lamb's book of Life, knows when and how the Jesus Movement began and that he saw my sweetheart as she went into the street with cancer eating through her body and took the Gospel to the hippies."

Frank looked up from his reading. "A lot of people got saved on account of this tract," he said. I told him that I didn't doubt it and kept to myself some further information about the business conference in which Tony met Jesus.

His unknown at the time was a singer-composer named Bobby Jameson. Tony had taken out ads in the music trade papers touting Bobby as the star of the century. At the conference, a very important one, Jameson says that Alamo leapt to his feet and shrieked to the man behind the desk, "You must give him [Jameson] all your money because he is Jesus Christ and if you don't he'll point his finger at you and you will die."

Billboard magazine claims that the bill for the Alamo-Jameson ads is still an unpaid account—$14,000 worth.

A week after I left the Foundation, I was back in one of the booths, talking to Tony and Susan Alamo. It wasn't the way I had planned it. "The press only tells one half of the story," Tony was saying. "If you want a story, you want the A side and the B side."

My original scheme had been to visit the Alamos in their controversial house. Biff Alexander, the deprogrammed

Alamo-ite who claimed to have been inside many times, told me what to expect: "three bathrooms. Three brand-new bathrooms with bath and shower facilities. On the lower level there's an office, about twenty feet by forty feet and it's got a fireplace in it. They've got a huge living room and a small section off to the end where they have a big grand piano. There's a dining room with a chandelier. And a kitchen and then two large bedrooms, say fifteen feet by twenty feet or bigger, and closets that are immense, running three-quarters of the length of the room." Alexander said that the older overseers sometimes stay at the house upward to a week at a time, "answering the phones for them, catering to them, and so forth."

According to Alexander, "Tony was instrumental in making the plans for the house, but one of the guys there who had some experience really drew up the plans, and I think it took two guys along with one of the county engineers, who was a tremendous amount of help." Alexander swears, "with God as my witness," that while helping to build the house, "we . . . got up at five in the morning every morning and we slept on the floor there with what blankets we could muster up and it was filthy. We wouldn't get to go home and wash every night . . . people who were really needed were forbidden to go to services . . . because that house had to be built." Alexander says he spent over a month, working twenty hours a day, on the house.

"A lot of times I would think, How could Tony and Susan have so much and we have so little? We were told that when such thoughts come to our minds to say, 'The blood of Jesus is upon you Satan' and 'Get thee behind me, Satan' . . . that that was an accusation brought by the devil."

Two of the Foundation men, however, couldn't quite get Satan out of their minds and brought this accusation to Tony. According to Alexander, Tony told them that a woman of the Lord should be dressed in fine clothes, linen, and silk. "As far as I'm concerned," Alexander remembers him saying, "the Bible says that Elders who do well are worthy . . . you should have built twice the size of the house you built for us. . . ." The two men were asked to leave the Foundation.

It is Tony who seems to be the disciplinarian, probably because he deals with the men, who are more numerous and more troublesome. "One time Tony got so mad," Alexander says, "that people were using too much toilet paper, so toilet paper wasn't put on the finance list that week . . . then another time he had the water shut off [on property number two where the women and children live] and neglected really getting it repaired quickly enough and the littlest babies and the women had to defecate in buckets and we actually had to bury it. . . ."

When I talked to Tony Alamo, he was wearing expensive cowboy-styled boots and slacks. Even in the church he wore dark glasses, and this, combined with a paunch he has developed since his crooning days, gave him the unfortunate appearance of the stereotypical nasty southern sheriff.

I had set the interview up the day before and driven up to Saugus that afternoon, calling the Alamos from a nearby phone booth, telling them I would be right up.

"Meet us at the Foundation," Susan Alamo said.

"I'll save you the drive. I'm about two minutes away."

"We're on our way over to the church now," she said breezily. "Just meet us there."

I had very little desire to meet her there since I had left under unpleasant circumstances—consigned to hell, actually—not a week before. Still, I drove up there and arrived the same time as the Alamos' Cadillac. There is probably some significance in the fact that not one of the people I spoke to (or saw) in my second visit recognized me. I was wearing different clothes, but probably more to the point, I was talking with Tony and Sue.

Susan Alamo was wearing slacks and a frilly blouse. Her hair was dyed stark white, Southern California style. She spoke with conviction, in a voice that might be called lilting were it a bit less pointed. She gave the impression of "just talking sense." When we agreed, she had the disconcerting habit of cutting in on the end of the sentence to say, "uuhv course," as if to suggest I might be the slightest bit dim, stating such an obvious point. She did most of the speaking, with Tony lounging at the far end of the booth, looking both wary and bored.

Susan was talking about Ted Patrick. "Tim, the man is criminally insane. He is taking people and *abducting* them because he doesn't agree with them. He uses force on them. My God, it won't be long before someone is murdered. Because he can't compete in the marketplace of ideas. . . ."

"You deny his charges of kidnapping and brainwashing?"

"Tim, that is such nonsense I wouldn't know where to begin to answer that. Why, Patty Thorpe here is in fear for her life because of that man."

Later, on the subject of the marketplace of ideas, I asked, "Is it true Tony screens the reading material?"

"Well, of course he screens it," Susan said quickly. "For heaven's sake, we wouldn't have a bunch of pornography passing around in here. Or we wouldn't have books advocating Devil worship . . ."

In contrast to Ted Patrick's muscular brand of argument, Susan Alamo seemed quicker, more nimble. She bobbed and weaved, ducking in and out of corners, taking a hard question on the chin only to come back with an apt Biblical quote. In the few times her answers were without substance, she had the knack of insisting on them passionately. She was clearly the spiritual leader. Tony sat silently; I suspected he had heard much of this before.

Susan had been born in Southern California, and, at the age of five, she had had a vision. "I was a little child." Here her voice lost its glibness. I gathered this was something she didn't often speak about, because for once, there was no practiced quality to her words, and she hesitated, waiting, I thought, for the most precise and honest descriptions to occur to her. "I saw Christ as he was coming back to earth again." She became, for a stunning moment, a wistful child: "I saw him in a beautiful bright red robe, long hair flowing in the wind and . . . his eyes were . . . very big and . . . very black. That's the one thing I remember most distinctly. That his eyes were big." Suddenly she became the Susan Alamo that deals with accusations. "It disturbed my family and they took me to doctors and the doctors said that they felt that it was because I had lost my father when I was two and a half years old and evidently someone had shown me photographs or talked to me about Christ and that he," she hesitated, "he had become a father image." A pause. "Which, of course, wasn't true." Her common sense voice: "Wasn't true at all."

She had met Tony just as the tract said. He joined her Bible class: one of about twenty-five. There was a romance. They were married. Susan wanted to preach to the hippies. One night a dealer named Ed, who lived in "an insidious crash pad right in the heart of Hollywood," called from jail wondering if the Alamos could bail him out. God told Susan to do it.

Ed became a Christian. He and some friends asked the Alamos to "come over to the dope den and talk to the kids down there." Susan said, "We told them that they had souls that were created by God and that they were destroying their minds, their souls, and their bodies. Everything they were doing was a sin, it was destruction. We said, 'You know the kinds of lives you are leading. Where can the next stop be: a marble slab, the prison yard, a mental institution? How far can you go like this?'

"We asked to see the hands of those that believed what we said, and all of them raised their hands and . . . so I looked at Tony and said, 'My God, where do we go from here? We just inherited a dope den full of hippies.'"

The first church was in the Dope Den. The "kids" flushed all the dope down the toilet and vacuumed the rugs. Soon it was too crowded. Tony and Susan begged the churches to take the born-again hippies, but it was no dice. Prejudice, Susan feels, was behind the refusal: too many were long-haired or black. They moved to a bigger building on Crescent Heights Boulevard. "Tony and I were going to the back doors of the bakeries and markets begging for food."

As Biff Alexander remembers it, the Alamos called the markets, and the brothers drove down to pick up spoiled food. "Is that feeding the hungry or is it feeding garbage?" he asked angrily. But as Susan Alamo was to say in a different context, she never met anyone who left a church without having a destructive attitude toward it. As a general rule, that seems to be true, and perhaps Biff Alexander's testimony should be tempered with that knowledge.

When Crescent Heights got too crowded in late 1969, the Alamos scraped $2,000 together and put a down payment on the old Wilson Cafe in Saugus, situated on seven-and-a-half acres of land. They acquired property number two, for the women's and children's dorms, soon thereafter. They now own both. The house, on five prime acres, was built during most of 1972. Men from the Foundation had built a needed set of bleachers for the high school, and the local jaycees had paid them back by pouring the cement for the foundation of a house in which none of them would live. Much of the lumber was donated, Susan says.

Biff Alexander says that Tony Alamo personally told him that the president of a Santa Clarita bank estimated the worth of the house at $100,000. Susan says they borrowed on it to make a down payment on some other property, and that, because they didn't fully own it, they could only get $20,000.

There is, in addition, a 160-acre ranch under lease with option to buy. It houses a small cattle ranch and, until recently, about two thousand laying chickens.

In a previous call to the local chamber of commerce, I learned that prices for nearby plots of land ranged from about $3,000 an acre to almost $9,000. I wondered where the finances came from.

Susan mentioned donations: an anonymous Newhall man had given $40,000. Some fundamentalist churches gave them money, as their missionary work. Virtually no money came from the people in the church, she implied, though Biff Alexander, a former finance overseer, says everyone was "pressured" to give to the Foundation. Tony, he said, suggested Biff turn a small trust fund—about $500—over to the Lord, in the keeping of Tony Alamo.

"Tim," Susan said, "you sit here until that bus comes in, and every hippie that comes in here holding money that gets off, I will eat every ounce of money he donates, if you will eat his shoes."

It sounded like a bad deal to me, and I told her so. "Anyway, what I'm trying to get at is the total worth of the Foundation, which I understand is a nonprofit California corporation."

"What is the net worth of the Catholic Church?" Tony shot back. "Why don't you come out and pick grapes with us. I want you dragging cotton bags!"

I directed my questions to Susan.

"Do most of your finances come from the Fundamentalist churches?"

"A lot of them, yes."

"The rest from donations?"

"From citizens . . . citizens' groups." She mentioned a Christian businessman's group in Orange County. In addition, there were proceeds from speaking engagements, and money from the sale of the Tony and Susan Alamo Big Band Gospel Sound Records.

"What are the names of some of the churches that pay—"

"I'm not going to tell you that, Tim, 'cause that's putting my business on the street. . . ."

"Well, that leaves a substantial mystery as to where—"

"If it's a mystery, then it's a mystery."

The conversation was getting heated and was leading nowhere. I changed the subject, asking Tony if he distrusted the press because he manipulated it so well at one time.

"Oh, those days," he said, describing a weary parabola with his right hand. "No, I was just shocked to find out that anybody would ever . . ."

Susan finished the sentence for him. "That they can't tell the truth!"

"That they can't tell the truth and not only that but . . ."

"They're looking for sensationalism, and if it isn't there, they're going to create it."

"The biggest story," Tony said, "is the *truth*. If they'd go out and tell the truth, that'd be the most sensational story that ever happened."

Later I made a call to the Los Angeles County Regional Planning Office in which I learned that the population of the Saugus-Newhall fringelands is sixty thousand and was projected to triple by 1990. Land prices could be expected to do the same. Biff Alexander had told me that the Alamos said that if they were to die, everyone would share in the church, but that they had never signed any papers to that effect. I reflected that if Susan Alamo were to pass on first . . . that would leave Tony Alamo—the man who used to take "complete unknowns" to stardom, who likes Cadillacs and "yes men," who met Jesus the Nazarene while borrowing money, who joined Susan's small Bible class when things were simpler, who allegedly skipped out on a $14,000 bill after being Saved—the pastor of a very wealthy church.

Holy Saturday evening at the Alamo Foundation: a tomato stuffed with beans for dinner, a brief chant in the ratbox, followed by some Bible study and a course in political science.

The communists, I learned, were harbingers of the Apocalypse: the very chaos the Bible prophesied for the last days. Frank had looked into politics "pretty deep below the surface." While the rest of us have been treading water, trying to assimilate a mass of conflicting facts and opinions, Frank told me that he had seen clear to the slimy bottom. A nice lady from the John Birch Society—very interested in the Bible—occasionally stops in on Monday afternoons to give a slide show and a talk.

The conspiracy, as Frank related it to me, was this: A group of international bankers got Nixon—a sympathetic dupe—elected so that he would continue the war and decimate America's great storehouse of young soldiers. Those that weren't killed would be rendered useless by heroin. With the nation teetering weakly on its depleted base, the commies could march right in and take over.

In the 1972 election, all the Christians at the Foundation had registered and voted for John Schmitz, who took the injured George Wallace's spot on the American Independent slate. "He was the one who came closest to what the Bible says," Frank informed me. I got the impression that,

in the end, Frank didn't think all this made too much difference anyway, what with the end of the world just around
the corner. He seemed resigned to imminent communist
takeover; and though he didn't say it, I think he felt the Fall
of America and the End of the World would likely happen
simultaneously.

I wondered how Frank had gotten to the bottom of
things—like the real reason for the Vietnam War—when, as
I had noticed, there was only the Bible to read. No Congres-
sional reports, no Washington newsletters, no newspapers,
no magazines. Aside from the speaker in the bathroom, the
only electronic device in the place was a grandpa's antique
tube-type record console that played scratchy Gospel records at 78 revolutions per minute.

Frank told me that he read certain carefully selected
books. "Tony screens our reading," he said offhandedly.

"Tony censors our reading?" I exploded.

"He just makes sure that what we read is the same as
what's in the Bible," Frank replied reasonably.

"He censors our reading?" I repeated, incredulous.

"We wouldn't want to have a lot of pornography up here,
you know."

I said I guessed that we wouldn't and asked Frank which
books Tony found in accord with the Bible. Two titles that
came up were *None Dare Call It Treason,* all about communist
spies in the very highest echelons of our government, and
None Dare Call It Conspiracy, concerning itself with overwhelming evidence of a massive secret plot on the part of
international financiers and politicos to overthrow the government of the United States of America. The book makes
the point that there have been conspiracies throughout history that have overturned governments; but that recently
there has been a very clever and subtle campaign to invali-
date the *word* itself. Today, even when one presents irrefut-
able evidence to the typical American dupe, he is likely to
be treated as an out-and-out raving paranoid crazy.

After another bout with the Bible, Frank told me that as
overseer, he had to prepare for the coming Easter sunrise
service. I wasn't to worry though, he'd find me another

older Christian straight away. He just didn't want me wandering around while he looked. "Stand right there," he commanded.

Since the beginning, I had been beset with short Christians. I am not an outsized man: I stand six foot one at the most. But I estimated neither my witness nor teacher had been over five foot six, a fact of no special significance in itself except that it made our teacher-pupil relationships somewhat awkward. This last of my Christians was by far the smallest. His name, fittingly enough, was Tiny.

Frank disappeared to his duties as I mentally sized up Tiny. Intensely sparrowlike, he looked like the kind of teenager who handed out towels to the high school basketball team and was forever being described as having "a lotta school spirit." He had a bright, chirrupy voice which had the same effect on my teeth as the sound of crushed Styrofoam.

Tiny pegged me straight off as a chronic doper with a bad wet dream problem. "I used to sit around and do dope, just like you," he said. "Boy, I never thought I'd be serving the Lord.

"You can give up dope real easy. If your friends don't like it, they're not real friends. If they tell you you're crazy, that's the devil talking through them. The devil is such a liar. You know what he does? He gives you filthy dreams at night and then in the morning he comes and sits on your shoulder and tells you you're evil. See what I mean, see what a liar he is? He's such a liar he—"

"Hey, Tiny," I interrupted, "I think I'll invite a friend to the service. Maybe see if I can get him born again."

Tiny started to object, but I was up and out of the booth, on my way to the phone. He fluttered up beside me, jabbering away about how the devil works through the unsaved.

"Yeah, yeah," I said, dialing.

Cardoso, my outside contact, sounded as if he were in an extraordinarily good mood. "Hey, Bill, I've been born again in the blood and there's going to be an Easter service here tomorrow at five o'clock in the morning. I want you to tell my friend Tim Page to come up."

"Jesus, it's twelve-thirty. He's at some drive-in movie with his wife. He won't be home till late. And he's sure not going to want to get up at three to get out there for any of that shit."

"Witness to him," Tiny whispered.

"Look, Bill, tell him it's an assignment to meet Jesus. An assignment. I'd *enjoy* it if he could be here. I'd be *disappointed* in him if he missed it: Tell him to consider it an assignment."

"Remember," Tiny piped in, "the devil might be working through your friend."

"I'll tell him you sound pretty frantic."

"Praise the Lord."

"I'll tell him to get his ass up there."

"I'd enjoy that."

"Tell him how it felt when God came into your heart when you were Saved," Tiny suggested.

"Who's that?"

"Just my older Christian, Bill. He wants me to tell you that God came into my heart the other day. Hey, didn't Tim just get his Brownie fixed? I'd enjoy it if he brought that one camera up." It had occurred to me that it might look suspicious if Page arrived decked out like a professional photographer.

"I'll tell him."

"Thank you, Jesus."

Later Tiny told me during Bible study that I'd make a better witness when I got more experience. It was about two-thirty, I was exhausted, and my temper was getting short.

"You know," I said, "I got about two hours sleep last night. I think I'll go over there and rest awhile."

Tiny smiled and shook his head. A definite no. "We don't punch a clock around here. We serve the Lord day and night. Sometimes it isn't easy, but it's pretty darn rewarding."

It was about that time when I began thinking of him as *the dwarf.*

"Look, I gotta get some rest." I curled up under a fluo-

rescent light in the back of the church area. Shortly thereafter Tiny was tugging at my sleeve, pulling me reluctantly
out of dreams of food: Visions of gluttony they were, raw
meat orgies. "Thank you, Jesus," I muttered and was inco-
herent for fully three minutes. The place was suddenly
empty but for Tiny, myself, and a Christian guard at the
door. Everyone else had piled into the buses, on their way
to the Alamo house and a nearby field where the services
would be held.

"It's four o'clock," Tiny announced brightly.

"Why," I asked with what I thought was icy self-control,
"did you wake me up? My friend isn't supposed to be here
for another hour."

"I thought we should talk." The dwarf's intention soon
became evident. "Your friend hasn't been saved, has he?"

"No," I said flatly.

"You know the Bible says that Light shall have no Fellowship with Dark. . . ."

"So?"

"Well, your friend is of the Dark. You are of the Light.
See what I mean?"

"No."

"OK." Tiny spelled it out for me. "The devil may be
speaking with his tongue. He may try to tell you you're
crazy. He'll say, 'Why do you want to waste your life up
here?' and it'll be the devil talking. I've seen times when
friends came up and people turned away from God! They
ended up in mental hospitals or the morgue."

"Not me."

This went on for an hour, Page becoming more and more
identified with the Weasel until it began to appear that we
had a date to meet the cloven-footed deceiver himself. At
precisely five, a Volkswagen pulled into the lot. "Remember now," Tiny said, "the devil isn't always the guy with
a tail and a pitchfork."

The car had a big American Society of Press Photogra-
phers sticker on the windshield and I cringed when Page
stepped out into the parking lot hoisting a leather bag containing $4,000 worth of Nikons. Tiny, however, was intent

on spiritual matters, and Page's first sentence confirmed his
Satanic suspicions.

"Bloody fucking five o'clock in the fucking morning," he
grumbled by way of greeting.

"Brother," the guard said, "we're Christian and our ears
are *not* garbage cans."

"Yeah," I said. "Do our ears look like garbage cans,
Page?"

He declined comment, and Tiny smiled a secret dwarf
smile. We piled into the VW and drove five miles to the
Alamo house. I got into an inexplicable witness binge while
Page stared at the road in a pained silence and Tiny beamed
from the backseat.

We were late. The band was hammering away at the
gospel favorites, shivering in their new blue uniforms.
Tony, dressed in a vanilla ice-cream suit, sang all the songs.
He held one leg crooked at the knee, bouncing slightly with
the steady mechanical *thunk* of the drum. His crooner's
voice sounded corroded in the fringeland stillness. Susan
stepped forth to deliver a ringing sermon. She wore a fine,
flowing white dress—Tony's fine lady—that reflected the
subtle colors of the Easter sunrise. Behind her, the hills, for
the first time, looked soft and sweet and untainted. And
Susan looked holy.

"Hallelujah," the brothers and sisters shouted, feeling, I
thought, exalted in the clear desert morning.

And yet, for all this, the house was no more than five
hundred yards away, and the sleek Fleetwood with ALAMO
plates rested in the parking lot. To the rear, there was a
much smaller house, built like a windmill where, I had
heard, select overseers lived. The main house was boxy—
pillared and plantationlike. It was big enough to contain all
that Biff Alexander said it did: immense bedrooms, a piano,
a large home-entertainment console, an office with a fireplace, sinks that worked. It was perched fat on a nearby hill,
there for all to see . . . seeming somehow symbolic to me,
in my exhaustion. But none of the brothers and sisters
shared my interest. They had, after all, seen it all before,
and their minds were focused on Jesus.

Immediately after the service, we drove back toward the
Foundation; Page and I in the front, Tiny once again in the
back. He was twitting on merrily, telling us about politics.
"We are all registered Republicans and voted for John
Schmitz," he said at one point.

Page didn't take the bait, so I couldn't resist asking Tiny
why he didn't vote Republican.

"Schmitz was the Republican. Anyway, the thing—"

"Tiny, Schmitz did not run as a Republican in the presi-
dential campaign."

"He did."

"What was Nixon then?"

Tiny hesitated, perhaps catching a note of challenge in
my tone.

"Oh, Nixon. He was just a loser. You want to know how
he got elected? He became Rockefeller's lawyer and Rockefeller got him elected."

"Rockefeller," I spluttered, genuinely amazed. "Governor Nelson Rockefeller? He got Nixon elected?"

"One of the Rockefellers. Or Rothschilds. They knew
that Nixon would continue the war and deplete . . ."

Tiny took us down under the surface, right to the bottom
causes of the war. Which brought him somehow to the
mansions of heaven and the fires of hell.

"I don't know how hell could be any worse than some of
the things I saw in Vietnam," Page offered, innocently I
think.

Tiny snorted, a short derisive sound. "It's so much worse,
you wouldn't even believe it."

"Were you there?"

"I didn't have to be. I know beyond the shadow of a doubt
that hell is the worst thing there is."

Page, who spent seven painful months in the hospital
after losing half his brain to a mine in some soggy rice
paddy, passed me a look that I read: maybe we could strangle him and no one would be the wiser. The look was not
lost on Tiny who likely began to feel some unholy alliance
between the two of us. He trotted out the vision of hell that
Frank had told me, ending up with the same hoarse croak-
ing effect on "mercy, Lord, mercy."

"I already heard that one," I said.

At this point, Page and I later decided, Tiny had worked himself into a dither that was reaching fast toward panic. I suspected he would have someone to answer to if he lost a soul entrusted to him, especially after the big Easter fandango.

"Your friend," he said sternly, "will have to go home."

"So will I," I added.

"What?"

"I'm going back with my friend."

"You can't do that after you've known God. It's just like pounding another nail into the cross of Christ!"

"No, it's not," I pointed out

"Why do you want to turn your back on God? Why?"

"For one thing, I prefer to sleep in a bed. For another, I came up here to see what your church was like, and you tried to tell me that it says in the Bible that John Schmitz was the Republican candidate for president."

"I didn't say . . . I said . . . you're just using politics, that's what you're doing. Using politics to cop out on God." We were pulling into the parking lot. "You'll go straight to hell," Tiny chirped bitterly.

"I don't think so."

"Where do you think people go when they leave the Foundation? They wind up on a marble slab, in mental institutions. They go to hell."

"Tiny," I said evenly, "we have a serious difference of opinion."

I got out and pulled the seat forward for the dwarf. We faced each other on the gravel beside the Volkswagen. "You are going to hell," he hissed with terrifying intensity, then turned and stalked up the steps of the House of God with the insensate fury of a very small man.

t was still early, before eight, when we reached Page's Los Angeles apartment. He cooked up a mighty breakfast of scrambled eggs, sausages, and a great mound of hashbrowns, which I washed down with a couple of icy Heinekens. There was plenty of time for me to grab a plane back to San Francisco, so we drank a few after-breakfast beers, and Page—an aficionado—offered to take me on a classic Los Angeles scum-bar tour. It seemed unwise after a couple of sleepless nights, but we quickly decided that it would be the best thing to do—a sort of personal deprogramming session.

By about ten o'clock that evening, we had worked our way to within three miles of L.A. International, to a nudie bar on Century Boulevard. It was no place to be exhausted and full of bourbon and soda on top of beer. Nonstop porno films bounced off great wall mirrors, surrounding the drinker with disconcerting images: giant erupting phalluses on poor color stock; unfortunate vaginal closeups like open heart surgery. There was a naked girl dancing on the platform, and I tried to draw a steady bead on her. It seemed very significant, this music, Stevie Wonder: "When you believe in things you don't understand, then you suffer. . . ." Impossibly, the girl who had been naked a few seconds before was standing at my side, carrying a tray with two more bourbons and sodas.

"You are a . . . very special person," I told her, suddenly sentimental.

She took our money and kissed me chastely on the cheek. "You're sweet," she said. That could very well be true, I thought, sinking into a sloppy, exhausted melancholy. I was thinking about Susan Alamo at the sunrise service. In my vision, I was floating above the crowd, like an angel, or a helicopter. The voices of the choir and the sound of the orchestra were a lost, discordant whisper in the stillness of the dawn. From above the crowd was a vague, bluish blotch on the green hillside. So very few had been chosen.

Susan stepped again to the pulpit, resplendent in her swirling white gown. I saw her, quite suddenly, as a Biblical matriarch—a prophet unheeded—preaching her brave Gospel of wrath and doom to an uncaring world. Her words pierced the sky, and I listened properly this time, as she told the bare hills about the signs of spring, and the summer that must surely come. She knew too, from the poisoning of our waters and from the death throes of our seas, that the Savior was at hand. She had seen it so many times there in the Book of the Living God who gave his Word to those with the courage to truly read it.

The tides of communism were at this moment washing our shores, I heard the voice of Susan Alamo say, and it trembled on the words, "America, this great eagle, going down for the last time." She paused and glanced upward, through me, for I had no substance in my vision. I wondered if she would ever know—really know—why the devils were coming at the Foundation. Or why so few seemed to listen. And in my vision, I imagined I saw Christ coming again to Susan, as he had when she was so young: the bright red cape, the dark hair flowing in the wind, the big black eyes. . . .

I imagined I saw Susan Alamo, sitting at the right hand of the Father, hearing him say, "Well done thou good and faithful servant," and "Susie, you were right all along."

I imagined I saw Susan Alamo, dressed in lace and linen, looking down from her heavenly mansion, smiling on her children.

Leaving Tony behind to carry on the Work.

Postscript: This story was written in 1973. Shortly afterward, Tony and Susan moved the Foundation to the Ozark region of Arkansas, because of its reputation for religious tolerance. Susan Alamo died of cancer in 1982. Tony refused to bury her. Instead he had the corpse embalmed and kept it in a casket in his living room where he held twenty-four-hour prayer sessions, sessions that were to last until she rose from the dead. The most requested song at a local radio station was "Wake Up, Little Susie."

After two years—and some thought—sources inside the Foundation said that Tony stood before the congregation and declared that God had appeared to him in a very special way and that he, God, was sending Susan back to Tony "in the body of a younger woman." Presumably one with great knockers. There were many defections.

Meanwhile, the U.S. Labor Department filed a lawsuit alleging that the Foundation exploited church followers who worked twelve to sixteen hours a day, sometimes seven days a week, for no pay. The U.S. Supreme Court ruled that workers were entitled to minimum pay, or its equivalent in food and board. Tony had followers distribute tracts asserting that the Labor Department and Supreme Court were controlled by the Catholic Church which, inexplicably, he said, was out to get the Foundation.

In 1985, the IRS revoked the Foundation's tax-free status. Tony and Susan, the IRS report stated, had accumulated tens of thousands of dollars worth of South African Kruger-rands, silver dollars, and gold coins. The Foundation had purchased scores of antiques, a grand piano, many pieces of jewelry—including a $49,000 gold nugget diamond ring and a five-karat emerald ring. The IRS said the couple had traveled in several Cadillacs and shopped for their fur coats at Neiman-Marcus. Tony, who is contesting the IRS action, said that the Cadillacs and diamond rings, the fur coats and $285 silk shirts, all of it, were investments on the Foundation's behalf.

In late 1987, there were reports that Tony had been bragging a little: "I am," he allegedly told a real estate agent, "worth over a hundred million dollars." This is not a clever thing for a man with tax problems to say. My guess, in the summer of 1988, is that the next episode of the Tony and Susan story will be heard in tax court.

The Weasel, as always, is ever present.

IN THE
VALLEY
OF THE
SHADOW
OF
DEATH

An On-the-Scene Report from Guyana

he others were already in Guyana. Stuck in the Miami airport, through no fault of my own, I paced. I was a journalist, a ghoul, with a desire to go where no sane man would wish to go. A smiling woman with large, syrupy eyes tried to pin a candy cane on my shirt. She explained that the Hare Krishnas were feeding people all over the world, and she had this record album and a book and a magazine—"Like, it's *rully* ecstatic"—and would I like to cough up a donation.

"Doesn't this Jonestown stuff make you wonder about yourself?" I asked.

"What?" She looked up at me in shock.

"Selfless commitment," I began.

"It's the oldest—"

"They killed the babies first," I said.

"—religion in the world. We have—"

"Potassium cyanide."

"—members in all—"

"Dead," I said. "Men, women, children, old, young, black, white . . ."

Her eyes glazed over and she turned from me, walking rapidly in the general direction of the United Airlines ticketing desk. I followed along after her, the way so many of them had hounded my steps over the years in airports all over America.

"They were people who couldn't look into themselves," I insisted. "Good people. People who fed the hungry. Who helped others. And now they're lying out there in that goddamned jungle . . ."

She stepped up her pace.

". . . swollen. Grotesque. Nothing more than thirty or forty tons of rotting meat."

She ran from me, her bag full of magazines and albums thumping against her hip. I felt both ashamed and full of fierce, brutal joy. There were a dozen of them at least, between concourse A and concourse H, and I got every one. All you had to do was "Jonestown" them and they fled like rats.

While I was raging through the Miami airport, Tim Chapman, a husky twenty-eight-year-old photographer for the *Miami Herald,* was doing some of the best work of his life. In Georgetown, the capital of Guyana, he had talked his way onto a flight to Jonestown, where the bodies still lay, three days after the massacre that culminated in the death of more than nine hundred members of the Reverend Jim Jones's Peoples Temple.

From the helicopter it looked as if there were a lot of brightly colored specks around the main building. At three hundred feet the smell hit. The chopper landed on a rise, out of sight of the bodies. Other reporters tied handkerchiefs over their faces. Chapman didn't have one, so he used a chamois rag. It turned out to be a good idea.

Chapman was telling me all this about three in the morning the day I arrived in Georgetown. He wasn't drinking, but his words slipped out in slurry bursts. He hadn't been able to sleep much.

"The first body I saw," he said, "was off to the side, alone. Five more steps and I saw another and another and another; hundreds of bodies. The *Newsweek* reporter was walking around saying, 'I don't believe it, I don't believe it.' Another guy said, 'It's unreal.' Then nobody even attempted to speak anymore. It was overwhelming. Bizarre."

Chapman talked about how he kept moving, shooting wide-angle shots of the hundreds of bodies. "There were colors everywhere: raincoats and shirts and pants in reds and greens and blues; bright, happy colors." Chapman saw two parrots on a fence, a red and yellow macaw and a blue and yellow macaw. He moved around to get that angle: the contrast of life and death.

"I started moving to my left," Chapman said, "and I was battered by the smell. It hit me. Went right into my chest. I started to gag and turned my back. Seeing it, plus the smell . . ." He wadded the chamois into his mouth, bit down, got some saliva into it, and tasted the leather. That helped some. "Then, I found if I kept my eyes moving and let my camera be my eyes, I'd never really see it. I shot verticals and horizontals, moving to my left. And then there it was." Chapman shrugged helplessly. "There were piles upon piles of bodies. What do you call it? There's no definition. Nothing to compare it to."

Outside our hotel, a tropical rain battered the windows. Inside, an air conditioner cranked up to full-high howled mechanically. The bodies, Chapman said, were in grotesque disfigurement. One woman's false teeth had been pushed out. He saw a child, maybe five years old, between a man and a woman who were swollen in death. He remembered that the child wore brown pants and a blue shirt. He wasn't as swollen as the man and woman. The children didn't seem to swell as much. Just for a moment Chapman stood there, hating the parents. They had a choice, and the child didn't.

When the other reporters left for Jones's house, Chapman decided to stay with the bodies, and he moved through them alone. He stopped for a moment, and in the stillness, he heard a body working. "It was . . . gurgling. And it came from a black woman in a red shirt with VIVA written across the front. She wore gold earrings and she was arm in arm with a black man. Her head was swollen to the size of a bowling ball. Her eyes had popped completely out of her head. The entire eyeball was resting outside the socket." Chapman paused. "It didn't bother me then," he said. "I knew it would get to me in a few days.

"This is going to change my life," Chapman said softly. He lost the thread of his thought momentarily and his eyes went blank. In Vietnam, they called it the one-thousand-yard stare.

I waited for a while, then asked, "What else?"

"Okay. I moved to my left. There was a vat, and then I saw Jones. As I moved toward him, I got a real bad whiff. I stepped away, almost tripped on a body, stumbled to get my balance, and as soon as I bent down, I was suddenly too close to one. There was a tremendous adrenaline shot, a fear." He had then stepped back and tried to tell himself that he had to go on, that he was an instrument of history.

"It was really sickening at this point. The bodies were all, well, they were oozing—literally. Fluids running out of the bodies on top of bodies. Some of them had guts hanging out. They had burst in the heat. Eyeballs, intestines, bodies virtually held in by clothing. Somehow it all reminded me of Salvador Dali's *Resurrection of the Flesh*. Did you ever see that? And I thought, 'What I'm doing here is a form of art.' "

Chapman told me he saw seven needles. One was sticking out of a man's neck. Another was totally bent, as if it had been shoved into someone or something with a lot of force. There was about half an inch of milky fluid in the syringe.

There were some dogs that had been shot and some dead cats. Chapman decided not to photograph them. He thought there were a lot of sick people in the world who would be more angry about them than "this mind-boggling, nihilistic thing, this questioning of the very value of human life."

Chapman chose not to shoot any photos of Jones. It had

been done, and besides, he felt that somehow any more photos would glorify the man. He never got closer than fifteen feet to Jones. "He was wearing a red dress shirt, and it looked to me as if it had burst open because of the swelling. From where I stood, it looked as if he wore a soaked white T-shirt. Either that or his skin was bulging out, because you could tell it was holding in liquids and goo.

"His head was all blown out of proportion. There was a wound under his right ear, and it was oozing. One arm was up over his head, stiff in rigor mortis. The skin was stretched tight over the hand, and it looked desperate, like a claw."

There was something else, something about the arrangement of the bodies that struck Chapman. Jones was on his back. Most of the others were face down, their heads pointing to Jones. "I could tell," Chapman said, "that it wasn't their final statement. It was Jones's."

Somehow that single thought was the most terrifying thing Chapman said that morning.

The Park Hotel is a big, faded, white, four-story frame building surrounded by palms. Someone in the Guyanese government had decided to put all the survivors of the massacre on the same floor with the survivors of the Port Kaituma ambush (during which Representative Leo Ryan of California and four others were murdered; he had traveled to Guyana at the request of some constituents who were troubled about relatives living in Jonestown).

On the second floor of the Park is a large ballroom. A white ribbed dome rises some seventy feet above the floor, where there are a dozen or so tables with three or four chairs apiece. Just under the dome is a balcony, which leads to the rooms. The ballroom is open to the wind on three sides. A white wooden railing keeps inebriated guests from stumbling off the floor and plummeting onto the gardenias below. In deference to the periodic downpours that last an hour or more, there is a green metal awning, hung with pots of various tropical flowers and ferns. I thought of the place as the Graham Greene Room.

Guyanese soldiers stood about conspicuously. Reporters occupied most of the tables. The survivors were confined to the third floor, sometimes two, three, and four to a small, un-air-conditioned room. They were forced to leave their doors and windows open for the breeze, and they lay sweating under yellowing canopies of mosquito netting. When they couldn't stand the rooms anymore, they came down to the ballroom, where the reporters swarmed around them like hungry locusts on a single ear of corn.

One afternoon a steel-drum band called the Pegasus Sound Wave took the stage and played lilting versions of popular songs. The musicians wore red baseball caps and enjoyed their own music. They liked Christmas carols in particular and smiled and laughed their way through "Jingle Bells" and "Jolly Old Saint Nick" several times, to the obvious delight of the local crowd.

Off to the side, over bottles of Banks beer, the survivors talked to reporters. You'd hear the most heartwrenching, bloody awful details—"Part of her skull landed in my lap"; "Lost five children out there . . ."; "My child was dead, and my wife was dying"—over the din of laughter and applause and Christmas carols.

t began to rain, cooling the room. Rain hammered on the awning, then let up. The sun burst through, and its light glittered on the wet palms swaying in the trade winds.

The survivors, some of them children, stared at the reporters with vacant, ancient eyes. There were literally hundreds of journalists from at least five continents in Georgetown. It was madness. Virulent lunacy. And when you tried to assemble bits and pieces of the story, none of it fit together. There was no perspective, no center. And so we assaulted the survivors in the Graham Greene

Room at the Park. There were three distinct groups. First came the voices of dissent: those who had gone with Congressman Ryan and survived the shootout at Port Kaituma. This group included the Bogue family, the Parks family, and Harold Cordell. They hated Jones and Jonestown. The press counted them as the most reliable sources.

The second group consisted of those who had escaped the carnage at Jonestown. Odell Rhodes and Stanley Clayton made up half of the total number. Both were articulate, both had witnessed the final moments.

On Saturday, the third group—Tim Carter, thirty, his younger brother, Mike, and Mike Prokes, thirty-one—came walking up the steps of the Park to the Graham Greene Room. Both Tim Carter and Mike Prokes had held leadership positions in Jones's organization. They were accompanied by several Guyanese soldiers, and they looked terribly frightened.

They sat at one end of the tables, and the press pounced. Lights, cameras, microphones, tape recorders, half a dozen people shouting out questions. Tim Carter, in particular, fascinated me. It was his eyes. He looked like a beaten fighter in the fifteenth round, one who just caught a stiff right cross he never saw coming. Tim Carter was a beaten man, and his eyes had the watery, glazed, and unfocused look of a boxer who can no longer defend himself and who is simply going to absorb punches until he falls.

"I heard a lot of screaming," Carter said, his voice breaking, "and I went up to the pavilion and the first thing I saw was that my wife and child were dead. I had a choice of staying there"—he continued, close to tears—"and I left. And these people [referring to the dissenters who had lived through Port Kaituma] are saying we are after them and it is ridiculous."

We heard a remarkably similar story from the dissenting survivors. Jim Jones had promised that anyone who left Jonestown would be tracked down and killed. And yet, leaders of the organization had left in the midst of the suicides. They had with them a suitcase containing $500,000 in American currency.

"The money was given to us by one of the secretaries," Prokes said. He identified Maria Katsaris, a top aide and mistress to Jones. "She said, 'Things are out of control. Take this.' We left. The money was in the suitcase."

Prokes and the Carters said they were running for their lives, and the suitcase was too heavy, so they buried it. When they arrived at Port Kaituma, they told the police about the suitcase and took them to it.

"You saw your wife and child take poison?" someone asked Tim Carter. His eyes swam. "I didn't see them take poison. My baby was dead. My wife was dying. I'm trying to forget about it. Everything you thought you believed in, everything you were working for, was a lie, it was, it was . . . a lie.

"All I can say is that it was a nightmare, a nightmare. It was the most grotesque thing I've ever seen. We were there two days later and I couldn't even recognize people I'd known for six years." [The Carters and Mike Prokes had gone back to help identify bodies.]

Prokes said, "We've all lost loved ones. We feel we've been more than cooperative. We would like to be alone for a while." They got up and sat by themselves at a far table. I saw one reporter label his tape PUNKS.

The band was still playing Christmas carols. I bought a beer and watched the "punks" from across the room. They were constantly checking the position of the Guyanese soldiers, and, I imagined, looking for an escape route. They feared the dissenting survivors and feared they might be killed because of the nature of their escape and their leadership positions. They refused to go to their rooms on the third floor. Escape routes were limited.

So the "punks" were forced to stay in the Graham Greene Room. Despite their wishes, reporters would still try to sit with them. When this happened, it triggered another rush of cameras and microphones. "The circumstances were different," Tim Carter said for the fourth or fifth time. "We were asked to leave. We were given a suitcase and told to take it to the embassy. I heard crying and screaming. And I went up, like I said, and I saw my wife and son . . . please, I don't want to talk about it."

But they had little choice. As long as they stayed in the Greene Room, one reporter, bolder than the rest, would approach them, and it would start all over again. I was reminded of the way a bitch weans her puppies. She may be sleeping when they waddle over and begin to suckle. Annoyed, she gets up and walks to the far side of the room. The puppies regard one another in dismay. Soon enough, one, bolder than the rest, waddles over to mother. The others, fearing that they won't get their fair share, make a mad comic dash.

And so it was with Prokes and the Carters. Through the carols and the rain and the moments of sunshine, we all stopped at their table to suckle more information. The letter to the embassy, for instance. The one in the suitcase with the money. It was addressed to the *Soviet* embassy. Mike Carter explained, "Jones told us the Soviet Union supported liberation movements."

The bits and pieces wouldn't fit. It was like trying to hold too many ball bearings in one hand. Every time you got something, everything else you held threatened to clatter to the floor and roll out of reach.

Odell Rhodes is a soft-spoken, articulate thirty-six-year-old, an eyewitness to the first twenty minutes of the massacre at Jonestown. The first time we met, he spotted a forty-ounce duty-free bottle of Jack Daniel's in my case. We drifted up to my room, where it was quieter.

We sipped the bourbon, strong and sweet and straight, out of Park Hotel water glasses. Odell had been a junkie for ten years. He'd been through two drug-treatment programs, and both times he had gone back to drugs and some sleazy hustle on the street. "They tell you an addict shoots junk because he likes it," Odell said. "I never liked it. I had to shoot it."

The Detroit street scene got more and more sordid. Once

an old friend of his dropped by with some drugs. "She liked to take it in the neck," Odell said. "I used to hit her." But this time Odell missed her by five minutes. Someone else had hit her up, and it turned out that the drugs were bad. When Odell found her, she was dead, the needle sticking out of her neck. "Five more minutes," Odell said, "and I would have hit her up and killed her. Probably killed myself too."

Odell was down and out, ashamed even to see his family. Once he was in jail on traffic violations, sick, wondering where he was going to get bail, knowing there were no drugs for him that night. Dozing, he felt someone "messing with my foot." It turned out to be a white businessman. The man explained that he had this thing for feet. If Odell would just let him sort of . . . fool around . . . the guy would pay his bail the next day. So Odell lay there in the dark, weak and sick, while some guy drooled over his feet.

"I hated being an addict," Odell said.

When the Peoples Temple buses came through Detroit, an alcoholic friend decided to join. The next time they came through, the friend looked up Odell. The friend was dry, sharp, well dressed. "He looked like a successful business-man," Odell said. And Odell, who had failed twice trying to kick his habit, decided to check out the Temple.

Jim Jones, he said, gave him a new self-image. He was intelligent. He was useful. Odell was given a job in the San Francisco temple. "The area it was in," he said, "was like where I had come from in Detroit. But I could walk down the street with money in my pockets and pass it all up."

When Odell first arrived in Guyana, things seemed fine. His job was teaching crafts to children, and he was good at it. He'd spend hours poring over books, looking for projects children could complete in a couple of hours. The kids teased him—"Hey, that'll never work, man"—and he'd bet them cookies that it would. They laughed a lot.

The children would throw their arms around Odell and call him "Daddy." He was worried about that at first. Jim Jones was Daddy. Jim Jones was Father. But the leaders in the organization appreciated his efforts. Odell, they said, was providing a stable image for the youngsters. His estimation of his own worth soared.

"I really loved those kids," he told me.

But then things started going sour in Jonestown. The food deteriorated. The workdays increased. It seemed, to Odell's experienced eye, that Jim Jones was developing a serious drug problem. Crazy things began to happen, and he made plans to escape.

Odell had been to Vietnam and attended something they called "hunt and kill" school. It was said that no one could survive in the jungle around Jonestown. Armed members of the Temple's security squad combed the roads and trails. Escapees were invariably caught. And punished. Odell figured he could steal one of the camp's crossbows. He'd hide it in the bush, then make off with it the next morning, before anyone noticed that he was missing. He'd stay off the roads and trails, hiding in the bush and living off the land until he was presumed dead.

But then the news of Congressman Ryan's visit hit Jonestown. Security was increased. Then came the incident at Port Kaituma, followed by the terrible night of screams in which more than nine hundred died. The children were first. Odell watched Larry Schact, Jonestown's doctor, measure poison into a syringe. Nurses squirted the liquid into children's mouths. Some of them were brought to Odell. He was their daddy, and they died in his arms.

"I watched them die," he said. "And I haven't cried yet. It's like I'm dead inside. Sometimes, I'm alone in my room, and I close the door and I wait to cry. Water comes to my eyes, but I can't cry."

Odell sipped at the bourbon and blinked several times.

t was a massive job, loading up all the corpses at Jonestown, and it took eight full days. On the ninth day, the government allowed about fifty news ghouls into the jungle enclave. We flew up to Matthews Ridge and were ferried the twenty or so miles to the ghost town in one helicopter accommodating twelve. There was a dash to be on the first flight. TV crews claimed they should get preference because they needed the light. Newspaper reporters were shouting, "Fuck that TV shit. I have to see, too." The boarding process looked like a Tokyo subway at rush hour. It was, all in all, a shameful disgrace that led several young Guyanese solders to laugh out loud.

At one thousand feet, the jungle seemed like a vast, gently undulating sea: forty shades of green stretched as far as the eye could see. And it was literally steaming: mist rose up from the low-lying areas and from the sluggish, tea-colored rivers. It was awesome, frightening, and my guess is that every reporter on the chopper, reminded of Joseph Conrad's descriptions of the jungle, scribbled *Heart of Darkness* in their notes, as I did.

We landed on the rise Tim Chapman had mentioned, walked down a dirt path through a neatly mowed lawn, crossed a gracefully arched wooden bridge over a turgid brown river, passed several wood buildings on stilts, and made our way to the pavilion, where the bodies had lain.

Everything was ironic. The last bodies to be removed had been in such a state of decomposition that bits and pieces kept falling off. Guyanese workers were plowing the whole area under, using tractors that had belonged to the people, bits and pieces of whom were being plowed under.

To get to the pavilion proper, we had to step across muddy rills, and the thought of that ocher-colored mud clinging to our shoes was unpleasant. The pavilion had a corrugated metal roof set on wooden columns and a hard-packed mud floor. Tractors had not yet been inside. The smell was bad, and several of us gagged. In front of the stage, along with a collection of musical instruments, were several bits of gore: blackened flesh, shriveled skin, all crawling with flies. On the walls were signs that said LOVE ONE ANOTHER, and the like. Red rubber gloves were lying about, dozens of sheets of paper reading, "Instructions for use; bag, plastic mortuary," mementos of the American graves detail.

I found a notebook containing "notes on the news," which consisted of a recapitulation of Soviet space triumphs and details of repressive actions taken by reactionary, American-supported governments around the world. The notebook must have been in among a pile of bodies because it stank of rotten meat, and I got that stink on my hands.

A soldier pointed out a pile of crossbows. They were Wham-O Powermasters, set on wooden rifle stocks. The arrows were short, lethal, razor-tipped. Forty guns had been found, but the soldiers wouldn't let us see them.

A short walk across the mud ended at a wooden cage with a corrugated metal roof and sign reading MR. MUGGS. Jones had started off in the Midwest as "the monkey preacher," selling imported monkeys door to door. He loved animals, and the Temple was always taking in strays. Mr. Muggs, the Jonestown chimpanzee mascot, had been shot in the back of the head. Patches of blackened fur littered the cage floor.

The path led down a shallow slope to Jones's house, a brown, wooden affair, slightly larger than the rest, surrounded by tangerine and almond trees. The place was locked up, but scattered on the porch was Jim Jones's mail, a collection of books and magazines, and his medicine cabinet: three things that reveal much about a man.

The books and magazines were about conspiracies, spies, political imprisonment, people who manipulate news, and Marxism. A large red book contained dozens of Russian posters; one showed Lenin speaking before a crowd of workers.

Near a footlocker full of health food and vitamins, I found hundreds of Valium tablets, some barbiturate-type pills, and several disposable syringes, along with ampuls of synthetic morphine. Next to the drugs, by a pile of blank

Guyanese power-of-attorney forms, was a great stack of letters addressed "to Dad." Most were labeled "self-analysis" and began with "I feel guilty because . . ." The self-analysis letters were confessions. No one admitted to being happy and well adjusted.

I read one from a young male: "I am sexually attracted to a lot of brothers and would rather fuck one in the ass than get fucked." After the original confession, the letters churned with hate. "I have feelings about going to the States for revenge against people." From an eighty-nine-year-old woman: "Dear Dad, I would rather die than go back to the States as there is plenty of hell there. I would give my body to be burned for the cause than be over there. . . . If I had to go back, I would like to have a gun and use it [she names several Temple defectors who worked with the anti-Temple Human Freedom Movement] and have them all in a room together and take a gun and spray the row of them. I am glad to have a Dad and Father like you. . . ."

Some letters seemed to be answers to questions posed by Jones, one of which concerned the writer's estimation of his ability to stand up under torture. The answers suggested that people felt that kidnapping and torture were very real possibilities. Most doubted that they could endure continual physical pain.

The letters were chilling, suggesting lives filled with guilt and hate and fear. More frightening was the tone of absolute submission to Dad, a man who, by all evidence, seemed to be a hypochondriac, a drug addict, and paranoid.

The soldiers clapped their hands and we were told to move along. No one wanted to leave the mother lode outside Jones's house. Everyone wanted to scribble down just one more letter or the name on just one more ampul of amber-colored drugs. Soldiers nudged one or two of us with their rifles.

We were shown a bakeshop, a machine shop, a brick-making area. We noted packets of a Kool Aid–like drink called Fla•vor•aid lying around. The illustration showed two children sipping Fla•vor•aid and smiling happily. There were shoes in the mud and on the grass and in the fields. A disproportionate number were children's shoes, sandals no bigger than the palm of your hand.

Across from the rise where the helicopter landed were forty or so cottages, painted in pleasant pastels. They were maybe twelve by twenty-four feet. Several doors were open, and we could see beds jammed together. The cottages seemed to be for sleep and sleep alone.

A guard tower stood above the cottages. Strangely, it wasn't near the roads in and out of Jonestown, but was directly over the area where most of the people lived. Someone had painted several bright seascapes on the tower, so that it appeared to be a contradiction of itself, like a .357 Magnum disguised as a candy cane.

As we stood on the rise waiting for the helicopter and looking down on the cottages, a rainbow began to form in the distance. It grew more brilliant. A second bow formed above the first, and together they stretched across the sky, encompassing the whole of Jonestown.

A soldier said the Guyanese might continue the communal agriculture experiment Jones began. We wondered who could work there, what kind of men and woman would be required to spend their nights in those awful, empty cottages. Someone else said that the Guyanese had considered making Jonestown a tourist attraction. A tourist attraction? What would they call it? Club Dead?

Later, back in Georgetown, I asked dissident survivor Harold Cordell about the guard tower with those painted yellow fish swimming all over it. He told me they had placed a wind-driven generator on top, but it had never worked. Finally, they had installed children's slides on the lower level. The guard tower was called the playground.

The whole process—this denial of the tower's function—reminded me of George Orwell's *1984*, in which the Party re-forms language in such a way as to make "heretical thought" impossible. The language is called Newspeak and makes abundant use of euphemisms. In Newspeak, a forced labor camp is called a "joycamp." The guard tower at Jonestown was the architectural equivalent of Newspeak.

Jonestown itself had become a joycamp in its last year. There was no barbed wire around the perimeter. It wasn't needed. Escape was a dream. The jungle stretched from horizon to horizon, thick, swampy, and deadly. Armed security guards patrolled the few trails, and it was their business to know where an escapee would look for food and water. Rumor had it that captured escapees had their arms broken. Toward the end, most of them were simply placed in the euphemistically named Extra Care Unit, where they were drugged senseless for a week at a time. Patients emerged from ECU unable to carry on a conversation, and their faces were blank, as if they had been temporarily lobotomized.

They were told that even if they could survive the jungle, elude the guards, and somehow make it almost one hundred and fifty miles to Georgetown, they'd be stuck there. The Temple held their passports as well as any money they might have had when they arrived.

[*The Party*] *systematically undermines the solidarity of the family, and it calls its leader by a name which is a direct appeal to the sentiment of family loyalty.*"—*1984*

It happened that way with Dale Parks, one of the men who tried to leave with Congressman Ryan. He had quit the church for some months, but Jones's wife, Marceline, had convinced him to come back and give Jonestown a try. He was given a round-trip ticket, which he was required to turn over, along with his passport, "for safekeeping." Almost immediately, he was "forced" to write letters to his family about how wonderful it all was. "I saw the guns around," he told me, "and I didn't want it to come to that."

Parks's family believed the letters and followed him to Jonestown. Soon after arriving, his father, Gerry, who had a stomach condition, mentioned that the food didn't agree with him. During the night's Peoples Forum meeting, in which "problems" were discussed, Gerry Parks was called up "on the floor." Jones humiliated him in front of the community, gathered in the pavilion. "How can you complain about food," Jones raged. "You, with a full belly, when two out of three babies in the world go hungry." Dale then watched his father being beaten.

When Jones called people on the floor, Dale Parks said, relatives were expected to confront them first. Defending a father, mother, or child could result in a beating. The family itself was expected to dispense the most vitriolic criticism. When the Parkses found themselves together (as when they were forced to write glowing letters home), they would whisper furtively: "You know I have to do it. If I'm on the floor, you do it too. I still love you."

"Every citizen . . . could be kept . . . under the eyes of the police. . . .—1984

There were informers everywhere. They got time off, extra food, extra privileges, sometimes even a pat on the back from Father. Children informed on their parents, parents on children. Senior citizens were prized as informers. In rare moments of privacy, one resident might express "negative" opinions to the other. It was unwise to reply with anything but criticism of such ideas. The person might be an informer, and any agreement would put you on the floor and result in a beating.

The aftermath of a beating used to be called "discipline," but the name was changed to the more euphemistic "public service." People in public service were transferred to a dorm patrolled by armed guards. They did double work duty, and food might be withheld if they didn't give their all. Security people would stop by the dorm to administer a beating. Often people in public service were allowed to sleep for an hour or two, then were roughly wakened and made to do some tedious chore, such as washing walls.

The only way to get out of public service was to express regret for your previous attitude, to pretend to like the work, to display a "good attitude." It did something to a man's mind, public service.

"Sexual intercourse was to be looked on as a slightly disgusting operation, like having an enema. . . . It was not merely that the sex instinct created a world of its own which was outside the Party's control . . . sexual privation induced hysteria, which was desirable because it could be transformed into war fever and leader worship."—1984

It had been pretty rough for Stanley Clayton in Oakland. He started stealing at the age of eight, and the only presents in the house on Christmas were the ones he stole. Clayton was originally attracted to the Temple because the women he met there were warm and "foxy." Later, he came to share a vision of economic and social equality. On the boat from Georgetown to Jonestown, he met a young, female Temple member. They talked about how they were home for the first time: home in a socialist country with black leaders. They were finally free.

The woman expressed her freedom by sleeping with one of the sailors. The boat's captain told Jones about it, and the second night Stanley was in Jonestown, the woman was called on the floor. The question was put to her: "Why did you do it?" She answered, "Well, because Stanley said I'm free." The community turned on him, shouting invectives. He was knocked to the ground, where security guards, trained in martial arts, shoved him and shouted at him and threw punches.

According to Stanley, Jones frequently railed against sex in marathon meetings. He said it was unhealthy and shortened the life span. When a married man was discovered having an affair, the two were called on the floor and made to strip to their underwear and pretend to make love—there on the floor in front of the man's wife. "Look at them," he said. "They're like animals."

When Stanley had sex with an older woman, both were called on the floor. "They beat the shit out of us," Stanley said.

At Jonestown, you didn't have a lover, you had a companion. One day Stanley's longtime companion told him it was over. "The way she told me," he said, "I knew it was put upon her." At one meeting, Jones's wife told Stanley's companion to sit by the doctor. "At that time," Stanley said, "Jim Jones tried to humiliate me, calling me all kinds of names. 'See what sex can do for you,' he said. 'Your companion is off somewhere else.' He even tried to humiliate her by saying all she wanted was a dick. He said, measuring a small space with his hands, 'Stanley's dick ain't no bigger than that.' "

"[A Party member] is supposed to live in a continuous frenzy of hatred of foreign enemies and internal traitors . . . the discontents produced by his bare, unsatisfying life are deliberately turned outwards."—1984

The public-address system was sometimes on all night, the survivors explained, so that people could learn in their sleep. At six A.M., someone knocked on the door. Breakfast consisted of rice, watery milk, and brown sugar. Promptly at seven, a typical resident reported to work in the field, which might be as much as a mile and a half away. A supervisor took his name, and the list was given to security. It seemed as if the weeds grew back to choke the crops in a single day, and workers were required to do heavy weeding in temperatures that often rose well above 100 degrees.

There was a half-hour break for lunch. Most often, midday meal was a bowl of rice soup.

The workday ended at six P.M. A resident had less than two hours to walk back from the fields, shower, and eat dinner, which usually consisted of rice and gravy and wild greens. At 7:45, the public-address system began blasting out "the news."

Jim Bogue took an adult education course from Jim Jones in Ukiah, California. At the time, Jones didn't believe in tests. In Jonestown, he gave one or two tests every week, and if you did poorly, you might end up on the floor. Sometimes Jones would read and interpret the news, sometimes another voice would supply his interpretation. The news outlined repressive measures taken by the South African government, and it implicated the United States. Tortures in Chilean prisons were described.

Jones became more and more radical in his opinions.

Charles Manson was misunderstood. The Red Brigades, who kidnapped and eventually murdered President Aldo Moro of Italy, had done a good thing. People took notes, dreading the tests.

About nine P.M., it was time for Russian class. Such phrases as "Good day, comrade," were practiced for an hour and a half. People paid attention, because supposedly they would someday visit Russia, a "paradise on earth" where the government "helped liberation movements."

At about eleven P.M., the community could knock off and fall exhausted into bed. Unless there were problems (and there were problems on the average of three times a week), at which point Jones would sit on his "throne" and ask leaders to describe them. Complaints about the food were always dealt with harshly. There were maggots in the rice, and you either ate in the light and picked them out or, if too exhausted, sat in the dark and ate a lot of maggots.

Jones's answer to the problem with the inferior rice had something to do with the CIA. They couldn't allow an interracial socialist experiment to flourish. And to complain about the food was to fall into the CIA's hands, to be in league with them, to be a traitor.

Beatings were often severe enough to require a stay in the infirmary. People wept uncontrollably on the floor as they confessed their crimes and negative attitudes. Some were whipped with a leather belt. Jones encouraged senior citizens to strike others with their canes. Victims lay unconscious on the ground until coming to, at which time they were expected to apologize to the community at large.

The Peoples Forum meetings might last until three A.M. Undernourished and exhausted, people took their three hours of dead, dreamless sleep.

"In her opinion, the war was not happening. The rocket bombs which fell daily . . . were probably fired by the government . . . itself, just to keep people frightened."—1984

Jim Jones said he was in constant danger. And he felt it was necessary the community know this. Once, he informed them that a curse had been put on his life. He confiscated all the children's dolls and later, burned a passport onstage. He said the passport belonged to the traitor who put the curse on him. The next day, an old man was found dead. Some of the survivors believed the old man died the day before and that Jones took the opportunity to display his omnipotence.

Sometimes, Jones would stumble and slur his words onstage. He'd go back to his cottage for an hour, somehow collect himself, and return full of fire. One day he stumbled out of his house in pain. He'd been poisoned. An infiltrator, a traitor or the CIA, had gotten to his food. Jones managed to heal himself.

In September 1977, shots were fired at Jones from the bush. They were real shots. Tim Carter, who was standing with Jones at the time, swears to it. The shots were said to come from mercenaries, mercenaries hired by the Human Freedom Movement (the Berkeley group of Temple defectors). The Human Freedom Movement, Jones told the community, was funded by the CIA. They were out there, in the bush. He could hear their military vehicles, could see white men in uniforms at the tree line, hear them on the shortwave radio.

It seemed absurd on the face of it. Mercenaries, hired by the shadowy hand of the CIA, make their way to Jonestown, level their sophisticated weapons, take one shot, and miss? Jim Bogue and Harold Cordell concluded that the shots were "self-inflicted," that they were fakery and theater.

Nevertheless, the atmosphere of fear was such that people rose in the morning, checking the tree line for mercenaries. Jones said there were sophisticated bugging devices on the trees. There weren't enough children's shoes because, as Jones explained, the customs department had broken into a shipment on the docks in Houston and taken them. The rains came early, and Jones told the community that the CIA had seeded the clouds. He reminded them of the time he was driving in California and a driverless car tried to run him off the road. Who has a device *that* sophis-

ticated? The answer was obvious. And now there were
mercenaries in the trees.

Jones despaired of defending the town. Originally, during alerts, people were to ring the perimeter with guns,
crossbows, pitchforks, and hoes. But what could they do
against trained mercenaries? Jones began to talk of revolu-
tionary suicide as a final statement. The early suicide drills,
most people felt, had been loyalty tests. But now he was
talking about reincarnation, about how death was only a
step to a higher plane. Suicide was tricky. If you did it
selfishly, by yourself, you'd revert five thousand years to the
Stone Age. But killing yourself for and with Father, that
would be a glorious protest against repression.

*Medically, paranoia refers to extreme cases of chronic and fixed
delusions that develop slowly into complex, logical systems. A paranoid system may be both persecutory and grandiose. "I am great,
therefore they persecute me; I am persecuted, therefore I am great."
True paranoids sometimes succeed in developing a following of
people who believe them to be inspired. An essential element in the
paranoid personality is the ability to discover "proof" of persecu-
tion in the overinterpretation of actual facts.*

In the past, Jim Jones *had* real enemies. They were, for
the most part, louts, bigots, and segregationists: the kind of
people who referred to him as a "nigger lover" and who
spat on his wife when she appeared on the street with one
of their adopted black children. Sickened by racist attacks,
Jones moved his ministry from the Midwest to Brazil, then
to northern California, where the hostilities began anew.
Vandals shot out the windows of the Redwood Valley temple, and dead animals were tossed on the lawn. In August
1973, a mysterious blaze devastated the San Francisco
temple.

Legitimately harassed, Jones began making connections
between events, part real, part delusion. In 1976, Unita
Blackwell Wright, a black woman and mayor of Meyers-
ville, Mississippi, spoke at the San Francisco temple. Two
men were seen holding a satchel outside the temple.
When approached, they got in a car and sped away. The

license plate was traced to a Sacramento rental agency, and the names to a Mississippi air force base. Jones concluded that Mississippi Senator John Stennis, chairman of the Armed Services Committee, was spying on him. The story was released to a newspaper. The fact that no one would print it seemed to confirm the awesome power of the senator.

"All our troubles," one of Jones's aides tried to convince me, "stemmed from taking on Stennis. After that, the attacks on us seemed more coordinated." The temple was being bugged. A couple of reporters started nosing around for information for a smear campaign. One of the reporters was named George Klineman, and, according to Jones, he came from a big-time German "Nazi" family.

(George Klineman is a freelance reporter, a former student activist whose parents were born in America. He got wind of the story through the man who was to become his father-in-law, David Conn. Conn was an elder in the Disciples of Christ, a loose confederation of churches that included the Peoples Temple. In the early seventies, Conn heard strange rumors about Jones: guns at the Redwood Valley temple, beatings, fear in those who left the Peoples Temple. Klineman interviewed temple defectors and took the information to one of his sources in the Treasury Department, which encompasses the Bureau of Alcohol, Tobacco and Firearms. Klineman had simply asked his source if he knew anything about a northern California religious organization that was arming itself.)

The Nazis hated the Temple. They sent notes, on their letterhead, with ugly messages, such as: "What we did to the Jews is nothing compared with what we'll do to you niggers and nigger lovers." Now, somehow, Stennis had turned the Nazis loose on the temple.

The connections were made: Stennis, Nazi reporters, the Treasury Department. Now, an even more sinister force was against Jones. A group of Temple defectors were telling "lies," speaking to the "Nazi" reporters, and for publication.

Klineman provided research material for another "Nazi"

reporter, Marshall Kilduff, who, along with Phil Tracy, wrote a blistering exposé of the Temple in the August 1, 1977, issue of *New West* magazine. Various defectors told stories of false healings, humiliations, beatings, and financial improprieties. The article contained a sidebar arguing that the temple should be investigated. Jones used all the political clout at his disposal in a vain effort to kill the story. He fled to Guyana shortly before it was published.

The Art of Brainwashing
According to experts, the following six techniques are commonly employed on political prisoners.

1. Isolation from all vestiges of former life, including all sources of information.

2. An exacting daily regimen requiring absolute obedience and humility.

3. Physical pressure, ranging from deprivation of food and sleep to the possibility and reality of severe beatings.

4. The engineering of situations in which freedom and approval by the group are contingent on successful reform.

5. "Struggle meetings" in which recalcitrant members are interrogated and required to confess. Interrogation could be gentle and polite, but more often involves harassment, humiliation, and revilement.

6. Doctrinaire daily study groups.

The phenomenon of folie à deux *was noted in medical literature as early as 1877. It is a "psychosis of association," most often paranoid in nature, occurring frequently among people who live together intimately and in isolation.* Folie imposée *is a kind of* folie à deux *in which the delusions of a dominant individual infect*

one or more submissive and suggestible individuals who are depen-
dent on and have a close emotional attachment to the infector.

In the isolation of the jungle, in the intimacy of the pavilion, Jim Jones raged against the defectors. They were
organized now, and the traitors called themselves the Concerned Relatives. They were plotting against him, smearing
him in the media, and in league with the shadow forces
arrayed against him.

One of the defectors, Grace Stoen, had a six-year-old son,
John Victor, living in Jonestown. Jones claimed he had
sired the boy and that he would never give him up. Stoen
hired a lawyer to start custody proceedings. For Jones, it
was just another measure of how far they would go. Traitors were playing with children's lives, using a six-year-old
as a pawn in their plan to bring down the Temple. They
would take a boy away from his Father.

He was Father to all of them. He had taken the junkies
and prostitutes off the street. He took in lonely old folks and
fed the hungry. The young idealists had been floundering,
unsure of how to make a better world. And he showed
them. Without him there was nothing. Without him they
would be back on the streets or lying on a slab in the
morgue. The community was totally dependent on him.
Without him they were nothing, and he told them so. It
frightened them to realize he was ill.

Jones told the community he had cancer, a kidney dis-
order, diabetes, hypertension, and hypoglycemia. He was
God, "God manifested a hundredfold," the only God they'd
ever known. The God of the Bible had been used to oppress
people for centuries. He was building a socialist utopia,
providing economic and social equality to the oppressed
and scorned. And now traitors were killing him with their
plots. One top aide saw him "crying hysterically, as if his
whole life was a failure."

His hate and fear were contagious. Elderly women united
to kill the defectors. He held his hands up for the people to
see, and they were running with blood. "I'm bleeding for
the people," he said. ("Ground glass," a surviving Jonestown nurse told me later.)

Sometimes during Peoples Forum, when members spoke of being homesick or wanting to leave, Jones would have a "heart attack." The community could see what it was doing to Father, and they'd turn on the speaker in a fury. It wasn't just people leaving. That might be acceptable. But no one ever left and remained neutral. They sold out. They told lies. They joined the traitors. Perhaps those who spoke of leaving were infiltrators. Everyone could see what their words did to Father. He had to protect himself. "No one leaves Jonestown unless they're dead," Jones said.

In May, Deborah Blakey, one of Jones's top aides, left the Georgetown temple headquarters, obtained a temporary passport from the American embassy, and fled to the United States. The day was May thirteenth, Jones's birthday. When Father heard of the betrayal, he called a "white night," a crisis alert, and the community sat stunned in the pavilion as he raged. They were betrayed. Wasn't it better to die? He challenged anyone in the community to speak for life. When they did, he battered them with arguments. He said he was "the alpha and the omega," the beginning and the end. He said it over and over again. The white night lasted twenty-eight hours. No one was allowed to go to the bathroom without an armed guard. Anyone who tried to run, he said, would be shot. Meals were brought into the pavilion. Finally, everyone in Jonestown voted to die.

Harold Cordell told me most of the details of this meeting. I asked him if he too had voted to die. He nodded glumly and said, "I figured if we just quit arguing with him, we could get some sleep."

The Temple hired Mark Lane, a lawyer and conspiracy theorist, in the hope that he could help unravel the mystifying web of harassment. But by early November, it seemed as if it was already too late. The shadow forces were squeezing the lifeblood out of Jonestown.

The *National Enquirer* was preparing an article. It would be another smear, like the one in *New West*, full of lies. Jones became more isolated, and his dependence on drugs increased.

On November first, Leo Ryan wired Jones and informed him he would be visiting Jonestown on a fact-finding mission. Ryan had been talking to traitors all summer.

Shortly after the wire arrived, Terri Buford, Jones's most trusted aide, left the Temple. She had been working in San Francisco and told Jones, by shortwave radio, that she "had some conflicts." Jones had often said that Terri was "the smartest person in the organization, besides me." It was three days before he could bring himself to talk about it, and then all he said was, "Someone left." All the survivors I talked to, from those in leadership positions to dissenters, agreed that Buford's defection had a devastating effect on Jim Jones.

The conspiracy came to a head on Saturday, November eighteenth, during Ryan's visit. Some Temple members had deserted in the morning, when security was concentrating on the Ryan party. Now others were saying they wanted to leave with Ryan. Whole families—the Parkses, the Bogues—had turned traitor. They had lied on the floor, lied in front of the entire community when they confronted a father or mother or child. They were more concerned with blood relations than with the cause and Father. Jones looked beaten, defeated. A man named Don Sly flew into a rage and menaced Ryan with a knife, but he was subdued. Newsmen were present. There'd be more smears. Ryan would report to Congress, and the full weight of the United States government would fall on Jonestown.

When Ryan and his collection of traitors left for Port Kaituma, gunmen followed. The shadow forces had won.

An alert was called and the community rushed to the pavilion. Jones told them the congressman's plane would "fall from the sky." He could do things like that. Hadn't he killed the man who put a curse on him simply by burning a passport? At Port Kaituma, a Jones loyalist named Larry Layton, who left with Ryan, pulled a gun. Although Layton later denied it—saying it was his idea to go after the congressman's plane—Jones may have instructed him to shoot the pilot when the plane was airborne. But the party was too large and they were going to take two planes. Layton wounded two, leveled the gun at Dale Parks's chest and fired. Dale fell back, thinking he had been shot, but the gun had jammed. He jumped Layton, and, with the help of another man, wrestled the gun away.

Meanwhile, gunmen arrived from Jonestown and began firing at the other plane. Ryan, Patty Parks, and newsmen Bob Brown, Don Harris, and Greg Robinson were killed. Others were wounded. The gunmen retreated to Jonestown.

"Those people won't reach the States," Jones told the community. Then he said it was time for all of them to die. He asked if there was any dissent. An older woman rose and said she didn't think it was the only alternative. Couldn't the temple members escape to Russia or Cuba? The old woman continued to plead with Jones. She had the right to choose how she wanted to live, she said, and how she wanted to die. The community shouted her down. She had no such right. She was a traitor. But she held her ground, an elderly woman, all alone.

"Too late," Jones said. He instructed Larry Schact, the

town doctor, to prepare the poison. Medical personnel brought the equipment into a tent that had been used as a school and library. There were large syringes, without the needles, and small plastic containers full of a milky white liquid.

Jones told the community that the Guyanese Defense Force would be there in forty-five minutes. They'd shoot first and ask questions later. Those captured alive, he said, would be castrated. It was time to die with dignity. The children would be first.

A woman in her late twenties stepped out of the crowd. She was carrying her baby. The doctor estimated the child's weight and measured an amount of the milky liquid into a syringe. A nurse pumped the solution into the baby's mouth. The potassium cyanide was bitter to the tongue, and so the nurse gave the baby a sip of punch to wash it down. Then the mother drank her potion.

Death came in less than five minutes. The baby went into convulsions, and Jones—very calm, very deliberate—kept repeating, "We must take care of the babies first." Some mothers brought their own children up to the killing trough. Others took children from reluctant mothers. Some of the parents and grandparents became hysterical, and they screamed and sobbed as their children died.

"We must die with dignity," Jones said. "Hurry, hurry, hurry." One thirteen-year-old girl refused her poison. She spit it out time after time and they finally held her and forced her to take it. Many people in the pavilion, especially the older ones, just watched, waiting. Others walked around, hugging old friends. Others screamed and sobbed.

Jones stepped off his throne and walked into the audience. "We must hurry," he said. He grabbed people by the arm and pulled them to the poison. Some struggled, weakly. One girl put up a fight and she had to be injected.

After an individual took the poison, two others would escort him, one on each arm, to a clearing and lay him on the ground, face down. It wouldn't do to have bodies piled up around the poison, slowing things down.

Stanley Clayton watched as "one of the brothers came

into the pavilion. He was running. When he came in, he
started stumbling. He turned and flipped over and was just
lying there. He was suffering. He was shaking and carrying
on, spitting up his last spit, eyes turning up in his head. All
of them were suffering. I was terrified and looked for a way
to get out." Security men with crossbows circled the pavilion. Men with guns guarded the periphery.

Odell Rhodes made himself inconspicuous. He even held
his students, the ones who called him Daddy, as they died.
And he saw that the only people who were allowed through
the circle of crossbows were medical personnel. He heard
the doctor ask a nurse to get his stethoscope. Odell fell into
step beside her. The guards stopped them, but the nurse
said, "We're going to the medical office." As they stepped
beyond the crossbows, Odell realized he would have to kill
the nurse. Fortunately, she instructed him to look in one
building while she searched the other. Odell entered the
nursing office and made his way to the back of the building,
where there was a senior center; most of the people there
were bedridden.

"Are you the man who is going to take us up there?" an
old woman asked.

"You know what they're doing up there?" Odell asked.

"We know."

"I'm not the man to take you."

Stanley too decided to risk arrows or bullets rather than
take poison. He sorted through the bodies, pretending to
look for people who might still be alive. There were only
one hundred people left alive when he saw his chance and
took it. He was lucky. It will never be known how many
people were murdered, how many saw there was no escape
and chose poison to arrows or bullets.

The security men were found with the rest. They, certainly, must have died voluntarily. In the end, it appears as
if Jim Jones put a pistol under his right ear and ended his
own life.

missed the flight back to Miami and ended up spending a night in Curaçao. There was a television in the hotel room, and I found that, after staring into the face of horror for two weeks, all I could do was sit there and watch Popeye cartoons in Spanish while my mind spun and slipped gears.

Jones was a contradiction of everything he stood for. He denigrated sex, but he slept with any woman who pleased him.

He brought homosexuals to the floor for beatings, but had sex with men.

He stood for social equality, and ate platters full of meat while others ate rice.

He preached racial equality, and yet the leadership of his primarily black organization was mostly white.

He railed against slavery, but he forced his followers to work twelve hours a day in the fields. He fed them maggoty rice and they called him Father instead of Massa.

He feared oppression but became an oppressor.

In the end, he put a bullet through his brain, killing all those things he hated with such vehemence.

There was nothing to feel for Jim Jones but a sure, steady loathing. It was harder to think about the people of Jonestown. Many of them had suffered in America, and they had turned to Jim Jones for help.

I remembered sitting with Odell Rhodes just after he had come back from identifying bodies. Another survivor asked him if he had seen a certain woman who had been very special and very dear. Odell said he hadn't seen her. The lie was transparent.

Later, Odell told me about it. She had written on her arm in ball-point pen, "Jim Jones is the only one." It was better to think she had been murdered.

Having a theory about it helped some. Mine was that

Jones was paranoid, in the clinical sense, and that he infected others. The mechanism of *folie imposée* was magnified
by the classic techniques of brainwashing. The mass suicides of history—Masada (the hilltop fortress where, in 73
A.D., nearly one thousand Jews killed themselves rather than
surrender to the Romans) and Saipan (under invasion from
American forces, one thousand Japanese took their lives in
1944)—had occurred when a people were under siege and
surrounded by enemies. Jones and the people of Jonestown
were no exception: for months they had been harassed,
persecuted, surrounded, and besieged by shadow forces.
When the final attack was imminent and undeniable, they
chose to die.

assumed in Curacao I might finally get more than two
hours of sleep. Since Tuesday, November twenty-
eighth, the day after the planeload of newsmen visited
Jonestown, there hadn't been much to do except sit
around the Graham Greene Room and touch bases for
the third or fourth time with the survivors. The problem
was that we had been pushing so hard, we'd been so charged
with adrenaline, that it was hard to break the inertia. One
network TV crew was filming a cockroach crawling across
the floor. They had the lights on it and the camera going,
and the soundman was crawling along next to it with a
microphone.

A few of the survivors were charging for interviews, and
it seemed to me that some of them sold their exclusive story
several times. (When one reporter phoned his editor in New
York and asked, "What am I authorized to offer?" the editor
replied, "Offer him a glass of Kool-Aid.") I didn't pay anyone, but I didn't begrudge them the money. It was the first
time many of them had had cash in their pockets in years,
and some hired prostitutes from a nearby brothel to stay
with them, there at the Park Hotel.

Some people—other survivors and newsmen—were outraged by the situation. It struck me differently. I remembered the attitude toward sex at Jonestown, and I saw that these men and women treated each other with affection. In some way it seemed to me a bittersweet affirmation of the resilience of the human spirit.

VISIONS
OF
TERROR
AND
PARADISE

CAST
FROM THE
GARDEN
Thoughts from Behind a Rock

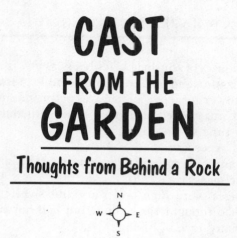

n William Boyd's bright novel of exquisite embarrassment, *A Good Man in Africa,* the protagonist, a British foreign-service official, finds himself, for a series of convoluted reasons, naked in the jungle, voiding his bladder on a column of ants, and listening to the "moronic unvaried *churrup* of crickets. . . .

" 'One man against nature,' he said to himself in a deep American accent, 'nood, in the African farst.' For a second or two he tried to imagine himself thus exposed, a creature of pure instinct. The setting was right: dusk, heat, foliage, animal noise, mysterious crepitations in the undergrowth. But he was wrong. What would anyone think if they saw him? A naked overweight freckled white man . . ." ludicrously nude and barely human.

So it is with noodity in the farst: the fragile illusion of omnipotence and grace collapsing in the presence of a single witness, even the mere thought of one.

I know this for a fact. One summer day in Innsbruck, Austria, I was the only passenger on the chairlift to the top of the mountain. From the top of the lift I hiked for several hours, walking alone above the tree line until I found a sunny spot for lunch. There was no one about, and I stripped off my clothes and sprawled on the hot rocks, soaking up the sun. Sometime after eating, I remember standing on a boulder, looking down on small spots of color that were the houses of Innsbruck, far below. How insignificant were civilization and its discontents. And I . . . I was a giant of a man, towering above all that was petty and small; a man naked and unashamed; a man in tune with the power of nature, in tune with—

"Fal der reeeeeeee . . ."

The singing was coming from some short distance below.

"Fal der raaaaaaaa . . ."

The voices were high and pure and sweet: children's voices. I had thought I was alone but had not counted on the Austrians' love of hiking.

"Fal der reeeeeeee . . ."

The song was louder now, and the children were very close. The trail passed directly under the rock where I stood, and my clothes were twenty yards away, somewhere on the other side of the rocky path. I considered a frantic dash, then discarded the idea, certain that my body, such as it is, was not one of the wonders of nature these children had climbed a mountain to see. Soon they would be topping the ridge and coming around the bend. Miserably naked, I crouched behind a rock, holding my breath. And here they came, a kind of Scout troop, twelve-year-old boys and girls together, led by a stout, muscular man in lederhosen and knee socks.

"FAL DER RA HA HA HA HA HA . . ."

An entirely naked man, crouched in shame and fear behind a rock, is obliged to consider the symbology of Genesis. In the second chapter of the Good Book, before their expulsion from the Garden, Adam and Eve were "both naked, the man and his wife, and were not ashamed." Good for them. But soon they began humanity on its passage from a state of innocence and bliss into the knowledge of evil, misery, fast food, and North Dakota. Driven from the Garden and possessed of guilty knowledge, Adam and Eve gathered up fig leaves and made themselves aprons. (Try that on a talus slope a few thousand feet above Innsbruck.) When God called them, they hid, because, as Adam later explained, "I was afraid, because I was naked . . ."

All of us, religious or not, seem to have some dim vision

of the Garden, an archetype that lives in the racial memory as surely as the fear of falling or the hatred of lawyers. Nearly five thousand years ago, in what is now southern Iraq, the people of the land of Sumer developed the world's first written language. One of the grand Sumerian epics concerned an earthly paradise—probably located in southwest Persia—where the first man and woman went proudly naked. According to cuneiform script scratched into rock five millennia ago, the first couple was persuaded by a fox to eat one of eight fruits that had been specifically forbidden to them. Big mistake. The landlord evicted the couple, and their descendants were forced to wear message T-shirts and designer jeans.

Ever since, cultured individuals have equated clothing with civilization. Once, in Africa, I talked to a colleague who had applied to visit the pygmies of the Ituri forest. The bureaucrat who denied the application, my friend discovered later, routinely forbade journalists to visit the Ituri. He believed that depictions of the pygmies' lives would be detrimental to the image of Zaire and make it appear less than completely civilized to the rest of the world. "They wear few clothes and you will surely be offended, *n'est-ce pas*?" the bureaucrat had said, frowning intently. The bureaucrat, my friend told me, wore a double-knit leisure suit.

When supposedly civilized individuals are discovered nood, in the farst, charitable people simply assume they are insane. Something like this happened to the writer Farley Mowat when he traveled up above the Arctic Circle to study wolves several decades ago. In his memoir of a season with the wolves, *Never Cry Wolf*, Mowat writes about a warm August day on the tundra: "I decided to take advantage of the weather and have a swim and get some sun on my pallid skin, so I went off a few hundred yards from the Eskimo camp (modesty is the last of the civilized vices which a man sheds in the wilds), stripped, swam, and then climbed a nearby ridge and lay down to sun-bathe."

In Carroll Ballard's brilliant cinematic version of *Never Cry Wolf*, Charles Martin Smith, the actor playing Mowat, dozes, then wakes to find himself in the middle of a huge, migrating caribou herd. Rather than lose the opportunity to study the interaction of wolf and caribou firsthand, Smith, entirely naked but for his boots, runs with predator and prey, a scene of beauty and splendid savagery.

What Ballard chose not to film was the aftermath of the chase. "I gave it up then," Mowat wrote, "and turned for home. . . . I saw several figures running toward me, and I recognized them as the Eskimo woman and her three youngsters. They seemed to be fearfully distraught about something. They were all screaming, and the woman was waving a two-foot-long snowknife while her three offspring were brandishing deer spears and skinning knives."

Mowat sprinted back to his camp, pulled on his pants, and picked up his rifle. Later, when things had quieted down, he learned that the woman had heard from one of her sons that the wolf man had gone galloping out over the hills, quite naked. "She, brave soul, assumed that I had gone out of my mind (Eskimos believe that no white man has very far to go in that direction), and was attempting to assault a pack of wolves barehanded and bare everything else. Calling up the rest of her brood and snatching up what weapons were at hand, she had set out to rescue me."

I was thinking about this story, about the Garden, and about conditions inside Austrian jails, as the parade of revoltingly cheerful children marched by my rock, singing like little banshees. It took them weeks to pass. I yearned for dwarfdom and wished the children of Austria mortification and porridge for dinner.

"Fal der reeeeeeee . . ."

When the little cretins were finally gone and I could hear them only faintly, I found my clothes and started trudging mournfully down the mountain, thinking uncharitable thoughts. The Garden is a secret spot and one not gladly shared. It took me fifteen full minutes in a pair of pants before the situation began to seem even vaguely amusing.

IN THE
SHADOW
OF THE
MOON

Searching for Grand Terror in Big Sky Country

eattle in the sun is splendid, but Interstate 5 this day
was slick and the rain fell like a fine mist. To say it
was raining in Seattle is like pointing out that bears
tend to relieve themselves in remote wooded areas.
People who live in Seattle have a puddle on the back
stoop 365 days a year, and some experts attribute a
significant portion of the city's suicides to its damp and
pearly, sunless skies. I have always imagined that Venus,
under its cloud cover, would look like an infrared Seattle.
Grappling with these morbid and otherworldly thoughts, I
turned east, where the weather got worse.

Snoqualmie Pass was closed for an hour because of an
avalanche, and the sun's light was a dead-gray glow that
barely filtered through the falling snow. I-90 eastbound out
of Spokane was a trucker's nightmare; big rigs were either
jackknifed in the ditches or sitting safely on the side, defeated by some snow-packed pass. In Idaho, at 3 A.M., the sky
simply collapsed, and wind-driven drifts spread across the
icy pavement. Dawn in Missoula, Montana, consisted of a
certain hazy brightness under glacial skies. The last total
eclipse of the sun in the continental United States in this
century was due in three days, and meteorologists working
on special forecasts set the chances of heavy cloud cover at

about 90 percent. The odds for actually seeing the phenomenon were dismal.

Locals took that news much better than those of us who had spent considerable time and money to be in Montana in the dead of winter. I was sitting in a bar all festooned with lumberjack paraphernalia, bitching over a beer, when a three-hundred-pound log peeler suggested that I could go through the door marked GENTLEMEN, turn off the light for several minutes, and get the same effect.

Not exactly true, I thought. There just isn't all that much in the way of Grand Terror in the men's room. Eclipses ought to be awesome, as they were for our distant ancestors. When the lights went out at noon, those folks surely figured it was a message from Mr. Big that He wasn't entirely happy with the way things were going.

The sun-worshipping Aztecs liked to sacrifice hunchbacks and dwarfs during an eclipse, which was apparently their way of saying, "We're sorry." In 840 A.D. when the moon got between the earth and the sun and its shadow fell on Louis of Bavaria, son of Emperor Charlemagne, his heart clogged up with a greasy sort of fear, and he fell to the ground, lifeless as a rock. Louis of Bavaria, like a lot of big-time kings of the day, interpreted everything personally.

The ancient Chinese were able to predict eclipses, but they preferred not to take any chances. Moonshadow or no, the appropriately forewarned populace hammered away on drums and fired arrows at the sun to frighten a celestial dragon bent on dealing with the sun as if it were a macaroon. Legend has it that in 2134 B.C. two astronomers, Hsi and Ho, sampled local wines to excess and failed to predict an eclipse. They were subsequently beheaded for incompetence.

These days incompetents are seldom decapitated, and there are a growing number of people who go out of their way to be in the shadow of the moon as it sweeps across the earth somewhere on the average of once a year. I know three of these self-proclaimed eclipse addicts personally. One, an award-winning science writer, traveled to Africa—

to Mauritania—to witness a total eclipse visible there in 1973. Now, Mauritania is one of the most Godforsaken places on the face of the earth, a scorching, poverty-stricken, sandstorm-wracked desert hellhole where his lips cracked and his brain boiled and where he lost twenty pounds after getting amoebic dysentery. He returned to the States a shriveled, wind-burnt hulk who babbled, not entirely coherently, about the transcendental experience of totality.

The other two eclipse addicts I know have no special interest in astronomy. One is a lawyer, the other a Sierra back-country guide. None of the three has ever been able to explain to me just what it is they find so fascinating about an eclipse—or why they are willing to spend hundreds, sometimes thousands of dollars for a few minutes' thrill. All agree only that a total eclipse is worth the effort; beyond that, they say, it's a situation in which "ya hadda be there."

This time I had arranged to be there, viewing it all through a glass darkly. After the dragon ate the sun and spit it out, I figured I'd know if there was anything to this eclipse-addict business.

The trouble was, the weather didn't seem to want to cooperate. My science-writer friend and I had conferred on this point. He had been collecting a lot of material from people who spend a lifetime studying something called "eclipse meteorology," and had decided to go to a little town in the rainshadow of the Cascades. The path of totality was a band of darkness about 170 miles wide, north to south. It would sweep in out of the west, hitting Portland, Oregon, then curve gradually north through Walla Walla, Washington, and up to Missoula, Helena, and Lewistown, Montana.

Montana looked best to me. Mobility would be the key. If short-range forecasts showed clouds west of the Continental Divide, I'd run for the east. If there were clouds there, I'd head up to the high plains of north-central Montana. I suggested to my friend that if the Cascades were socked in, he'd have no alternative viewing site. He smiled smugly and waved his sheaf of eclipse forecasts. As it turned out, forecasts three days before the event indicated that a big Pacific storm was riding in on the jet stream and that both of us were shit out of luck.

The Eastgate Liquor Store and Lounge in Missoula is a good place to have a drink and complain about the prevailing cloud cover. But the bar chatter there wasn't about the weather; it was about some poor guy from Seeley Lake who had died an awful death the day before. He had been plowing the lake in preparation for a snowmobile race, and his thirteen-ton Allis-Chalmers road grader had cracked through the ice like a bowling ball through the top of a glass coffee table. It was, everyone agreed, the kind of thing you have nightmares about. Imagine coming up under the ice, searching for the hole, feeling the burning in your chest, trying to control the overwhelming desire to gulp that frigid water into your lungs. The ice is no more penetrable than a layer of solid steel, but you hammer against it, weakly, knowing then, with horrifying certainty, that you are dead.

The peculiar thing about the entire tragedy, they said at the Eastgate, was that the driver, Edward V. "Mike" Kelley, didn't have to go out on the ice. Everyone in town had told him not to. A much lighter bulldozer had gone down only two weeks earlier, and the operator had been lucky to escape with his life. I wondered why someone would take a chance like that—money, machismo, job pressure, what?

Grand Terror was what I had come to Montana to experience, and since it appeared that the weather was going to get between me and my attempt to unravel the mystery of eclipse addiction, I decided to make a quick forty-mile run up to Seeley Lake. Darkness under the ice was going to have to substitute for darkness under the Big Sky, and one man's terror would have to do for everyman's.

The road runs by the lake, which is long and narrow and deep. Mountains rise on either side. The winter community at Seeley Lake is quite small, and if you sat long enough in Barney's Bar and Cafe, you'd likely meet everyone in town. The first person I ran into there was Roy Brown, a husky, slow-talking man who had been on the grader with Kelley when it went down.

"Yeah," Brown said, "I went out with him because I didn't want him to go. Everyone told him not to do it. But he was determined, and I decided to go along and keep an eye on the ice. As soon as we hit the lake, there were all these popping noises, from the ice contracting. We began working the snowmobile course, but on the first turn we started to go through. The wheels dropped through the first layer of ice."

The Montana winter had been especially severe, but there had been a few thaws. By late February the ice was honeycombed with air pockets and was perilously thin. There were two major layers separated by air and slushy snow. The back wheels of the grader dropped through the first layer, but the second layer held.

Brown and Kelley decided to get off the ice—fast. Kelley brought the plow blade up and rammed the accelerator down, but before they reached shore, the grader broke through the ice again. This time it didn't stop at the second layer.

"Both doors of the cab were open," Brown said, "and I was standing on a little four-inch ledge outside. I shouted that we were busting through and yelled at Mike to jump. I jumped off, and the last thing I saw was Mike still sitting at the wheel, being thrown backward. When I landed, the front wheels of the grader were just going under. The thing went down like a concrete block dropped in a bathtub.

"There were bubbles coming up and a sort of whirlpool

effect, sucking down big chunks of ice. I thought about going in after him, but I thought I'd be pulled down by the suction of the sinking grader. It was pulling all sorts of stuff down with it, like the draft behind a big truck on the highway."

Brown lay out over the solid ice and cleared slush and float ice out of the hole so Kelley could get up. He began pounding big chunks of ice around the hole to direct Kelley to the surface. (Because sound underwater seems to come from everywhere, this was not an effective strategy.) "I started clearing away snow from around the hole to see if he had come up under the ice," Brown said, "but it was a cloudy day and you couldn't see through the ice at all. So I waited by the hole, hoping to pull him out when he came up." But Kelley never surfaced, and when the bubbles stopped, Brown ran for help.

Over coffee at Barney's, I asked Bruce Copenhaver—a reserve deputy, a member of the search-and-rescue team, and a snowmobile racer—why it was necessary to have *anyone* clear snow off the race course. On a straightaway, he explained, hopped-up snowmobiles can do 120 miles per hour, and loose snow on the track can be extremely dangerous. Powder thrown into the air by the drive belts can cut visibility substantially. A clear ice track makes for a faster, safer race.

That's why Copenhaver had been out on the ice with a bulldozer several days before the Kelley tragedy. Unlike Kelley, Copenhaver is an accomplished scuba diver with experience in the arcane art of ice diving. When his Cat crashed through the ice, Copenhaver took a long, deep breath. But the Cat sank so fast that he found himself pressed tightly to the canopy over the driver's compartment, unable to free himself. The bulldozer settled in the silt at a depth of about forty-five feet.

In the sudden stillness, Copenhaver struggled free of the canopy. He was in big trouble. The sudden shock of the cold water had upset the delicate membranes of his inner ear, and he experienced a sudden burst of vertigo from the rapid pressure change. His ears ached, and the cold water sapped his will like juice being sucked from a section of orange. There was no visibility at the bottom of the lake; it was as dark as Dracula's crypt down there. In the icy blackness, Copenhaver thought of the lesson instructors drum into every new diver: Panic kills. There is always time to think.

"Luckily," Copenhaver told me, "I found I was positively buoyant." He had been wearing thermal underwear, jeans, and snowmobile pants. Air was trapped between the layers. Ordinarily, the pressure at that depth should have compressed his clothes and forced the air out of them, but he had gone down too quickly for that to happen. Still, he knew he had to ascend in a hurry, before the pressure turned his clothes into a dozen or more pounds of dead weight.

Assuming that the Cat had dropped straight and a perfectly vertical line could be drawn from the machine to the hole, Copenhaver began kicking, moving as well as darkness and vertigo would allow along that imaginary line. There was a thick layer of snow on the ice, and the sunlight did not penetrate it. At thirty feet, Copenhaver saw the hole. Sunlight on the water made it look dimly fluorescent. It was like being in a huge, windowless, unlighted warehouse with one small skylight, just at dusk. A shaft of dying light penetrated the water.

Copenhaver was on a slight angle to the light and kicked rapidly toward it. His confidence grew. He even exhaled a little air and saw with satisfaction that he was ascending faster than the bubbles. Every scuba diver knows that smaller bubbles rise at about sixty feet per minute. Making a quick almost unconscious calculation, he knew he'd be on the surface in fifteen seconds. He could do it.

It wasn't quite that easy. Copenhaver came up under a huge chunk of floating ice. He sank back down, tried another section of the hole, and once again hit ice. He was as close to panic as he had ever been when he burst through the water on this third attempt. He pulled himself to an ice ledge and gulped great drafts of frigid air.

Lying there with his wet clothes freezing on his body, Copenhaver couldn't stop coughing and spitting up a bloody, pink froth. The pressure of the water at forty-five feet had ruptured some blood vessels in the back of his sinuses, but the injury wasn't serious.

Mike Kelley had been an older man, and one untrained in the art of ice diving.

Copenhaver and others on the search-and-rescue team had made several dives, looking for their friend's body. They wore wet suits and boots and hoods worn in cold-water ocean diving, and they coated the exposed areas on their faces with lanolin. The dives were meticulously planned. They went down in teams following a descending line, each team of two connected by a close-quarters buddy line. One member of each team was tied to a line held by a tender on the surface. Fanning out for the search, they tied a pivot line to the descending line, and when they worked their way around an obstacle, one team held the point. Three sharp tugs at any time and the diver was pulled rapidly to the surface.

They found the grader at sixty feet, sunk into a soft layer of silt. Even with high-powered diving lights, visibility was a mere thirty-six inches. A thick cloud of mud and silt hung over the bottom to a height of about ten feet. One diver worked his way into the cab of the grader. Kelley's body wasn't there.

A former Navy diver who had seen too many bodies and who no longer worked with the search-and-rescue team devised an ingenious method of dragging the area where the grader had gone down. They hooked the body on the third pass. It was some fifty feet from the grader.

Another team dived to the grader and attached a cable. Five hundred yards away on the shore was a huge heel-boom crane, anchored to other heavy machinery and trees.

The cable was dragged over the ice and fixed to the crane, which strained against the weight of the twenty-six-thousand-pound grader. The cable sawed a line through the ice, and when the grader was close enough to shore, volunteer labor from the community cut huge blocks of ice and pulled them up with tongs. When the hole was large enough, they pulled the grader out of the lake. It came up front-end first, then twisted ponderously on its back wheels. Blue-black lake mud dripped from it, like some monstrous and alien thing.

The owner of the grader, Fred Drew, of D&D Logging, stopped into Barney's and sat down with Copenhaver and me. He was a short, compact, tired-looking man. A few days ago an anonymous caller had asked him why he had "ordered" Kelley out onto the ice. Drew wasn't angry, just saddened, and it showed clearly in his eyes.

"I didn't order Mike to do anything," Drew said. "He was in charge of the heavy machinery. He told me he was going to take the grader out, and I told him to use his own discretion." Drew turned to Copenhaver. "That was my Cat you went down in. Do you think I wanted another one down?"

The proprietor, Barney Bowles, a longtime friend of Kelley's, sat down with us.

"Was Mike being paid to plow the ice?" I asked.

Barney laughed, and Drew quietly said, "No, of course not."

"What then? Was he a snowmobile enthusiast?"

"He didn't own one," Drew said. Barney added, "He was a community enthusiast."

Barney explained it like this: In the winter, the population of Seeley Lake runs around one thousand. In the summer, vacationers swell that number to as much as ten thousand. People like Barney, and many others in Seeley Lake, make most of their money from tourists and local recreation seekers. The winter had been especially severe, and the weather had reduced the number of cross-country skiers who normally visited the area. The community had felt the pinch.

But the fine, warm weather of late February had coincided with the Montana State Snowmobile Championship Races, which would have attracted more than 125 racers from seven western states and Canada. At least one thousand people were expected to crowd into Seeley Lake for the two-day event. Economically, it was the most important two days of the winter season.

The racers needed clear ice. Drew donated the use of his equipment and Kelley donated the labor. When people warned Mike to stay off the ice, he realized that they were asking him to take food off their table in exchange for his safety. He took the grader out on the lake for everyone in the community. For Mike Kelley, taking that chance was a sort of sacred duty.

The championship races were canceled after the tragedy. Barney Bowles would help organize a benefit for Kelley's wife. It was volunteer labor that got Drew's machines out of the lake, and volunteer labor that would help build a new landlocked snowmobile course to be named after Mike. There would be no more snowmobile races on Seeley Lake.

"I knew Mike since he was eleven years old," Fred Drew said. "He was my brother-in-law. I think about this all the time. I'll have to live with it for the rest of my life."

"We all will, Fred," Barney Bowles said softly.

Things began looking up the day before the eclipse. A slight northerly shift in the jet stream and the storm riding in on it doubled the chances of clear weather in Missoula from 10 to 20 percent. East of the Continental Divide, along a line roughly from Great Falls to Livingston, meteorologists expected a chinook, a warm, dry wind that could rip big holes in the cloud cover. The chances of clear skies in that area were 40 percent.

In Livingston, at 3:30 A.M. the day of the eclipse, I could see stars shining through the cloud cover off to the north. Up that way, over some pretty substantial hills, was an area of high plains. I ran for it.

The sun rose off to the right, coloring the sky a pale pink and orange pastel over snowy fields. There were high cirrus clouds, wispy and insubstantial. The mountains dropped away, and the roads rolled out over the prairie, straight and dry, only now and again dipping into shallow river bottoms. Once, at 80 m.p.h., I hit a two-hundred-yard patch of black ice and had rocketed over it before I realized how nearly fatal that little ride had been. I had a strong urge to pull over for a minute to let my hands stop shaking, but there was no time; I shot along the black rib-bon of highway thinking about Mike Kelley and machines on ice and how death and destiny make no allowance for good intentions.

Diarrhea doesn't either, for that matter. I was clutching an open, economy-size bottle of Pepto-Bismol between my thighs; it served as a blunt reminder of a solemn oath I had taken the night before: I will, forevermore, avoid restau-rants advertising "Mexican Cuisine" when they are situated near the Canadian border. Just before that oath I had con-sumed, to my almost immediate dismay, what the special menu described as an "eclipse enchilada" and a "totality taco." At present they lay in the bottom of my stomach like a pair of poison army socks.

Towns, restaurants, and motels along the track of totality were cashing in on the eclipse the way Seeley Lake pre-pared for the snowmobile races—and for all the same rea-sons. In Manitoba, for instance, locals had built an ersatz igloo village to draw more eclipse addicts. In Winnipeg, the Colonel was selling eclipse-viewing goggles along with fried chicken. And at the Big Sky Resort near the entrance to Yellowstone Park, 550 people had paid $385 apiece to stay for the weekend and make a run for clear skies in a caravan of buses.

At Harlowton, where U.S. 191 crosses U.S. 12, I passed seven or eight of those same charter buses, parked on the side of the road. They were obviously trying to decide whether to run north toward Lewistown or east to Roundup. There were several CB-equipped cars and trucks parked along with the convoy; I tried them on the road channel.

Of course, I hadn't paid a cent for the services of the convoy's eclipse meteorologist, and the answering silence let me know that quite clearly.

Switching to AM radio, I caught a forecast that confirmed what I could see with my own eyes—the weather was looking good around Lewistown. Deejays on the Lewistown station proclaimed their city "the eclipse capital of America." Local stores, they said, would be closed for two hours and would reopen when the lights came back on. There would be incredible savings. At one store, I was intrigued to hear, bras and panties would be half-off.

I took 191 north. There were folks in the fields now, and you could see them tinkering with telescopes and cameras mounted on sturdy tripods. Just outside Lewistown, I pulled over and walked out into a flat, snowy field, where I met a half-dozen students from Arizona. They had driven up to Montana stuffed into a wheezing 1964 Chevy Impala. Other small groups dotted the field. In one there was a short, dark-haired woman with wandering eyes, who called herself Meadowlark and who had seen a total eclipse in the Caribbean—"It was rully, rully amazing," she said. She had dragged several scruffy-looking and less-enthusiastic friends with her. They were all from Boulder, Colorado, and except for Meadowlark, they sat around smoking hash in a bored and desultory manner.

At 8:30 A.M., the moon took the first nip out of the sun. The students had set up a four-inch reflecting telescope and were projecting the eclipse on a large, sturdy sheet of white cardboard. They spoke of sunspots and shadow bands and coronal prominences in an entirely giddy manner. On the cardboard, the dark ball worked its way over the shining ball with all the inevitability of a Greek tragedy.

Meadowlark's friends became interested, and they drifted over to ask a few questions of the students. It was getting undeniably strange out, and now they wanted to savor the weirdness.

It was about twenty degrees with high cirrus clouds sketched across the sky like strands of angel hair. A fuzzy, indistinct, red-orange rainbow formed around the sun, covering a fifth of the sky. In that field outside Lewistown you could feel the tension all around. It was like a wire being drawn taut, a wire that was near the breaking point. When the moon had covered 90 percent of the sun's disk, the light began to die. At 95 percent, it was much darker and colder.

At 99 percent, the band of totality, that 170-mile wall of darkness, erupted out of the west. From all over the field, you could hear a low, moaning sound, the kind of sound people in a roller coaster make at the top of the first high dip.

There was a range of mountains far to the west and I could see the sun setting on those craggy peaks. Then the mountains were gone, lost in darkness. The band of totality came roaring over the snow-covered plain. There was nothing you could make out as a distinct line of darkness. It was more like a huge, rippling wall of strange purple-black. The deeper you looked into it, the darker it was. As the eclipse reached totality, the wall of darkness—moving at about two thousand miles an hour—loomed up over all of us like a great, silent, inky tidal wave.

In the sky, the dark disk of the moon completely covered the sun, except for a single spot on the high rim where bright, golden sunlight poured through a deep crater on the moon. Surrounding the blackness of the moon's disk was the sun's corona, yellow with tinges of pink. The circular corona and that one bright crater full of sun created what is called the "diamond ring" effect. Then it was gone.

At Goldendale, Washington, in the rain shadow of the Cascades, it got especially dark because the skies were shrouded in clouds. My science-writing, eclipse-addict friend muttered curses amid the howls of the assembled meteorologists and astrophysicists. Near Roundup, folks from the eclipse convoy got their money's worth; the moon, like an inky thumb, blotted the sun out of a nearly cloudless sky. In Missoula, novelist James Crumley stepped into the parking lot of a bar called the Elbow Room, and the clouds parted briefly, giving him a perfect view of totality. In Bozeman, two thousand people gathered at the Museum of the Rockies, and, as John Woodenlegs chanted a prayer in his native Cheyenne, the clouds parted. "You're the Creator of us all," Woodenlegs said in English. "Bless all the people here." In Livingston, out by the Raw Deal Ranch, the chickens stopped scratching and went into the henhouse to roost. Confused dogs howled, and the horses got skittish in their stalls.

The darkness itself was like nothing I have ever seen. It was not quite black, but rather an iridescent indigo—a glowing, science-fiction sort of color. All over the field people were shouting and cheering. Meadowlark hugged everyone, and her friends rolled in the snow like puppies.

Totality lasted almost two and a half minutes, and though the darkness was not the bitter, impenetrable sort one finds at the bottom of Seeley Lake, I thought of Mike Kelley fighting the blackness and the cold in the most brutally hostile environment imaginable.

It occurred to me, in the inky iridescence of that field, that eclipse addiction has much to do with mortality; it is a shared premonition of death, enacted on a vast scale.

The first sensible monotheistic religions worshipped the sun as the giver of life—"the Creator of us all," as John Woodenlegs would have it. There is a truth there so deep and obvious we seldom acknowledge it, but it helps explain the suicides in Seattle's sunless seasons and why an eclipse has the power to stop the heart of a king. What we know intellectually—that totality is a transitory phenomenon—is not something we share with our emotions. The eclipse is a sudden, sharp view of the apocalypse.

The moon swung slowly through the sky, and a salmon-colored sunrise glittered on the mountains far to the west. In the sky we saw another diamond ring, and then the wall of darkness rushed out over the plain to the east. Cocks crowed. I found I had been holding my breath, like a man trapped under the ice, and I let it out in a great, braying rebel yell. I hugged Meadowlark, she hugged me, the students hugged each other and me and Meadowlark and her friends, and we were all laughing and shouting, and it seemed, for the moment, as if we'd live forever.

THE
MARQUESAS
Beauty, Terror, and Sublime Seclusion

"**B**ut I reconfirmed with you, personally," I said. "Three times." The woman from Air Polynesia shook her head sadly. "We have no record of your reconfirmation."

"But I was here. I talked to you. Two days ago you said I was on the flight."

The woman showed me a handwritten list. There were five names on it, and mine was not among them. "You see," the woman said patiently, "we have no record of your reconfirmation."

Outside the office, the island of Hiva Oa sighed under the weight of a heavy tropical sun. In the shade of the mango trees, the air itself was golden, as sweet and thick as honey. The sea was the cobalt blue of deep water, and it glittered in the hard brittle light of unfiltered sun. Breakers eight feet high thundered onto an expansive beach of black volcanic sand. Above the town of Atuona, above the tiny airline office, volcanic peaks rose in immense green velvet spires that caught and collected drifting South Pacific clouds so that rain fell on various summits, and the high peaks shimmered in impressionistic shades of blue and gray.

There were worse places to be stranded, to be sure, but few that are farther from home. Hiva Oa is the southern administrative center for the Marquesas island group, which is about a thousand miles from anywhere: 3,500 miles west of Peru; 2,500 miles southeast of Hawaii; 740 miles northeast of Tahiti. The Marquesas, a part of French Polynesia, are, in fact, the most remote islands on the face of the earth: the island group that's farthest from any continent. This isolation makes tourism rare, and as a consequence, a visit to the islands is rewarding and frustrating in equal measure.

"You could reconfirm for next week's flight," the woman said brightly. There was, of course, no reason to believe that another series of reconfirmations would be recorded.

Ordinarily, in such a situation, I might be tempted to batter my way onto the flight using journalistic clout. However, claiming that I was a big-deal travel writer from the United States would cut no ice whatsoever in Atuona, where there are exactly three tourist bungalows. The accommodations are more a matter of Polynesian courtesy than an attempt to cash in on big tourist bucks.

"You could," the woman suggested, "go out to the airport. Maybe one of the confirmed passengers won't show up."

In another country, I could possibly bribe one of the five passengers: offer a free ticket next week to anyone willing to give up a seat. After spending several weeks in the Marquesas, however, I knew better than to try. The islands are so provident, so rich in game and fruit, that reasonably able folks can live quite well off the land itself. This produces a cavalier attitude toward cash; money is best spent on toys, luxury items, travel. A Marquesan might give up a seat on the plane because he or she liked me, or felt sorry for me, but never for money.

At the airport, all five passengers showed up for the flight. I was destined, it appeared, to enjoy the Marquesas for another week. Or more. There was just enough money left to rent one of the bungalows in Atuona. Oh well, I could hang out on the black beach. Drink cheap rum. Do a lot of writing: hard-hitting, sinewy romantic stuff, full of adventure. . . .

The Marquesas have always been a good place for this sort of creative work. Herman Melville and Robert Louis Stevenson both lived for a time on the northern island of Nuku Hiva. Belgian-born singer and songwriter Jacques Brel moved to Hiva Oa to live the last years of his life when he discovered he had cancer. Paul Gauguin came to Atuona in 1900, looking for inspiration in uncorrupted savagery. Gauguin and Brel are buried in a small cemetery on a hillside overlooking the town of Atuona. Most of the graves there are draped with seashell necklaces and are neatly tended. Brel's stone features a bas-relief of the man. Gauguin's simple grave is headed by a sculpted female figure—Oviri, a disturbing, hollow-eyed symbol of the savagery the painter hoped to find in the Marquesas. A plumeria tree grows beside the figure of Oviri.

At the airport, I found myself thinking about these graves as the small, single-prop plane took off without me. The day I visited the cemetery, Gauguin's plumeria tree had been in full and fragrant bloom. It had bothered me then that roots surely must protrude into the grave itself. Now, standing alone on a vacant airstrip 740 miles from anywhere, I began to think of those profuse and fragile white plumerias as an expression of the artist's soul. It was a romantic and melancholy thought. Perhaps I would be buried in that pleasant cemetery along with Gauguin and Brel. My tombstone would read: "Tim Cahill: We Had No Record of His Reconfirmation."

The Marquesas Islands are volcanic peaks that rise two to four thousand feet above the surface of the ocean. Six of the islands are inhabited, and the population stands at about six thousand. Hiva Oa is the administrative center of a southeast cluster of islands, while Nuku Hiva, the main island, is the economic and administrative center of a northwest group. The single weekly flight from Tahiti lands at Nuku Hiva, where the first-time visitor is immediately introduced to the difficulty of travel in the Marquesas.

Nuku Hiva's airstrip is on the northeast shoulder of the island, in a dry rolling grassland that looks something like the wind-whipped high plains of Wyoming, and is called Terre Déserte, Deserted Land, because little that is edible grows there. The main town, Taiohae, lies directly over the spine of mountains that bisects the island, and a dirt road runs from the airport to the village. It is a narrow, dangerous, sometimes boggy affair; a twisting, rockstrewn washboard of a road in which every other turn features heart-stopping dropoffs. The rutted path passes near the highest point on Nuku Hiva, 3,865-foot-high Mount Ketu. It is probably less than thirty miles to Taiohae from the Deserted Land, and the drive takes all day.

Anyone in a hurry takes the ferry, a clattering sixty-foot, twin-diesel vessel that docks at a small cove called Haapoli. Boarding the ferry is an adventure in itself. Because the Marquesas are volcanic in origin—the islands simply erupted out of empty ocean—they are not protected by a fringing reef, and the full force of the Pacific Ocean batters them ceaselessly. There is no breakwater at Haapoli, which means that the ferry, docked at a small cement pier, rises and falls as much as eight feet on swells and breakers. Passengers try to step aboard as the deck rises to the level of the dock. To stumble at this point could be catastrophic: a passenger in the water would be crushed between the lurching boat and the cement dock.

It takes about two hours to get to Taiohae, and the boat sails by rocky cliffs, crusted with ancient lava, that rise eight hundred feet above the surface of the sea. Oceanic swells explode into polished rock. The thunder and spray of high sea meeting solid rock is a constant spectacle: water rises against the rock in immense sheets, reaching twenty-five feet or more like moving molten silver under the high tropical sun.

There was no one living above those cliffs on the Deserted Land, and Nuku Hiva was as it always had been, as it was two thousand years ago when the first of the people who were to become Marquesans landed on the island. They had come out of the west, in dugouts filled with coconuts, breadfruit, chickens, pigs, dogs, and heroes. The people, the first Polynesians, ranged as far south as New Zealand, as far north as Hawaii. The Marquesas are the farthest east they came, and the Marquesans' mystic culture—terrifying, brutal, and beautiful—developed in the splendid isolation of these most lonely of Polynesian islands.

As the boat rounds a point by the bay of Hakaui and moves to the windward side of Nuku Hiva, the scenery begins a sledgehammer assault on the sense. The mountains rise sheer, impossibly green, and waterfalls thunder down the drainages, carving out narrow valleys where the people live. The valleys are separated one from the other by high, vegetation-choked ridges. In the time before the first Euro-Americans visited the Marquesas, the people who lived along the streams in those valleys called themselves The Men. Their coconut and breadfruit thrived in the fertile volcanic soil; the chickens and pigs multiplied beyond counting. Feasting was a way of life—there were feasts for marriage and death and birth—and The Men, to Western eyes, were among the most beautiful people on the face of the earth.

Art was integral to the life of The Men. They carved human images of wood and filigreed tiny representative scenes on ear ornaments and tortoiseshell fan handles. Males sometimes decorated their entire bodies with tattoos in contrasting bands of light and dark, in swirling circular patterns that followed the contour of a buttock, the curve of the biceps or thigh. There were ritual tattoos that marked the large events of life, such as puberty and marriage. Since the process of tattooing was extremely painful—the colors were made of ground candelnut, ash, and water and were generally applied with a sharpened piece of bone—some body decorations were simply signs of courage: those that swept across the eyelids, for instance, or the genitals.

The most fearsome tattoos served to frighten enemies. The Men were always at war, valley against valley. Groups of warriors would trudge up over the ridges and descend upon those in the neighboring drainage, looking to capture a suitable sacrifice, a man to be killed in the name of the gods. The great stone terraces that The Men built in dark groves above the beach rose to the sculptured stone figures called *tikis:* large, squatting statues with huge empty eyes and scowling mouths. To consecrate the holy place, the bones of victims were hung nearby, in the branches of the sacred banyan tree. Sometimes, The Men practiced ritual cannibalism.

The first European to set foot on the Marquesas was Spanish explorer Alvaro de Mendaña, who landed at Hiva Oa in 1595 and named the islands for the Marquesa de Mendoza. In 1813, American naval officer David Porter claimed the islands for the United States. President Madison declined the offer, and France declared the Marquesas a part of its empire in 1842.

That was the same year that Herman Melville sailed into the bay of Taiohae aboard an American whaler. In *Typee*, the novel he wrote about Nuku Hiva, Melville described the horseshoe-shaped bay: "From the verge of the water the land rises uniformly on all sides, with green and sloping declivities, until from gently rolling hillsides and moderate elevations it insensibly swells into lofty and majestic heights, whose blue outlines, ranged all around, close in the view. The beautiful aspect of the shore is heightened by deep and romantic glens. . . ."

As the ferry from the airport enters this bay, the view is precisely as Melville described it, which is to say, awe inspiring. Taiohae is, arguably, the most spectacular bay in the world. "Very often when lost in admiration at its beauty," Melville wrote, "I have experienced a pang of regret that a scene so enchanting should be hidden from the world in these remote seas." The staggering beauty of the bay bursts upon the eye like privilege.

Taiohae hasn't changed much since the days of Melville. There are no high-rise hotels, no condos or "planned resorts." There are three good reasons for this happy state of affairs. First is the remote nature of the islands. Second, land in the Marquesas is generally owned by family groups that may number in the hundreds. To acquire a legal deed, a developer must obtain the signature of every owner. This sometimes means tracking down a cousin who is living in Bakersfield or Borneo or Bimini. Often, by the time the last owner signs, one of the first signatories changes his or her mind. The third good reason that there are only two small hotels on all of Nuku Hiva is the existence of a nasty little sand gnat called the nono fly. The nono's bite is painless, but, over a period of several hours, it raises an ugly red welt that itches like fury. Scratch the welt and it is likely to burst, bleed, become infected. The nonos are a plague, and the lack of condos in the paradise of Taiohae is a tribute to the gnats' vicious ubiquity.

In the town of Taiohae, I stayed in one of the Keikahanui Inn's three bungalows. The inn is owned by an American couple, Frank and Rose Corser, who taught me how to deal with the nonos. A mixture of five parts water to one part liquid bleach is splashed on the body in the shower, then rinsed away. The bleach prevents possible infection and also kills the itch for up to five hours. While in the Marquesas, I generally bleached myself three times a day.

My first Sunday in Taiohae, I went to mass at the Catholic church. Sitting in the pew, smelling faintly of Clorox, I listened to the bishop speak and recalled the passage in *Typee* in which island maidens swim out to the American whaler and do things with the sailors that Melville felt he "dare not mention." The practice of trading sexual favors for such precious items as fishhooks and iron nails was common throughout Polynesia at the time, and the French, through their Catholic missionaries, strove to put an end to the practice.

The missionaries believed that the sins of licentiousness and ritual cannibalism were endemic to Marquesan culture, which they therefore systematically set out to destroy. In this they were aided by the French military, and more significantly, by the diseases they had brought with them. The population of the islands, which probably stood at fifty thousand in the 1700s, fell to under five thousand. There was a brief period of revolt against the French—against the death that had come to the islands aboard the big ships, against the killing of the people and its culture—and in the late 1800s, this pathetic revolution erupted into a period of defiant and orgiastic cannibalism. By 1900, the revolt had been crushed, the culture destroyed. Today, the Marquesas are the most staunchly Catholic islands in all of French Polynesia.

After mass, I talked with Bishop Hervé-Marie Le Cléac'h at his home. He was a tall, aristocratic Frenchman who had been in the Marquesas for fourteen years. "The people here," the bishop said, "are as they were in the olden time. Nobody obeys chiefs because no one ever did. If the people work together on a project, they do so because they want to and not because someone told them to. They are very individualistic. The motto here is 'mind your own business.'" The bishop seemed to think that this was a good thing.

He was critical of the kind of Catholicism that decimated the culture of the islands a century ago. "Even now," he said, "the Marquesans are governed by foreigners; they learn a language in school that is not their own. They don't know their ancestors, their legends, their history, their art."

What the missionaries had taken from the people, the bishop wanted to give back. "I want them to be proud of their heritage," he said. "I feel I was sent here to make the people proud to be Marquesans. When a man is proud and happy, when he is content with himself and understands his place in the history of his land, then my job is made easier. He has conquered his confusion, you see, and is then free to accept or reject God as he pleases."

Later the bishop and I visited Damien Haturau, a handsome and imposing man who is probably the best-known sculptor in the Marquesas. The church had commissioned Damien to carve a life-sized wooden Madonna in the Marquesan manner. He had worked on the sculpture for three weeks, but now he thought there was a fault in the wood, and he told the bishop he wanted to start over.

Damien lived above the beach in the Meau Valley, sometimes called Sculptors Valley because so many good woodcarvers had chosen to live there. The artist took me into the open-sided shed where he kept his chisels and mallets. On the table, recently completed, was an exquisite carving of an elaborately tattooed Marquesan warrior. Beside the sculpture was a scholarly work on the archaeology of the Marquesas that had been written by a German around the turn of the century. Damien was using the sketches in the book to be certain that the tattoos were absolutely authentic. He was, it seemed, in the process of reinventing his own culture using the archaeology of another.

The bishop studied Damien's carved warrior for several minutes. "Wonderful," he said. "Brilliant, beautiful."

Nuku Hiva is an island that bombards the sense, numbing the mind with its constant and unrelenting beauty. The mountains behind Taiohae rise through groves of coconut and mangoes. A cruel joke of a road threads through papaya, banana, and passion fruit trees. Semiwild goats challenge cars for the right-of-way. A sudden squall blows in from the sea, bringing ten minutes of heavy rain. When the sun breaks through the clouds, light and shadow race across the green slopes below.

Descending from the central plateau atop the mountains into the valley called Taipivai, our car passed two boys carrying a rooster with a long string attached to one leg. If the boys came upon a wild cock in the jungle, they'd set their rooster on it. Both birds would become entangled in the string, and the boys would have themselves another fighting cock.

There are wild horses in the jungle as well, horses originally brought to the island by the French. Marquesans use a mare in heat to draw wild stallions, and the horses are easily broken by riding them belly-deep through the surf. They are small horses, sturdy climbers perfectly suited to the steep, jungled slopes of the Marquesas.

Everyone, it seems, owns a few stallions. In the village of Taipivai, I watched a family of six ride up into the hills, followed by five riderless horses. In less than two hours they were back, and each of the five horses carried over one hundred pounds of ripe bananas on its back.

Just above Taipivai, near a wide pool in the clear river

that runs through the village, there is a small trail that winds a mile or so through the jungle to the largest of the ancient ceremonial sites in the valley. The great stone terrace, called a *me'ae*, was perfectly square, twenty-five by twenty-five feet. Off to one side was a one-hundred-foot-high banyan tree. Aerial roots had dropped from its branches and they had, in turn, become new trunks so that the tree covered perhaps half an acre. The banyan and the thick groves of coconut trees filtered the sunlight, breaking its power. The sacred site was cool and spectral, shadowed in gloom.

A *tiki*, one of the ancient gods of the valley, squatted before the platform. It was six feet high, but three times wider than any human being. Blue-green algae grew like leprosy across the idol's immense head and obliterated one of the huge, round, empty eyes. The figure was clearly female, its genitals swollen as if in sensual excitement.

It was a simple matter, in the gloom, to imagine sacrifices committed by torchlight, to hear the screams and see the blood flowing over the holy stone. The people of Taipivai, the Typee, had been the most notorious cannibals of Nuku Hiva, the most feared tribe on the island. There had been skulls hanging from the branches of the sacred banyan tree; there had been human sacrifice and ritual cannibalism perhaps as late as 1900.

Later, I sat on a vista point overlooking the valley of Hatiheu and let the afternoon sun bake away the vague, sickly sad sense of dread that had descended on me at the *tiki* above Taipivai. Hatiheu was the valley where Robert Louis Stevenson had lived. The gentle beauty of the place suited my mood. The hills, alive with soft, calf-high ferns, spilled down toward the sea in waves of variegated green. The sound of the surf rose faintly from the bay below and mingled with the lazy hum of insects, the sigh of the breeze through the trees, the thunder of the waterfalls and the constant symphony of bird song that was punctuated at odd intervals by a single strangled prehistoric croak.

Below, a series of jagged black rock spires, too steep to carry vegetation, rose like sentinels just above the bay. They might have been the parapets of some alien civilization, or so I thought, and then the idea of blood flowing under the lurid light of torches hit me again so that the contrast of beauty and terror, of life and death, seemed especially vivid.

The *tiki* had been female, but perhaps the swollen organs were not meant to indicate sexual excitement. Perhaps the god that stood over the place of death was in the process of giving birth.

O n the island of Hiva Oa, I stayed for a time in Puamau, a village of some two hundred souls. As is the case almost everywhere in the Marquesas, there is no commercial hotel in the village. A visitor simply asks to see the mayor, who makes it his business to provide shelter. The mayor of Puamau decided that I could stay in his village, and I was given a comfortable room in his own house, a poured concrete dwelling with a working toilet and shower. Meals were provided along with the room for a cost of about thirty dollars a day. I ate well on roast pork, passion fruit, platters of raw tuna fillets marinated in coconut milk and lime, and French bread that was baked daily in a wood-fired oven.

I had come to Puamau to watch the single most important event in the economic life of the village. The copra schooner was about to make its monthly visit. Copra is dried coconut meat. The islanders collect coconuts, husk them, and leave the meat to dry in large wooden beds. The dried meat is stuffed into burlap sacks and taken to the beach for loading.

The copra is transported by ship to a factory in Tahiti, where the meat is cleaned and crushed. The coconut oil is used in soap, shampoo, synthetic rubber, glycerin, hydraulic brake fluid, margarine, and vegetable shortening.

Copra is the single source of income for most Marquesans, and the arrival of the copra schooner is cause for celebration. People who live up in the hills bring down strings of horses loaded with copra. Everyone gathers on the beach as the boat steams into Puamau Bay. Women play a kind of bingo that may only otherwise be played on Sundays. Young boys strum guitars and sing. Children play in the surf. The able-bodied men hoist 150-pound sacks of copra on their shoulders and trudge out through the pounding surf to the schooner's "whale boat," a twenty-foot-long craft designed to carry heavy loads through the breakers and out to the anchored ship.

The schooner is Puamau's link to the outside world. When the whale boat returns from the schooner, it is full of consumer goods ordered by the villagers and paid for with the thirty cents per pound they earn for their copra. I saw the men offload a few stoves, a refrigerator, and some furniture; but for the most part, the copra schooner delivered stereo systems, dirt bikes, motorcycles, and televisions. In the two days it took to load and unload the schooner, I saw at least half a dozen Sonys and as many VCRs invade Puamau.

The French Polynesian government installed television transmitters in Taiohae and Atuona in 1979. Relay stations on the mountaintops beam the signal down to smaller villages like Puamau. The programs are recorded in Tahiti and broadcast, commercial free, for two hours a day. In Puamau, at the mayor's home, I saw *Towering Inferno*, an episode of "Shogun" and some kung fu epic out of Hong Kong.

A French official, who would rather not be quoted, told me that the government provides television because the people love it. They love it so much, according to this man, that many of them might move to Tahiti simply to watch "Dallas" once a week. In Tahiti, however, jobs are scarce and there is a growing problem of overpopulation. "The idea is," the official said, "that if Marquesans have TV at home, we won't have to provide food and homes for them in Tahiti."

The fact that television exists in so remote a land, in a place littered with the artifacts of the old times and the old beliefs, sometimes staggers the imagination and presents the traveler with a number of truly remarkable culture crosscurrents. The day after the copra boat left, for instance, the mayor led me on a short walk through the jungle to a *tiki* that stood above his house. There are more than twenty-five *tikis* in the Puamau valley, but this one was eight feet high: the largest *tiki* in all of French Polynesia.

Above the ceremonial site there was a steep, rocky spire that rose to a needlelike summit. We began climbing this spire, the mayor and I, using rope he'd brought along. After a stiff hour's climb, we reached the summit. The mayor moved down a few feet among the ironwood trees and reached into a small cave about two feet in diameter. He pulled out a human skull and began telling a long, incredibly involved story about how a man—or more properly, a man's head—came to be buried there.

It seems that some time ago—I later placed the date at about 1900—there was a queen in Puamau who lived in a house on the large stone terrace not far from the mayor's house. In this time, said the mayor, a prolonged drought threatened the staple breadfruit crop, and there was danger of famine. The queen requested a human sacrifice to appease the gods, and three men took it upon themselves to perform this duty. They pulled all the hair out of their heads and hung their machetes around their necks, which was a dead giveaway to everyone else in the village that they were looking for someone expendable. The people of Puamau gathered together on the beach for mutual safety.

The three hairless men were forced to find a victim in another drainage. "It was over there," the mayor said, pointing to a small ridge, "where they saw a man in a coconut tree." The story became very detailed here. The mayor wanted me to know precisely how many shots were fired (three), how many times the man was hit (twice), and which was the fatal shot (the one that passed through the right kidney).

The dead man's head and long bones were carried to the top of the spire, where they were placed in the cave. The rains came immediately, of course, and Puamau was saved. The French heard about the murder, however, and sent a gunboat to Puamau Bay. The queen was imprisoned on the ship until the village surrendered the killers. The three men were taken out to the ship at gunpoint and were never seen again. The queen was released.

The mayor pointed down to a house in Puamau and said the name of the family that lived there. "That is this man's family," he said, holding up the skull. The mayor stared into the empty eye sockets, in the manner of a man who is mentally adding a set of figures. "This is the great grandfather," he said at last.

"And the family knows he is up here?" I asked.

"Yes, of course."

"And they don't want to get this skull and bury it properly?"

"No," the mayor said. He seemed to regard the question as both strange and mildly offensive. "Why would they?"

It was late in the afternoon—the mayor's story had taken almost two hours to tell. He carefully placed the skull back in the cave and said we would have to hurry back down to the house. The television would be coming on soon, and he wanted to watch "Dynasty."

I am living in Atuona, in a bungalow near the black sand beach where Gauguin painted many of his most famous oils. The bungalow stands on the site of Gauguin's house. In recent years, the place sometimes has been the home of travelers whose reconfirmations were not recorded. Perhaps these hapless visitors reacted as I did; perhaps they spent a day or two trying to figure out how to change their schedule or contact the people they were supposed to meet at home. Over the space of days, perhaps others also felt the sun burn away their anger, and maybe they settled into the gentle rhythm of life in the Marquesas.

These days I rise at six o'clock, just as the five or six roosters who seem to live under my window explode in paroxysms of ear-shattering bravado. The old man who lives next door is generally up already, sitting on his porch and playing taped Tahitian laments on his immense JVC boom box.

I pull on my shorts and step out onto my own porch. The old man and I nod to each other, but he expects me to ignore him for the rest of the day, just as I expect him to ignore me. Mind your own business, as the bishop said, is the motto here.

About seven-thirty, I walk five blocks to the bakery and buy a loaf of good French bread fresh from the oven. I keep forgetting to bring money, but the woman behind the counter recognizes me and runs a tab under the name of "M. Américain."

The dog that has adopted me follows at my heels. He strolled into the bungalow several days ago and I shouted one of the few phrases I know in Marquesan: "Keer aw." The words, generally addressed to invading dogs, chickens, horses, or pigs, mean "get out." I had the misfortune of running into a dog who thought his name was Keer Aw. He gave me one of those open-mouthed looks of keen canine anticipation, the kind that seems to say: "Oh boy, wanna play, got something for me to eat?"

So Keer Aw lives on my porch. He sleeps at my feet while I type and tips over the garbage whenever he thinks I'm not looking.

About eleven-thirty, when it gets too hot to work, I walk down to the Gauguin beach for a swim. I am trying to improve my French with the aid of a French/English dictionary and a French comic book I found about the American cowboy, Stormy Joe, and his comical sidekick, Sardine. Already I have learned to say, "Drop your gun or I'll kill you like a mad dog."

Keer Aw lies in the sand while I read. After an hour or so, he gets up and slinks off down the beach, looking back over his shoulder in the most guilty fashion imaginable. "It's not what you think," he says. "I'm not really sneaking back to the bungalow to tip over your garbage."

About two-thirty, I walk back home and clean up the garbage. Keer Aw, skulking under the picnic table on my porch, eyes me cautiously. I step into the bungalow, bleach myself down, take a cold shower, and lie down for a brief nap. Outside my window, chickens are lunching on some ants that are feeding on spilled garbage. I find the pluck and cluck of contented poultry curiously soothing.

Some days, I borrow a stallion from a lady who lives nearby and ride over the ridge to a bay called Taaoa where there is a beach that seems devoid of nonos. There is something almost unbearably romantic about riding alone, galloping bareback across the sand as the breakers thunder into the shore.

Some evenings I go to a Chinese family's home on a hill above Atuona's hundred lights. The family runs an informal restaurant. I'm particularly fond of the river shrimp dinner.

Strangely, I've stopped my habit of visiting the airline office and reconfirming my flight every day. I think I'm becoming almost Marquesan in my attitude: if I'm on the next plane out, fine. If not, what the hell. My work is going well, the food is good, the land is vibrant. I'm content and my dog loves me for no very good reason. Money is no problem. There is plenty to eat growing on the hills above town if it should come to that. Worrying about something I can't control, something like another missed flight, would simply spoil an otherwise perfect day.

WET WORK

IN
DEEP

Seven Good Reasons Why You, Too, Should Consider the Scuba Escape

iving doesn't upset your stomach, as aspirin often can: I got firmly and incurably hooked on diving several years ago when I was doing the pool work necessary to become a certified diver. It was early one Monday morning. The day before I had attended a wedding where I was forced, very nearly against my will, to drink massive quantities of champagne for hours on end without surcease. I woke up that Monday in my own bed, but I was still wearing the rental tux, and the overhead light burned like an ugly accusation. My tongue was made of sandpaper. I felt diseased.

That very day I had an appointment to go lie in ten feet of water, at the bottom of the pool in the scuba school. I would be down there for about an hour. The exercise was designed to help a student become familiar with the sensation of being underwater for long periods of time and to help him learn proper use of the scuba gear.

I pulled on the wet suit and put on a fifteen-pound weight belt, which weighed somewhere in excess of two hundred pounds, then fell into the pool, the tank on my back, the regulator in my mouth. At ten feet I took the regulator out of my mouth and blew a little of the pressurized air I had been breathing into the vestlike piece of equipment known as a buoyancy compensator, or BC. That was the extent of the exercise: put enough air into the BC so that its lift precisely equaled the downward drag of the weight belt. I lay a foot and a half off the bottom of the pool, very nearly comatose, like a man in a sensory-deprivation chamber. Each time I took a breath, I'd rise a few inches; each time I exhaled, I'd sink a like amount.

I was neutrally buoyant, completely free of the gravity that had seemed a cruel and unreasonable force only an hour before. The silence sang, and the moral aspects of my condition began to recede. I really wasn't such a bad guy, and it probably wouldn't cost all that much to get the tux cleaned and mended. The pain in my joints, which had made my arms and legs feel the way trees growing at the edge of the tundra look, had begun to subside. Each time I exhaled, another portion of my pain arose inside the bubbles and burst on the surface of the world, leaving me feeling stronger, healthier, more morally staunch.

And so it came to me, as I lay on the bottom of the pool, exhaling ailments, that scuba diving cures hangovers. And I was hooked.

We can learn from the wacky antics of our underwater friends and even apply these lessons to our everyday life: a single example should suffice. In tropical waters, especially around coral reefs, one often sees small blue-and-black or yellow-and-black fish known as wrasses. They usually hover close to coral heads and escape into small niches when big, predatory fish approach. A few of the smaller species of wrasse, however, stay well away from any protection. Out in the open water, in what is called a cleaner station, these cleaner wrasses twitch about in such a way that their colors catch the sun and attract the very fish that habitually eat most wrasses.

The predator in question may be a two-foot-long grouper. It approaches the cleaner wrasse and opens its mouth wide. The wrasse swims directly into the grouper's open mouth, an apparent suicide, but there it eats the tropical parasites that accumulate and annoy the grouper. This is an example of a good business deal: the wrasse gets a meal; the grouper gets rid of its parasites. Symbiosis. Mutual advantage.

In these same waters there is another fish that looks very much like the upright and businesslike cleaner wrasse. The blenny, however, is an entirely different type of fish. The sly blenny finds a wrasse in full dance at its cleaner station, and there it sets itself up for wicked business by imitating the dance of the honest fish. When the grouper approaches, mouth open, the blenny darts in, tears off a hunk of flesh, and escapes to a nearby niche the enraged grouper can't penetrate. The blenny is a fish that lives in treachery and feeds off the flesh of those who would freely feed it. It is sometimes called a false cleaner, though I prefer to think of it as a lawyer fish.

D iving makes you feel so good you could just die: rapture of the deep is a wonderfully poetic name for nitrogen narcosis, an intoxication produced by breathing nitrogen gas under pressure. The only time I've been noticeably "narked" was in the Blue Hole, a four-hundred-foot-deep pit off the coast of Belize (formerly British Honduras). The hole is set in shallow water, about an hour by light plane from the coast, and it contains structures that help prove a long-held scientific theory. It is thought that during the ice ages so much water was concentrated in the form of ice at the polar caps that the seas of the world were actually shallower by some four hundred feet.

To see the structures that support that theory, I was going to have to dive deeper than the maximum safe sport-diving depth of one hundred thirty feet. There are several dangers involved in exceeding recommended depths, and to understand them you have to know a bit about gas laws. The air in your tank is just ordinary air. But it is packed in there at somewhere between two thousand and three thousand pounds per square inch. The genius of the regulator is that it feeds air into your mouth at ambient pressure: if the water is pressing on you at five times the surface pressure, then you are getting air that is five times as dense as surface air.

You *need* this pressurized air. Your body is mostly water, and for diving purposes, it is best to think of it as a sealed plastic sack full of water. The lungs are two air-filled balloons inside that sack. The deeper you dive, the more pressure on the sack, and the more the balloons want to collapse. Breathing ordinary air at a hundred feet would be as difficult as trying to suck that air into your lungs from the surface with a narrow straw.

At one hundred feet, a diver is breathing air that is four times as dense as sea-level air. Each breath contains four times the normal component of nitrogen. Nitrogen is pretty much inert, and it is passed into the tissue and fluids of the body without being utilized. The fatty tissues of the brain and nervous system, however, seem most susceptible to nitrogen absorption. All this excess nitrogen banging around in your brain can make you perilously goofy. Divers use martinis as a rough measure of narcosis: each thirty-three feet of depth makes you feel as light-headed as one martini on an empty stomach.

To see for myself the reason that the Blue Hole is an object of scientific study, I was going to have to go about two hundred feet, or a little more than six martinis' worth. At that depth some divers have felt a euphoria so intense they've given their regulator to a fish and died laughing.

The hole is shaped like an hourglass, and I sank past its high waist at about ninety feet. The wall sloped inward then, forming a "ceiling" over me. At one hundred thirty feet I saw the first structure. It was a stalactite, hanging from the roof of the wall. There were others, deeper down, twelve to fifteen of them. They were huge, twenty-five to thirty feet long, and there was no oceanographic explanation for them. Stalactites can only grow in terrestrial caves, which meant the Blue Hole must have been a dry cave or sinkhole during the shallow-water times of the ice ages.

I remember floating upside down, looking at the stalactites, pleasantly aware of a growing euphoric narcosis. The stalactites pointed down, deeper down, and they were of a shape I remember from church. They looked like statues of the Virgin in her robes. The sound of my exhalations was symphonic, and the Virgins hung there, pointing into the darkness far below. Inexplicably I thought of Atlantis. If the legendary island had been an oasis of culture and knowledge *during the ice ages,* then *the flood* that destroyed it must surely have come *when the polar caps released their water.* The thought seemed monumental, earthshaking, historic in import. Bubbles rose up my body and rolled up a Virgin's robe, so that in one small corner of my mind I knew I was still upside down, and I was shining a light on the end of a stalactite, and there were crimson blotches, like carnations, where the face of the Virgin should have been. She was pointing down into the darkness, and oh, I wanted to dive deeper. Even deeper.

My buddies, professionals all, and I ascended according to plan, and we hung off on the anchor line for twenty-five minutes. Hanging off, or decompressing, is not nearly as much fun as reading *Silas Marner.* The purpose of hanging there at two hundred feet for all that time with nothing to do or see is to let all that excess nitrogen bleed out of your system.

Remember, the nitrogen was absorbed under pressure. If you shot straight to the surface from a hundred feet, all these nitrogen bubbles in your brain and nervous system would expand to four times their size, and you'd spend the rest of your life in a wheelchair explaining to people why they call it the bends.

So I hung there, bleeding nitrogen, and no longer narked in the least. Atlantis seemed a long way off, unimportant now compared to the realization that the Blue Hole had acted like a psychological syphon, had tried to pull me down into its darkest depths. Another fifty feet and I never would have stopped diving. I would have died happy in the warm womb of the hanging Virgins.

Diving is a sport for the lazy: there are sets of tables that tell you how deep you can go and how long you can stay, and if you follow the table, you will never have to decompress. Safety in diving is largely a matter of cerebration. Plan your dive, and dive your plan.

Here's the plan for my most recent dive: a guide and I anchored over a reef just opposite Rum Point, on the north side of Grand Cayman, an island about one hundred fifty miles northwest of Jamaica. Toward shore the reef drops off to a shallow floor, which slopes up to the shores of the island. The outer section of the reef fronts the Cayman Trench, which at its maximum depth is a little more than 4.7 *miles* deep. We're talking abysmal depth here.

The outer section of the reef forms a vertical wall, a wall that seems to drop off forever. We were anchored over the reef proper, and about forty feet below us, on the top of the reef, was a small opening. Long Tunnel runs down on slant. It is about sixty feet long altogether and empties out on the wall at a depth of about ninety feet.

Checking the tables, we found we could stay at ninety feet for thirty minutes without decompressing. Call it twenty-five minutes, just to be safe. A very gentle current was sweeping to the west along the wall; so we'd swim east for the first half of the dive, then turn around and let the current float us back to the boat. We decided to hang off for five minutes at ten feet, for no other reason than that it made us both feel smart.

We dropped over the side and entered the tunnel, which was so narrow we had to go single file. The oval passageway was dark and so smoothly sculpted with strange and grotesque shapes that it seemed to have been purposely crafted, but by forces unseen and inhuman.

At ninety feet the tunnel spit us out into the brilliance beyond the wall. The sensation there, with the wall dropping away forever into the abyss, was precisely that of dream flight. There was a euphoria there too, the emotion

I feel in my dream state when I realize how silly I've been all these years for not using my powers of flight. All this was touched by the sweetest tinge of purple narcosis.

Visibility—I swear it—ranged to one hundred fifty feet, and off to my left the open water was deep blue, like the Montana sky on the clearest of days. I looked to the wall. Every niche and ledge was overlaid with bizarre and unearthly shapes: purple pagodas from some alternate universe, barrel sponges a man could stand in, sea fans bluer than a baby's eyes. And all about, swimming purposefully, like citizens of a busy city, were hundreds upon hundreds of fish: the regal moorish idols, angelfish, long-nosed butterfly fish, sad-eyed squirrel fish, blue-and-black wrasses.

Every minute or so I'd check my watch and pressure gauge and depth gauge. After fifteen minutes of deep diving along the wall, we rose to the top of the reef—forty feet or so—and let the current urge us back toward the boat. No reason to swim if the ocean will do it for you. The top of the reef was choked with color, like an alpine meadow in spring. Blue and green and black and yellow crinoids—fernlike invertebrates that feel like Velcro to the touch—were interspersed with all manner of soft corals. There were green and gold and purple-red sea fans, there were flowering corals, and long golden sea whips swaying in the gentle surge.

We rose to examine a spire that jutted steeplelike from the top of the reef. Near the top of the spire and nicely centered in it was a particularly baroque niche or window. Set deep back into the middle of the niche was a flattish green barrel sponge, like a child's chair. To the right stood a long purple tube sponge that looked like the kind of floor lamp a color-blind person might buy at Woolworth's. To the left of the little green chair was a small white octagonal sea fan, which looked like a doily set against the gold-flecked plate of green-red sheet coral that formed the wall of the niche. All in all, it looked like a tiny room built by an aquatic hobbit with a psychedelic habit.

We rose to the anchor line and hung off on the rope. The most physically demanding part of the dive had been the two minutes it took us to don our equipment.

There is no record of any diver being eaten by a giant squid like the one that got Captain Nemo's sub in that movie: the diving industry blames the movie *Jaws* for a perceptible dip in sales, and I'm sure they'd like me to point out that not all sharks are particularly scary. In Australia the small epaulet shark tries frantically to escape divers and snorkelers. The little fellow feels safely hidden if he can get his head into a coral niche. No matter that his body is completely visible; the epaulet shark, this ostrich of the sea, can't see you, and he lies still as a stone, thinking he is a very clever fish. Incidentally, the epaulet shark has no teeth. He is affectionately referred to as a "gummy."

The carpet shark is a sedentary fish, and he is often seen loafing on a circular plate of coral. His coloration is intense in a mottled, ancient sort of way. He looks like the most ornate carpet in Grandma's house. A little fringe of beard, like white lace coral, hangs from his chin, making him look like an elderly dandy. The carpet shark simply sits and waits, snapping up the occasional unwary parrot fish. Once at Heron Island, on Australia's Great Barrier Reef, I watched as a woman, posing for a picture, sat on a carpet shark's head. The shark bucked in an irritable manner, and the woman came off her perch like someone shot from a cannon. The carpet shark glared up at the divers with its widely spaced, milky-white eyes. I thought of a grouchy old man forced to dress as a teenager.

Reef sharks, such as the blacktip, are considered harmless animals. I've seen them five and six feet long, and I've swum with them on patrol. They are beautiful, in the manner of a samurai sword—form follows function—and they make good diving buddies if you can keep up with them.

There are sleeping sharks off the Caribbean coast of Mexico, sharks so docile that divers have been known to pull their tails. Caribbean nurse sharks are large enough to generate a full-scale adrenaline rush, and they are the ones local divers look for when they want to watch sharks. In Cozumel, Mexico's premier dive resort, I talked to a woman named Rita Shess, who sometimes works as a shark handler for feature films. She told me about her work on a film called *The Zombie II*. The zombie, an underwater sort in this trasher, likes to grab topless female divers. These are rare off Mexico, but the zombie perseveres. In the end the zombie is carried off by a shark, and the Caribbean is again safe for starlets.

The zombie stood on the ocean floor in his weighted boots. Rita and her team of three stood just out of camera range to the left. Another team of three stood to the right. Rita's team pushed the shark out toward the zombie and in front of the camera. It drifted lazily by the guy in the rubber mask, indolent and indifferent. The second team caught the shark, turned it around, and Ping-Ponged it back to Rita's team. They did this dozens of times while the zombie waved its arms and spouted great gouts of artificial blood. The film would be cut in such a way that sales of diving equipment would be sure to suffer.

Experienced divers often choose a dive site where they know they will see sharks. They *want* to see sharks. Some diving guidebooks specify areas where sharks are usually present. Here's Nancy Sefton in *Dive Cayman*: "Shark Alley . . . a moderate depth site . . . noted for the frequent sighting of reef sharks. . . . Chances of seeing sharks are fairly good. . . . In Cayman waters these have proven to be harmless creatures, even shy."

I do not mean to suggest all sharks are shy or harmless. There are more than two hundred species of shark extant, and some—hammerheads, great whites, tigers, grays—can be dangerous. But even if you do come upon one of these bad guys, your chances are something on the order of half a million to one against being attacked. Knowledgeable divers consider such sightings a privilege.

There is good diving near you: while I like diving big walls, I feel obliged to point out that there is great diving all over the world. The cold waters off northern California could never support a reef, but diving the kelp beds there is like dropping into a series of ice-water cathedrals. A strand of kelp anchors on a rock, and a bulbous head on the other end floats on the surface, so that the bed itself is a forest of long, green strands. Diving a kelp bed feels very much like walking through the redwoods. Sunlight scatters throughout the bed, just as it does in a redwood forest, and the feeling is equally Gothic and mysterious.

Even in Montana, where I live, there are a number of interesting dive sites. The Firehole River in Yellowstone Park is fed by numerous geysers and thermal springs. The water stays relatively warm all year round, and a popular dive site is set in a spectacular canyon. The water pushes a diver through smooth rock corridors, shoves him up over the top of a small wall—the water is about thirty-five feet deep here—then rockets him over an odd grouping of humpy, sculptured volcanic boulders. The pool at the end of this fast, roller coaster run is full of cutthroat trout, and they can often be seen feeding voraciously on a sudden snow-fly hatch.

Not far from where I live, there is a pond fed by a thermal spring. The water temperature never drops below sixty-nine degrees, and someone has stocked the pond with colorful freshwater tropical fish. You can cross-country ski to this unusual site.

On the other end of the state, a railroad track runs along a ledge above a mountain lake. Many years ago a train derailed and rolled into deep water. I know of no other place in the world where you can dive to see a train wreck.

The point is this: if there's good diving near me, then there just has to be good diving near you.

You get to go around wearing tight rubber suits, and nobody thinks you're weird: this is our little secret.

HAREM
FANTASY

Vertigo Turns an Old Dream Upside Down

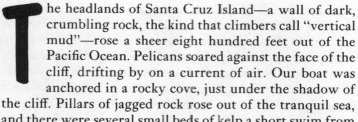

The headlands of Santa Cruz Island—a wall of dark,
crumbling rock, the kind that climbers call "vertical
mud"—rose a sheer eight hundred feet out of the
Pacific Ocean. Pelicans soared against the face of the
cliff, drifting by on a current of air. Our boat was
anchored in a rocky cove, just under the shadow of
the cliff. Pillars of jagged rock rose out of the tranquil sea,
and there were several small beds of kelp a short swim from
the boat.

The pelicans, with their long beaks and pouched, oddly
shaped necks, looked vaguely reptilian in flight, miniature
versions of the Japanese movie monster Rodan, that boxcar-
sized, Tokyo-stomping pterodactyl. Off on a rocky beach,
not far from the boat, a large group of sea lions discussed
our arrival. "Ark, ark, ark," they said.

There were several hundred of the beasts sunbathing on
the rocks. The animals are dark brown, almost black when
wet; but on the beach they took on the color of the sun. The
eight-foot-long males can weigh up to six hundred pounds.
The females, a couple of feet shorter, seldom weigh more
than two hundred pounds. The males fight among themselves to establish harems of up to twenty females. Unlike
true seals, sea lions can rotate their rear flippers, and they
moved from the beach to the rocks with an endearing awkward waddle. Humans seem to find this mode of locomotion
cute, in the same way they consider penguins cute. Most of
the trained seals you see on television or in the circus—the

181

guys who honk bicycle horns for fish—are actually California sea lions.

Out in the dark water, near the kelp beds, a few of the sea lions lay on their backs, floating there in lazy immobility like vacationers in the Great Salt Lake. Their flippers, which projected out of the water, looked like the fins of small sharks, makos perhaps, or blues.

I dropped into the water and swam for the nearest kelp bed. I was wearing scuba gear and a black hooded wet suit, and I expected to pry a few scallops off the rocks for dinner. Sea lions can be playful diving companions, but they are thieves as well. So awkward on land, they can swoop and dive like pelicans in the water, and they can make off with a goody bag full of abalone or speared fish in a manner that makes a diver feel furiously helpless, like an elderly and arthritic woman victimized by a purse snatcher on a city street. It is therefore prudent when diving in the presence of sea lions—or in waters where there may be sharks—to tie the nylon mesh or goody bag to your weight belt with a long rope, secured by a slip knot, an offering to these fat lords of the Channel Islands. If you have no choice but to cooperate, better to do it on your own terms.

I reached the kelp bed and dropped beneath the entangling mass of green blades on the surface. This particular variety of seaweed attaches itself to a rock on the ocean floor. A kind of air bladder forms on the upper leaves, allowing them to float to the surface. Diving in a kelp bed is like walking through a triple-canopy jungle or a redwood forest. Sunlight filters through the thick upper vegetation in the pure shafts that ought to be accompanied by an angelic chorus.

The beds are full of life. A cold-water current rushing down from the Arctic runs out of power here off Southern California, and the sea life is an amalgam of cold- and warm-water organisms. Little animals hide in the depths of the kelp, pursued by hungry, larger life forms that, in turn, are careful not to stray too far toward the edge of the bed where the really big predators lurk.

I was twisting through long stems of kelp, thinking of scallops (sauteed in butter and garlic), but the bed was small, and I decided to swim to another, larger stand that was closer to shore and the sea lion colony. It was there, just out of sight of both beds, in the open sea, with the sandy floor opening up like a desert on all sides, that the vertigo hit me.

ivers and pilots, even experienced ones, suffer from complete disorientation on rare occasions. It happens to pilots in no-visibility situations, on instruments, when they suddenly realize they no longer know up from down. The same thing can happen to divers moving through open water where there are no points of reference. There is a sense of dizziness and nausea, compounded by irrational thoughts and confusion.

I reminded myself that bubbles rise and managed to orient myself in two dimensions. There was nothing I could do about the confusion, though. I found myself thinking about sea lions, about the things that Karen Straus, who has spent years diving the Channel Islands, told me before this trip.

"Is it safe to dive with sea lions?" I had asked.

"Oh, sure," she said. "It's fun."

"Any danger?"

"Not from the females, generally. If the males think you're another male, there could be trouble. It's rare."

"What do they do?"

"They beat you up."

"Oh."

"Of course, since you're not nearly large enough to look like a male, it's more likely that they'd think you were a female." I was thinking about this because, at six feet and two hundred pounds, I was about the size of your basic female sea lion. The black wet suit looked like the slick and shining skin of a wet seal. Vertigo presented me with the unsettling thought that a powerful six-hundred-pound beast could just possibly fall in love with me, here in eighty feet of water.

"What happens if he thinks you're a female?" I had asked.

"Well, he'll try to separate you from your diving partners. Try to drive you out to open sea."

"Okay, but once he gets you where he wants you, what, uh (I wasn't sure I wanted to know this), what does he do?"

"He beats you up," she said.

Did I look like a female sea lion? What if one of the big fellows decided I was some desirable exotic, a worthy addition to his harem?

It was not a salubrious image: a life spent on the beach, wallowing around fatly with the other females. Knowing the shame of being the ugliest wife: the sad slow one who keeps getting her scallops snatched away, the outcast with the far-off, wistful look in her eye. Imagine lying there on the rocks trying to chat with the other wives, those complacent lard-buckets, secure in their own blubbery allure.

"Looks like we're in for a storm."

"Ark, ark, ark."

And every once in a while, every month or so, a freighter would steam by a few miles off the coast and there I'd be, standing in the wet sand, waving my arms, screaming for help, a damsel in distress, an innocent imprisoned in the sheik's seraglio. "Help me! For the love of God, they think I'm a female sea lion, and the big guy wants more kids."

No answer from the ship, but here comes the male, this six-hundred-pound tyrant, huge, dominant, terrifying. He's sliding rapidly over the beach, using his flippers and leaving a furrow in the sand the size of an irrigation ditch. The big guy is moving fast now, not nearly so cute as he might in the circus, and instead of honking a bicycle horn, he is growling deep in his throat, making the message abun-

dantly clear: "Siddown and shaddup." He glances around
at the other wives as if to say, "Yeah, she's ugly, but ya gotta
admit, she sure smells different." A chorus of sarcastic
laughter here: "Ark, ark, ark."

And then I was moving into the second kelp bed and the
vertigo dropped away from me like a rock kicked over the
lip of the Grand Canyon. The relief was primal, instinctive:
back to the trees and safety. What the hell: trapped in some
blubbery harem? What had been going through my mind?
Could such a thing really happen? Or was it the fact that I'd
just seen *Tootsie*?

At the far reaches of my vision, in open waters beyond
the kelp, a sea lion began slicing through gray waters in my
direction. It looped toward the surface and the tangle of
vegetation there, then dived straight down, disappearing
into the cathedral of light in the depths of the kelp. I
couldn't tell if it was a male or a female.

DRUNKEN DIVING
FOR
POISON SEA SNAKES

recently traveled to the Philippines and chanced on a
unique employment opportunity in the diving industry.
The following is an outline of what you will need to
know in order to get started in the glamorous and excit-
ing field of drunken driving for poisonous sea snakes.

Where: From California, follow the Pacific Ocean
west and south to the Philippine Sea. Make a sharp left turn
and stop at the island of Cebu, in the Vasayan Sea. At the
northern tip of the island is a jungle town called Daan
Bantayan, and a tad to the north is the village of Tapilon.
Stand on the sandy shore and look west. That hummock
standing dark against the setting sun is Gato Island. Gato
is honeycombed by caves. Sea snakes spawn in the caves.

The Snakes: *Fasciata semifasciata* is an aquatic snake about
four feet long and as big around as the business end of Dave
Kingman's bat. The snake weighs over ten pounds and has
alternating black and bluish-gray stripes. The skin is used
to make purses and shoes. The meat and entrails are used
as slop for hogs.

Fasciata semifasciata is definitely venomous. There is no
argument on this point. In recent years, one diver died from
a *Fasciata* bite. Generally, a bitten diver suffers only some
swelling and numbness.

"My arm became the size of my leg and I couldn't move
it for days because I couldn't feel it," is the way one diver

described the result of a bite. The single recorded fatality may have been due to the victim's severe reaction to the venom. If you know you have an allergy to sea snake venom, perhaps drunken diving for poison sea snakes is not for you.

Equipment: The craftsmen of Daan Bantayan can make you a pair of goggles. These are carved from wood to conform to the contours of your face and they will fit no one else. Glass is glued to the wood and a headstrap is fashioned from an old automobile inner tube.

You'll need a flashlight and a clear plastic bag. The bag is placed over the flashlight and secured with tape, twine, tire-strips, and glue. This is your underwater light. Get an old tire and make two rubber bracelets, one for each wrist.

Preparing for Work: The snake divers believe that alcohol, taken internally in sufficient quantities, thins the blood and renders a bite less harmful. Any liquor will do, and the stronger the better. Rum, either Anejo or Manila, is good, but coconut wine flavored with anise, called malloroca, is favored by most of the divers. They particularly like Green Parrot brand. The wine is clear and thick and tastes like licorice. It comes in a clear beer-type bottle; the cork under the cap is usually black and a little crumbly.

The last resort is called tuba. This is the rapidly fermenting sap of the coconut palm, colored with mangrove bark. In the morning, the tuba gatherers bring in the daily crop. Fresh, the liquor is sweet, orange, and there's a white frost on the top. It is not very alcoholic and of little use to a snake diver. Tuba of a more aristocratic vintage—say three days—is more suited to your purpose. It's bitter as a lemon and will set you howling at the moon.

The Work: A few hours before sunset, you will head out across the bloodwarm Vasayan Sea in a dugout outrigger called a banca, powered by an eighteen-horsepower Briggs & Stratton engine. You'll relax in the bow and have some more rum—it takes an hour to cover the twelve miles to Gato.

The island is a little over an acre and perhaps two hundred feet high. Sheer rock walls rise about eighty feet, then give way to an inward-sloping tangle of dense brush. At water level, you will see many caves set deep into the rock walls. The water inside the caves is a deep blue—the same shade of blue you see inside of fastidious people's toilet bowls.

The snakes hide in little nooks and crannies during the day. You will do your diving at night, when they swarm inside the caves in their serpentine mating ballet.

Take one last sip of tuba, switch on your flashlight, slip into the dark water, and duck into the cave. Train your light on the water. Drop down about twenty feet to a ledge and hang there. On a really lucky night, you'll be in the midst of a maelstrom of snakes. Grab one just behind the head. The skin will be dry to the touch, not at all slimy.

To train yourself in the proper technique, grab your left thumb just below the knuckle with the thumb and first two fingers of your right hand. The snake is larger of course, but there is a knucklelike swelling just below the head where you want to grab him.

Now take the snake and slip his head under one of the rubber bracelets on your wrist. Find another snake. A good diver will surface with three snakes on either wrist.

What To Do If You Get Bit: Review Preparing for Work. Whether your medicine is rum, wine, or tuba, ingest an improbably excessive quantity. The boatmen will take you back in the banca. You will be lying on your back, drinking three-day tuba and singing some song half-remembered from your childhood. There will be a nasty paralytic numbness in your arm and it will swell like a goiter. You will probably not die. Snake divers seldom die. Keep repeating, "I will probably not die."

MONSTERS
AND
HOAXES

BIGFOOT

An Historico-Ecologica-Athropoidologico-Archetypal Study

Believers theorize that he came down from Mt. Hood, the 11,250-foot blizzard-shrouded peak just outside Portland, Oregon. Massive, standing nearly nine feet tall and weighing all of nine hundred pounds, he strode down the wooded ridges, north and east to the seven-thousand-foot level where the spring snow lay wet and heavy in forests fifty miles from the nearest road. At the four-thousand-foot level, the thick coniferous forests thinned and the deep mountain gorges leveled out. It was late June 1971, and the lower rivers raged with the waters of the melting snow pack.

At the three-thousand-foot level the first growths of douglas fir and oak gave way to a few scrub oak, growing singly. From a high point on the ridge that runs down from Mt. Hood called Seven Miles Hill, he could see the lights of The Dalles, Oregon, where eleven thousand people lived.

Fifteen miles upriver the Wy-am Indians, roped to their platforms perched over the boiling river, netted spring chinook salmon by the hundreds with their long poles. This they had done every spring since prehistory. The Great Food is what the Wy-am called salmon; and perhaps he had come down to the semiarid insecurity of The Dalles to scramble on the banks of the river for the Great Food during one of the largest salmon runs on the North American continent. Some who theorize about him think that he came down to this narrow point in the river where there is little current because an island breaks the swim to Washington and the Cascade Range—where the deer and huckleberries are plentiful in the summer.

To the east the land opens to treeless rolling hills. Great high-tension towers converge on the Chenowith Converter and scar the land as far as the eye can see. There was no cover for him there. But to swim the river from here, four miles west of The Dalles, he had only to cross two roads: the old highway to Portland, US 30, and the new Interstate, 80N.

Things had changed since he had last been down to the river. There was an aluminum plant nearby, a new shopping center, a Rocket gas station, a new and used car lot, and—strangest of all for him during the nights—The Dalles drive-in, which specializes in films like *Deathmaster* and *The Two-Headed Thing*. In the early daylight hours of this first day of June 1971, he stood in a small meadow above what had been a large foothill apple orchard. It was now filled with flat electrified platforms and called The Pinewood Mobile Manor.

Joe Mederios, maintenance man for the trailer court, was watering flowers near his trailer that morning. Directly across US 30 is a large fenced meadow. At about one hundred fifty yards a rock ledge of perhaps thirty-five feet banks a higher meadow. Mederios caught a movement along the edge from a corner of his eye. He assumed it was George Johnson, the owner of the land, and went back to watering his flowers. But his mind was engaged in a curious and unconscious arithmetic. He had seen Johnson on the land previously—it wasn't unusual—but this figure was too big . . . the arms were too long . . . the shoulders too broad.

Mederios turned to the ridge for a longer look. What he saw was a shaggy, gray figure he took to be at least ten feet tall. It had an oval face and crest or dorsal ridge along the top of its head. The face was flat, brown, and hairless.

The man turned back to his flowers and considered his situation. He was responsible to some Portland businessmen who would be down to The Dalles the next day. If he were to report the sighting, there would be deputies and curiosity-seekers tromping all over his carefully watered flowers about the time his bosses arrived. Mederios later told the sheriff's deputy Rich Carlson that he didn't report the incident for fear he'd "be called a nut."

The next day, around noon, the three businessmen met Mederios and were in the midst of discussions in a trailer-office fronting the meadow when Mederios again saw an erect apelike figure through a window. The four men ran outside and watched from across the road as it moved through a break in the ridge and came into the lower meadow, where it walked among the sparse scrub oak near the rocks. It stopped near a small tree, and from where the men stood, it appeared to be somewhat taller than the tree. The four men and the other creature stared at one another for perhaps a minute, before it turned, went up through the break in the rocks, and disappeared into the upper meadow.

This time the sighting was reported and deputy Carlson went out to investigate.

From Carlson's report filed on June second, 1971: "Mr. Mederios . . . described it as being about ten feet tall, greyish in color, real wide shoulders and arms that hung way down. He went on to say it looked like an overgrown ape. He stated it was not a bear. The creature was walking upright at the time of the sighting."

The Portland men, solid citizens all, confirmed the sighting and description.

The same night, about 9:30, when the last summer light was fading in the meadow, a man named Rich Brown, a high school music teacher, and his wife were returning from a choir practice he had been conducting. At the entrance to the trailer court, Brown's wife either shouted or screamed and pointed to a figure in the lower meadow. Brown swung his car around and put the headlights stark into the meadow. He was joined by a second car, and eventually Mederios, who stepped out of the office to see why the cars were blocking the entrance.

At a distance of about sixty-five yards the creature froze and stared into the lights. Brown sprinted for his trailer, grabbed a Winchester 30.06 with a four-power scope. He opened his car door and steadied the rifle. He considered a shot to the heart, then the head. With the scope cross-hairs squarely between the thing's expressionless flat black eyes, he released the safety. Like any good marksman, Brown squeezes the trigger slowly. In the moment between the final squeeze and the shot, Rich Brown, who had just come from a church, made a complicated moral decision.

"I couldn't shoot it," he said later, "because it looked more human than animal."

Aside from Indian legends, which are virtually timeless, the Bigfoot saga on the North American Continent begins in 1811 when the explorer David Thompson noted in his daily journal the track of "a large animal . . . the whole is about fourteen inches by eight inches wide," in the Canadian Rockies by the site of what is now Jasper, Alberta. Several months later Thompson found similar tracks which he followed for nearly one hundred yards. "Reports from the old time," he noted offhandedly, "had made the head branches of this river and the mountains in the vicinity the abode of apes or more very large animals."

In July 1884, a Victoria, British Columbia, newspaper, the *Daily Colonist*, published an account of the capture of a gorilla-type animal the miners called Jacko. About four foot seven inches tall and weighing about 125 pounds, the animal may have been born a Bigfoot. No other mention can be found of Jacko in the *Daily Colonist*.

The *Seattle Times* reported a series of bizarre great ape sightings around Mount St. Lawrence near Kelso, Washington, in July 1918. In 1924, a group of miners camped near Mount St. Helens in Washington claimed a horde of giant apelike creatures attacked them in the middle of the night. One was shot and rolled into a deep canyon that is known today as Ape Canyon. Also in 1924, a prospector named Albert Ostman claimed that while camping near Vancouver he was picked up in his sleeping bag and carried twenty-five miles by a giant hairy ape. They arrived in a sheltered valley where he was curiously observed for several days by a family of four Bigfeet. He eventually fed them chewing tobacco and escaped while they were sick.

In 1940, the Chapmans, an American Indian family living near the Fraser River in British Columbia, claimed a giant hairy ape walked out of the woods and turned over a massive barrel of salt fish in the shed. Footprints were left, and local residents reported they were sixteen inches long and eight inches wide. The stride length was about four feet. Mrs. Chapman said the creature was about eight feet tall.

American sightings made national headlines in the Bluff Creek area of Northern California in October 1958. On the ninth of that month, the *Humboldt Times* reported that Jerry Crew, a road builder for the Granite Logging Company, made a cast of a huge footprint—sixteen inches long—he found on the damp bed of a newly built lumbering access road. The stride was fifty inches long, he said, and ran along the road for a distance of about three quarters of a mile.

Five days later two construction workers for the same company were driving along a remote mountain road late at night when they saw what they took to be the owner of the prints. Ray Kerr, then forty-three, said, "It ran upright like a man, swinging long hairy arms. . . . It looked eight to ten feet tall to me." Tracks found the next morning were identical to the first set.

Interviewed in the *Humboldt Times*, Ray Wallace, a partner in the logging firm, denied that he had perpetrated a hoax. "Who knows anyone foolish enough to ruin their own business," he said. Fifteen men had quit their jobs since the sightings. Workers reported that they saw nothing during the day but that every morning they found huge and apparently curious prints around the equipment. Huge gasoline drums had been turned over. Some workers had the uncomfortable sensation that they were being watched during the day. "I've got three tractors up there without operators, man," Wallace complained. "And all my brush-cutting crew has quit."

Dr. Maurice Tripp, a geophysicist from Los Gatos, California, made casts of the prints which proved that the toes showed mechanical function. After studying the soil and the depth of the print, Tripp estimated the probable creature's weight at eight hundred pounds. None of his casts showed impact ridges, which would have indicated that they were made by some kind of mechanical stamping machine.

Another series of prints, 1,089 in all, were discovered near Bossberg, Washington, in October 1969. The tracks measured seventeen and a half inches by seven inches. The right foot seemed twisted inward and calluses on the outside of the foot and the extrapolated bone structure indicated the creature who made the prints had a clubfoot. Dr. Grover Krantz, a physical anthropologist at Washington State University, studied casts of the Bossberg prints and concluded that if the tracks were hoaxed, the fakers were "absolute experts in human anatomy."

Since the 1958 Bluff Creek sightings, hundreds have been recorded, some less credible than others. While Albert Ostman only claimed to have been kidnapped by Bigfeet, one Helen Westring confessed right on the front page of the *National Bulletin* (July 1969), I Was Raped by an Abominable Snowman. Seems that while Helen was out hunting one day in the Minnesota woods she was attacked by a giant horny ape who stripped her of her flimsy clothes in a trice and had his hairy way with her right there on the mute forest loam.

There are many men hunting Bigfoot on a more or less regular basis, and one of the most impressive is a forty-six-year-old, Dublin-born former big-game hunter named Peter Byrne. Financed by Ohio businessman Tom Page and several others who wish to remain anonymous, Byrne has one paid assistant, two young volunteers, two International Scout jeeps, a pickup truck, a helicopter on twenty-four-hour notice, and a plethora of equipment including infrared nightscopes and sophisticated tranquilizer guns.

Byrne, who does not take a salary from expedition funds but lives off his own income, has a Hemingwayesque history. In World War II he flew for the RAF and subsequently ended up as assistant manager of a tea plantation in Nepal. He once effected the rescue of an Everest expedition stranded by an avalanche at twenty thousand feet. For fifteen years he led big-game hunts in Africa.

In 1968, with the game thinning out (more from poachers than hunters), Byrne wearied of leading bumbling clients through the brush and pointing them at the animals he had come to respect. He organized the nonprofit International Wildlife Conservation Society. As executive director, Byrne spent two years creating two large tiger sanctuaries in Nepal. The project was completed in November 1970.

While in Nepal Byrne had become fascinated with the legend of the Yeti (the perhaps mythical Abominable Snowman, cousin to the perhaps mythical Bigfoot). He disputed the findings of Sir Edmund Hillary's 1960 Yeti-hunting expedition, insisting that a month's search didn't constitute a real effort to find the beast. The Yeti scalp Hillary took from a Tibetan monastery had been analyzed as a goat- and antelope-hair fabrication, proving, to Hillary's satisfaction, that none of the sacred Yeti relics in any of the monasteries were authentic. Byrne felt that the scalp Hillary found was a copy of an original he never saw. Byrne himself had visited half a dozen of the monasteries and in one secretly cut the thumb from a mummified hand. He wired a mummified human thumb to the palm and sent the relic to scientists in Paris, then London, then the United States. In all cases the scientists came up with the inconclusive conclusion that the thumb was not human, that it was animal, and that further, it was unclassifiable.

In the Himalayas, only two Europeans have claimed Yeti sightings. Byrne, fascinated with the hypothetical creatures to a point just short of obsession, knew that there were hundreds of sightings in the Pacific Northwest. In 1971 he organized the present three-year search. He has, to date,

logged hundreds of thousands of miles on the jeeps, interviewed hundreds of claimants, talked at length to the Indians about their legends and knowledge of the apes, and
camped in the woods in various sighting areas nearly a
year's worth of elapsed time. Byrne regards as his strongest
piece of evidence an eighteen-second piece of film taken by
one Roger Patterson near Bluff Creek in the early afternoon
hours of October seventh, 1967.

Patterson, a small rancher and weekend Bigfoot hunter
from Yakima, Washington, had spent four years and thousands of dollars on his search. He claims to have been on
horseback in the Bluff Creek area with Bob Gimlin, his
tracker, when they caught sight of a female Bigfoot
crouched by a stream. Patterson's horse spooked and nearly
threw him. He pulled his camera from his saddlebag and
ran toward the creature, trying to focus simultaneously.

The 16mm color film begins with a wild, jerking view of
the manzanita underbrush. The camera steadies, pans right,
and focuses in on an erect, apelike figure which appears to
be about thirty feet away. It walks, at a slight angle to
camera, into a thickly wooded area and disappears. It turns
once toward the camera and its face shows large black eyes,
a small nose, a massive jaw, and a crest or ridge on the head.
Muscle movement can be seen in the upper right thigh.
When the right arm swings back, large, hair-covered breasts
become visible.

Patterson, apparently anxious to validate his film, took a
lie detector test, which he passed. He submitted the film to
the Smithsonian's director of primate biology, John Napier
(now visiting professor of primate biology at the University
of London), who had expressed his doubts in the recently
published book *Bigfoot*.

The walk seems to Napier "self-consciously" fluid. The
stride is essentially that of a human male while the filmed
creature is female. The crest is a male feature on orangutans
and gorillas, seldom seen in females. The heavy buttocks
seen in the Patterson film are a human feature, out of place
on the apelike superstructure. Furthermore, the fourteen-
by-seven-inch-prints—on a human scale—would indicate a

creature nearly eight feet tall, while both Byrne and Napier have estimated the height of the Patterson creature at about six foot six. Napier concludes his discussion of the film by saying that he won't proclaim it a hoax almost solely because, "I cannot see the zipper."

Byrne respectfully disagrees. "Napier is using human formulas to deal with an unknown quantity," he says.

(Patterson died of cancer in 1972. Byrne visited him in December when he was a gravely ill man. Patterson continued to insist on the validity of his film. For what it's worth, to my untrained eye, the film is very convincing.)

Byrne published the results of a year's investigation in the prestigious *Explorers Journal.* His case for the existence of the Giant Apes (which he calls Omah, after the local Indians), briefly and inadequately summarized, is as follows:

1. There are hundreds of thousands of virtually unexplored and roadless wilderness areas in the Pacific Northwest. The habitat of the Omah might be in the steep, thickly wooded gorges of this region.

2. These same areas support black and brown bears. If the Omah were an omnivore, with a diet roughly similar to that of a bear, the forest could easily support a small Omah population.

3. There have been few sightings, because like most primates, the Omah is wary of man. (First reports of African gorillas in the early seventeenth century were treated as folklore. Not until the middle of the nineteenth century did Europeans succeed in tracking down the shy beasts.)

Byrne does not speculate on the origin of Omah, though when pressed he will mention the fossil remains of a Chinese primate anthropologists call Gigantopithecus. "Its estimated height was between ten and twelve feet, and the fossils were discovered in an area of China scientists think provided the native American population, the Eskimos and the Indians." The theory, of course, is that nomadic tribes migrated across the frozen Bering Strait. "A case, I think, can be made for Gigantopithecus as an ancestor to Omah," Byrne says.

Currently living in a trailer in The Dalles, Byrne is still deeply involved in the hunt. If he should come on one of the animals, he plans to dart it and keep it subdued for several days. A team of scientists have agreed to fly in at any time at his expense. They would land in Portland and take a helicopter to the site. There they would take photos, measurements, urine, stool, and blood samples. The Omah would then be set free.

I asked if a tranquilizer capable of bringing down a beast that could conceivably weigh up to 1,000 pounds wouldn't kill a man hoaxed up in a gorilla suit.

"No," Byrne says, and adds wryly: "Unfortunately, the safety margin is quite high. The drug has been tested on volunteer prisoners. It simply puts a man under for quite a long period without harming him. You can, however, quote me as saying I would be delighted to put a dart in the ass of any jerk wearing a fur suit for my benefit."

I am indebted to Sergeant Jack Robertson of The Dalles's sheriff's department for a bit of woodsy Omah lore.

"If you should be out in the woods without a weapon," he said, "and you see Bigfoot, just throw some crap in his face and he'll run away. They hate that."

"What am I going to do if there isn't any crap around?"

"Listen," Robertson said, "if you're out in the woods alone and you see him, there'll be plenty of crap around."

lora Thompson is seventy-four years old, a Wy-am Indian who lives at Celilo Falls, the prime salmon netting spot on the Columbia River, which her tribe calls Wauna. Flora studied and learned the legends of the Wy-am from her late husband, the great chief Tommy Thompson, who died at 108 in 1951. She can tell about the time before men when all the animals were people and were giants. Coyote was the Changer. He dug a trench from the great eastern lake to the ocean so the salmon could swim upstream. In this way Coyote made the earth fit for man.

In the Changing Time, just after there were men, there was another beast. As Flora Thompson describes it, it is very much like the Omah in the Patterson film. It was a female and its name was Tlat-ta-chee-ah.

"We use Tlat-ta-chee-ah as a scarecrow," Flora says. "We tell the bad children that she will come to eat them if they don't behave."

The Wy-am are not the only tribe that have legends about giant, apelike creatures. Many tribes call him Sasquatch.

In British Columbia, the Salish call him Stwanitie. The Quamault of the Olympic Peninsula call him Seeakwa. In Alberta he is called Tsonqua and Ghaga, and in Northern California, the Hoopa call him Kadonkwa. In the Central Pacific Northwest many tribes call him Omah.

Peter Byrne in his investigation has talked to many of the tribes in the general sighting areas. Two elderly Indians on the Colville reservation located in Northeastern Washington told him that their grandfathers spoke of seeing up to twenty Omah catching salmon during a run on the Columbia River. In the 1850s, they said, the Omah caught the white man's disease and died.

Another legend prevalent in the Northwest is that there were once many Omah and they lived not only in the forests, but also far to the south and in the plains of the east. The Indians warred with them, and by the time the white man came, they were all gone.

tem: At twilight in a small mountain town in Northern California, a clerk in the general store thought she saw a large, hair-covered animal she took to be Bigfoot. Within an hour a large armored crowd had gathered in front of the store, ready to hunt the beast. Investigation showed that the beast was actually a prankster, a high school boy who had thrown fur over his head.

From a letter to Deputy Carlson, dated November twenty-fifth, 1972: "I believe from reading the article about the Bigfoot search that it is a man dressed in a gorilla suit so people do not kill him, he is probably getting a big kick out of doing his thing, scaring people. The article said it looked like a man. That's what it was—a man—in costume. If you attend a Halloween dance in Los Angeles you would see plenty of Yeti, dancing with the girls. I've seen plenty of these outfits, so *do not* shoot him, he's having fun."

The letter was signed "Miss Los Angeles."

Excerpt from a conversation with a deputy sheriff in The Dalles, Oregon: "Now I'm not saying that a critter like that actually exists. I've been hunting this part of the country for almost twenty years, and I've never seen hide nor hair of one. But if I did see one, you damn betcha it's a dead one. It'd be worth more to you alive, but even a dead one would bring you a million for a squeeze of the trigger. And how would you capture one? You couldn't, is all. Shoot it, is the best way. You'd have a million. I wouldn't even come to work tomorrow if I shot one tonight. I'd just sit back and start counting my money."

Sections of County Ordinance 69-01 Skamania County, Washington (located just across the river from The Dalles): "Prohibiting wanton slaying of ape-creatures and imposing penalties.

"WHEREAS, there is evidence to indicate the possible existence in Skamania County of a nocturnal primate mammal variously described as an apelike creature or a subspecies of *homo sapiens*, and

"WHEREAS, both legend and purported recent sightings and spoor support the possibility, and

"WHEREAS, this creature is generally and commonly known as 'Sasquatch,' or 'Yeti,' or 'Giant Hairy Ape,' and

"WHEREAS, publicity attendant on such real or imagined sightings has resulted in an influx of scientific investigators as well as casual hunters, many armed with lethal weapons,

"THEREFORE, let it be resolved that any premeditated, willful and wanton slaying of any such creature shall be deemed a felony punishable by a fine not to exceed ten thousand dollars and/or imprisonment in the county jail for a period not to exceed five years."

This ordinance was adopted in the spring of 1969. On the first day of April to be exact.

Excerpt from a conversation with The Dallas deputy Rich Carlson: "There are always fellows who go out to shoot it. There are people who said they would shoot it if they saw it. In the beginning, one sighting we had, the townspeople found out about it, and by jimmy, they went up there with rifles, ready to hunt it down. . . ."

Undoubtedly there have been many hoaxes in the Bigfoot saga. In 1968 a Mr. Ray Pickens of Colville, Washington, strapped a pair of sixteen-inch, foot-like plywood boards to his feet and tromped over the nearby woods. A small crowd gathered and a photo was sent to Peter Byrne, who dismissed the tracks as obvious fakes. Pickens later admitted the hoax. John Napier states in his book: "I have in my files photographs of a further set of tracks which were clearly made by a hinged wooden contraption which wouldn't fool the village idiot."

Another citizen of Colville, the Bigfoot hunter Ivan Marx, made a series of phone calls one night in October 1970. He was in a state of high excitement. A wounded Bigfoot had been sighted near Colville, and in the morning he was going to go out after it with his camera. As might be expected, a crowd gathered, and Marx stayed in radio contact with them. At one point he claimed to have sighted the beast and some minutes later said he was actually filming it.

Peter Byrne said Marx offered to sell the film to Byrne's organization for twenty-five thousand dollars. He agreed to buy on the condition that the film could be studied first for signs of a hoax. Byrne says his study showed that the film had been shot about a month previous to the date Marx claimed and that it had been shot in an entirely different area than that claimed by Marx. Armed with this information, Byrne, the sheriff, and some concerned citizens made a visit to Marx's Colville home. Marx was gone, and there was no forwarding address.

He resurfaced a few weeks ago on the television show "You Asked for It." He had shot a film, he said, of a large Bigfoot in a snowstorm and had come to "You Asked for It" because he was impressed by the show's reputation. To my layman's eyes, the film seems an incredibly clumsy fake. Peter Byrne said it was "ridiculous." In it, the creature is seen white in a heavy snowfall. It walks manlike, toward the camera, jumps around aimlessly, and gives us a view of his front and back sides. The white gorilla suit bags and wrinkles in the ass.

Most of the known hoaxers seem to be motivated by money, by a desire for notoriety, and by the desire to put one over on everybody, especially the bright boys, the scientists. Journalists, as everyone knows, are beyond these considerations. Through perseverance and knowledge of human nature, I personally obtained an exclusive interview with Bigfoot.

I had put notes up in the local supermarkets and laundromats asking anyone with Bigfoot information to call me at the Oregon Motel in The Dalles. About one in the morning on a dark and stormy night, I received a call. A hoarse voice with a heavy accent I couldn't identify asked me if I was the writer who wanted to talk to Bigfoot. I said I was. The voice said, "I am Omah." He stretched it out "Ohhhh-mahhhh." He said he would meet me in twenty minutes at the local Denny's twenty-four-hour coffee shop. He said I would recognize him because he would wear an ankle-length trench coat and a slouch hat, and because he would be nine feet tall. I suggested he carry a basketball so as not to attract attention.

I dressed quickly and doused my face with cold water. The restaurant was one of those bits of roadside Formica with zippy Muzak and menopausal waitresses on Mother Goose shoes. Two truck drivers discussed Peterbilt rigs near the door. Omah sat in the rear, hunched over a cup of coffee, the hat pulled over his forehead.

He looked up quickly, almost angrily, as I approached the table.

"Cahill?"

"Yeah," I said. "You Omah?"

"That's me."

"So why did you call me?" I asked.

He smiled strangely. "I need ink."

He wanted to know if I had done any interviews and what my approach to the story was going to be. I said that I saw him as a survivor, a self-reliant primitive in the midst of vast technocracy: a pleasant reminder that we haven't yet swallowed up all our wilderness. I said that I saw him as man's closest brother on the earth and that by knowing him, we could certainly learn to know ourselves the better.

Omah nodded absent-mindedly while I spoke. He called the waitress over and ordered five Lumberjack Breakfasts. "A stack of delicious buckwheat cakes with rich creamery butter and Vermont maple syrup, mounds of hash browns, a giant slab of Canadian bacon, golden brown toast, and an assortment of the finest jams: a breakfast fit for a lumber-jack."

While he ate, I pumped him with questions. He had been coming down to The Dalles from Fort Hood every spring for years to raid the apple orchard that is now The Pine-wood Mobile Manor. One fateful June, five years ago, he found the orchard gone. In his confusion, he had come to The Dalles Drive-in, which at the time was playing *Planet of the Apes*. He watched the film three times every night for two weeks. He learned to speak English. And an unshakable idea grew in his mind. Through the long, snowy winters on Mount Hood he considered. Every spring when he came down to The Dalles, there was a new ape sequel film. This year he was ready to act.

Suddenly he pulled the hat back from his forehead and turned his profile to me. The features were humanoid, but the nose was flattened and the eyes were flat black coals.

"What do you think?" he blurted.

"About what?"

"About me, Omah. . . . Do you think I could get a part in the next ape film."

He must have seen the look on my face because he stopped talking and stared moodily at his Lumberjack Specials. Mentally I scrapped my survivor story. A great, inexplicable wave of sadness washed over me. We sat in silence for several minutes.

"Been swell talking to you," I said and faked an expansive yawn. "Well, I better get back to the motel."

He looked up, and for the first time his humanoid face showed emotion. It seemed twisted into an expression of hopeless pleading.

"I need the ink," he began, then changed his tack. "Hollywood must know . . ."

I stood up, ready to leave.

His lower lip quivered, and for a terrible moment I thought he might begin to cry. We paid the bill and he followed me out the door where we stood for several minutes in the black and windswept Oregon night. He continued to jabber about ape films in his strange accent.

"Look," I said finally, "I gotta go."

"OK, sure," he said. There was a distant bitterness in his voice. "Ciao."

MOBY PIKE
LIVES
Ice Fishing in Wisconsin

T here are, in the state of Wisconsin, some ten thousand inland lakes. The lakes were created by glaciers
that advanced and retreated over the lowland plains
in the four major stages, modifying hills and dam-
ming valleys. In the current era, winter temperatures in the region reach thirty degrees below zero
and lower. Lakes freeze over, and a hardy subculture of
sport fishermen takes to the ice. Many of them are crazy. I
know this because I grew up with them.

A bitter north wind rolled down out of Canada and
howled over the frozen surface of Lake Nagawicka, a ten-
minute drive from the city of Waukesha, Wisconsin. It was
fifteen degrees below zero, colder even than the precise
scientifically determined temperature of a witch's mam-
mary measured on a Sunday morning after church. The
snow was almost two feet deep, and when you walk on such
snow it makes a bitter dry sound, like the crushing of a
Styrofoam coffee cup.

The old cottage was still there where I remembered it, on
a small hill overlooking the lake. It was abandoned now,
fallen into bleak ruin. As a boy, I spent my summers there,
fishing and swimming. My father tells me that I had no fear
of the water, ever, but I remembered differently. There was
a weedy patch off the south side of the pier where I fished
for perch and rock bass. Late one afternoon, alone on the
pier, I took my father's spinning rod and spent an hour or
so practicing casting. The plug, as I remember it, was about

ten inches long, painted white with dabs of red in front to
resemble an injured minnow. There were three sharp treble hooks spaced along the bottom of the plug.

I was casting out to a weedy hole about fifteen feet from
the pier, hitting it dead center every second or third try,
when something big hit the plug and took the line halfway
out with the star drag singing. I set the hook and started
horsing the monster in. He never broke water, and when I
had him next to the pier, I yanked him up onto the boards,
like the perch I was accustomed to hooking.

He was a huge, enormous, gigantic, mountainous, monolithic fish of about fifteen pounds, and I screamed. My father came tearing out of the house, down the hill, and out
onto the pier. He clubbed the fish, got a leather glove and
tried to work the plug out of the fish's mouth. Finally he just
cut the line and tossed it back, plug and all.

"It was a garfish," he tells me now, two decades later. A
garfish is a particularly repellent trash fish with a nauseous
oily taste. I do not believe that it was a garfish because I have
a very clear mental image of the fish, and the fish's mouth,
and my father's gloved hand in the fish's mouth. What I see
clearly are the teeth, like no teeth I had ever seen. They
were staggered in rough rows across the roof of the mouth,
and each of them curved toward the throat, so that any
living thing caught there would be impaled and driven back
to the gullet.

The fish, I know now, must have been a northern pike.
These are found in the lakes and rivers of the northern part
of the northern hemisphere. They are long, lethal-looking
specimens, and the Anglo-Saxons called them pike because
of their resemblance to a medieval weapon. A twenty-
pound pike will go over four feet in length, and the world's
record pike weighed forty-six pounds and two ounces.
There are bigger fish in the northern lakes—sturgeon and
muskie—but I am fascinated by pike. They are among the
meanest freshwater fish extant, a streamlined killing machine and the most satanic predator of the lakes. They take
small muskie, cannibalize their own kind, hit crayfish,
frogs, mice, small muskrats, ducklings, and any other birds

small enough to swallow. There are eyewitness accounts of pike killing and ingesting small swans.

I was out on the ice, alone on Nagawicka, because I wanted to catch a northern pike. It would be my first through the ice, and I imagined that, in that place, I could confront those fears of twenty years ago, turning them to my own advantage—to fun. Besides, I think it's silly to be afraid of a fish.

The first order of business was to drill a couple of holes. If you're after northern, you'll want to drill over about eight feet of water near the edge of a substantial bed of weeds. Pike skirt these beds and feed on the smaller fish that take refuge there. (If you don't know the lake, it is sometimes possible to obtain a hydrographic map of the bottom.)

Kids and muscleheads use a spud to chop the hole. This is a long metal pole with a chisel on the end, and it takes up to half an hour to drill a hole through three feet of ice with one. An ice auger, especially the thirty-dollar Swedish brand that I prefer, will drill a hole in two minutes flat, provided you keep the blades sharp. Some Winnebago-camper types—cretins and moral paraplegics—buy augers outfitted with gasoline-driven motors.

After the holes were drilled, I set up my tip-ups. These are wooden cross-shaped devices with a line and reel located near the end of one long arm. They cost about five dollars apiece. The crossbar is balanced across the hole, and the business end, spool and all, goes into the water. This way, the spool won't freeze over. When a fish hits the bait, a knob on the reel releases a long springy metal tip with a small red flag at the top. The tip and flag spring up, and the angler rushes over to deal with the catch.

If you're after northern, as I was, you'd probably be using live bait, like four- to ten-inch suckers. I hook them just behind the dorsal fin, let them drop until they hit bottom, then pull them up a foot or two. When a northern takes a sucker, it will usually hit it from the side—this is the conventional wisdom—break its back and run with it. This is where you must be especially careful. The smallest tug on the line will alert the fish that something is terribly wrong, and he'll spit the bait out. If you let the fish run, it will stop, turn the disabled bait around, and swallow it head first. Always head first.

Having swallowed the bait, the pike will make a second run. Watch the line: one run, a pause, the start of the second run. Here you yank back on the line—the proper amount of force is a matter of practice—set the hook and start pulling him in, hand over hand on the line itself.

Because much of the work must be done with bare hands—baiting the hook, pulling the fish in—you're advised to have two pairs of gloves or mittens. One pair always gets wet. Which was my problem that day out on Nagawicka. My right hand was numb. No feeling to it at all.

I decided to leave my three tip-ups in place and walk up to the old cottage to get out of the wind. The front door was open, hanging askew on the bottom hinge. Snow had drifted in through the broken windows and the floorboards were warped and cracked. It was smaller than I remembered it, and I wondered who my parents had sold it to, and why the new owners had let it fall into ruin. It was spooky and sad and colder than hell in the old place.

I had stuffed my right hand into my pants, under the belt, under the thermal underwear, and was holding it to the warmth of my groin. When a frost-nipped hand warms under these conditions, the first jolt of feeling is an intense, prickly sort of pain. It is a good pain because you know it will be over soon and because it means your hand will be all right. It was at this point—while I was feeling sad and spooked and hurt and happy—that I heard running steps on the porch outside.

It took no reflection at all to realize that my position was not a dignified one. I was standing there, motionless, trespassing in an abandoned house in the middle of nowhere, and I had my right hand sunk deep down the front of my pants. My face, I'm sure, reflected the pleasant agony of feeling coming back into my fingers.

The noise on the steps drew closer. Several people, it seemed, were charging into the old cottage at a frantic pace. Waukesha County sheriff's deputies, no doubt. Guns at the ready. They probably catch a lot of perverts this way. There would be unpleasant headlines in the *Waukesha Freeman*: PERVERT CAPTURED IN ABANDONED HOUSE: PARENTS MORTIFIED.

The noise reached the front door just as I was trying to yank my hand out of my pants in the most guilty manner imaginable. There were, however, no people at all, only two big dogs, both huskies, romping together in the snow. Both had icicles hanging from their snouts and their breath came in foggy blasts. They stopped in their tracks. We regarded one another in surprise and dismay. Precisely at that point, a tip-up, over my northern hole, sprang erect.

T hese days, whenever a little red flag is fluttering above the ice of a frozen lake I think of Old Hervey. Old Hervey is your archetypal old-timey ice fisherman. When I was a kid there weren't many people who braved the ice for fish. Those who did were guys like Hervey, a sixty-five-year-old retired welder who watches roller derby on TV when he isn't fishing. Hervey wore maybe six layers of clothes, wino-style, and caught more fish than anyone. Still does. But back in Wisconsin's dark days—before Vince Lombardi came to Green Bay—it didn't much matter because nobody tried to catch fish through the ice except a few Hervey types. They made bonfires and burned old tires and drank brandy for warmth. Decent home-loving folk considered Hervey and his ilk to be harmless masochists, rather like people who walk across hot coals or lie on a bed of nails for no particularly good reason.

Old Hervey has his reasons. He always catches fish. Always. Even if the bass and pike and walleye aren't biting. Old Hervey gets a catch off his jig pole. Jigging, he calls it. In jigging, you drop a line baited with mousies or yellow wax worms into shallow weedy water. You lie on the ice,

put your face over the hole, and cover head and hole with
the hood of your parka. Often as not, you'll be able to see
the little guys—perch and bluegill—swimming around
down there. If you don't, drop in some crumbled eggshells
or oatmeal for chum. The fish are very slow in the winter,
almost somnambulant, and they will approach the chum
in a ponderous and dignified manner. Jerk the bait up and
down in front of your fish. He'll likely hit it on the up-
take. Some days you can spend hours on the ice and never
have one red flag. And yet, on the same day you may bag
a score of foot-long perch on the jig pole, just like Old
Hervey.

Old Hervey doesn't bother to gut his perch. He cuts a
fillet from each side, soaks them in milk, powders them with
flour and bread crumbs or cornmeal, and deep-fries the lot.
The money he saves on food goes for brandy.

If you are new to ice fishing or if you don't know the lake,
it's always best to seek out a Hervey. A pint of brandy helps
immensely in this endeavor, and you are likely to learn
where the best holes are, what the lake bottom is like, and
any number of valuable tricks. The Old Hervey I know
does a thing with mousies. These are larvae of the drone fly,
plump little brown fellows, about half the size of your fin-
gernail, with a hairlike tail. On certain days the perch will
hit nothing but mousies. They will not, however, hit a black
mousie. Mousies turn black when they freeze, and they tend
to freeze rapidly. Old Hervey keeps a dozen or so warm in
his mouth, between the lower lip and teeth, like a plug of
tobacco. Hervey's mousies are always happy, fat, and
brown.

There is another thing Old Hervey does that disturbs
me. He refuses to kill the big fish fresh from the lake. Instead, he tosses them out onto the snow where they freeze
solid in a matter of minutes. When you take these fish
home and dump them into the sink, they clatter, but as
you're cleaning them, they tend to come to life and start
flopping around. This blurs the distinction between life
and death and makes for appropriately morbid funereal
dinners.

ce fishing is no longer exclusively the sport of pensioned lushes. Somebody tried driving his car out onto the ice and watching his tip-ups in comfort. Others discovered that you could construct a small shack and tow it out onto the ice behind a car. Then all you had to do was sit in the shack, by the cheap wood-burning stove, and drink and lie and play cards until a red flag showed. The advent of fashionable ski wear and snowmobile suits has even given ice fishing a bit of a chic look. Some hardy backpackers crate up their tip-ups and bait and jig poles on a sled and make for the more remote lakes where the fishing is best, but the majority of the new people on the ice choose to fish out of shacks clustered together, sometimes by the hundreds, on the more popular lakes, like Wisconsin's massive 215-square-mile Lake Winnebago.

It is a sociable scene. On weekends, entire families spend the day on the ice, and people can be seen tromping through the snow to a neighbor's shack to borrow some baloney and a cup of brandy. These people also band together to prevent vandalism to their shacks, organize fishing jamborees with prizes for the biggest catch, and elect honorary mayors of their tip-up cities.

One day, on Lake Winnebago, everyone was catching three- and four-pound white bass. Whatever mysterious system that tells fish to bite was operative, and operative for miles in every direction. The tip-ups would spring erect, and people would come whooping out of the shanties to haul up the large flat fish.

That night, the Otter Street Fishing Club gathered to celebrate at Jerry's, a bar near the waterfront in Oshkosh. The club is a service organization, and every winter they help plow a road ten miles across the frozen lake. They also construct bridges across the vast cracks that are created when the ice shifts. Everyone knows when this happens because the crack has the quality of a sonic boom and often it will rattle dishes in lakefront homes. When someone's car goes through the ice, the Otter Street boys are there with winches and tools to pull the vehicle up and, if necessary, save lives. The majority of the club members at Jerry's were avid fishermen in their thirties, and most of them seemed to own four-wheel-drive vehicles.

The night of the white-bass feeding frenzy, about thirty of the Otter Street boys got tired of their dank little bar with dead fish on the walls and decided to make a run over the ice to the town of Stockbridge. It was a relatively sober caravan that left Oshkosh about nine o'clock that night. Getting lost or stuck in the deep snow on the lake, miles from anywhere in the middle of a twenty-below night, can be deadly. Five miles out onto the flatness of the lake, with bitter wind whipping up the snow and cutting the visibility, it was possible to imagine oneself alone on some God-forsaken tundra well above the Arctic Circle.

The serious drinking began in a waterfront bar in Stockbridge. I ordered a Heileman's Special Export, which is a local brand and the best beer made in America. It tastes a bit like Heineken and, like Heineken, it comes in a green bottle. To order one in Stockbridge, you say: "Gimme a green hornet, willya."

Some fellows were drinking their green hornets with a shot of schnapps, the white peppermint kind and no other. To order this combination, you say: "Gimme a green hornet and a little white guy, willya hey." After a few green hornets and little white guys, the talk turned to fish stories.

"Remember when Dave and Mark speared that sturgeon, that two-hundred-pound sturgeon? Now that's a big fish."

During part of the ice-fishing season on Winnebago, it is legal to spear sturgeon. Rich guys fly their plane out onto the ice, set up a shanty, black out the windows, and saw a large hole in the ice. They sit there drinking green hornets and little white guys until a sturgeon swims by—happily, this seldom occurs—at which time they literally harpoon it. For some reason this strikes me as a repugnant and a stupid waste of time.

No matter. The proper response to "that's a big fish," is

"ainta," or more emphatically, "ainta hey." This usage corresponds to the French *n'est-ce pas* and means "is it not so."

Things seemed to blur over a bit after a few hours at Stockbridge, though I remember talking to a cabinetmaker named Mark, a short muscular guy with bowed legs who thought I was stupid.

"Anybody who fishes for northern is stupid and you're stupid and I've seen a hundred guys like you and they're all stupid and you're the stupidest of the stupid."

You can get into arguments like that over fish. Mark preferred to catch walleye pike, which is not a pike at all but a type of larger perch with strange, bulging milky white eyes. Walleye go six to eight pounds on an average, and they make for the finest eating fish of the northern lakes. Northern pike are more bony and the flesh tends to crumble rather than flake. Some people like them, but these people are considered by others to be stupid.

Mark was wearing a white sweater with three tiny mallards on it, winging their way across his chest. Whenever anyone walked by us, he would jab Mark in a mallard and shout, "Bang."

"If you're really a writer," Mark said, "which I don't believe because you're stupid, what kind of stuff do you write?"

I told him that I admired Gene Shepard, a turn-of-the-century timber man, city planner, and storyteller out of the Wisconsin north woods. Shepard once announced that he had captured an oxlike prehistoric monster in the big-tree country near Rhinelander. He called his find a hodag and he displayed it, half hidden in a dark tent, at various county fairs. The hodag had six horns on its back, two blinking eyes of different colors, and it occasionally breathed fire. Scientists from the Smithsonian Institution traveled to Wisconsin to examine the wonderful hodag. They found a large slab of wood, carved in the shape of a cow, covered with oxhide, with bear claws for eyebrows, curved steel spikes for claws, and twelve bulls' horns positioned along the backbone.

Mark shook his head in pained dismay. "If you really are

a writer," he said, "then you must right cockeyed, because you're cockeyed stupid."

"Yeah, and if you really are a cabinetmaker," I said—and this is rich, I have such a way with words—"you probably make cockeyed cabinets."

"Bang." Someone poked Mark in a mallard.

Suddenly, it seemed, we were back in the trucks. The plan was to run five miles south, to a bar at Quinney, and to make the run off the road, on the ice. We jolted over drifts, side-slipped through the snow, and pulled in at the lights of Chuck and Sue's bar, a large room with a horseshoe-shaped bar. There was a pool table and Foosball table and a bait shop in the back.

Mark and I continued to discuss fish relative to intelligence. This is no new subject, actually. Izaak Walton, in *The Compleat Angler,* praised the carp. Terrific fish as far as he was concerned. Great fighter, good eating, helluva all-around fish. In 1879 the Wisconsin State Fish Commission stocked lakes and streams with carp. They turned out to be prodigious breeders. The lakes are lousy with them. You bait a line with anything that stinks, drop it about a foot off the bottom anywhere, and you've got a carp. They like to stay on the bottom, and bringing them up is as much fun as hooking an old galosh. They are what they eat, and they eat garbage and fish shit.

Carp also like to flop around in the muck, roiling up the lake and spoiling the fishing. They take weeds off at the root and, since little fish need the protection of the weeds and the nourishment they provide, and since bigger fish need those little fish, pretty soon there is nothing but carp in the lake. The Wisconsin Department of Natural Resources sometimes kills all the fish in a lake, just to get rid of the carp. They then restock the lake with good fish: bass and crappie and bluegill and perch and pike and muskie. No carp.

I am told that in England the descendants of Izaak Walton still fish for carp as if it were a noble thing. The English, however, are known to keep bulldogs—ugly, useless beasts given to slobber and involuntary flatulence in their later years. In matters of taste, there can be no disputes. *De Gustibus non disputandum,* ainta hey.

This is the case I put to Mark, the cockeyed cabinetmaker, and, by a tortuous twist of logic, I attempted to identify him with carp fanciers. The argument was coming to a bitter head when someone asked if we wanted to join the minnow-drinkers club. I am now a member of that organization. I have a card signed by Chuck Lisowe, who is identified as the Imperial Minnow, which states that I am a member in good standing and will be as long as I continue to drink my minnow annually.

Here is what you do to earn such a card. The bartender pours you a seven-ounce glass of beer. He then goes to the bait shop in the back and scoops a three-inch minnow out of the bait tank. This minnow he places in your beer. You then drink the beer rapidly, and the live minnow as well.

Mark drank his minnow first, then demanded a beer and minnow for me. Anxious to prove my intelligence, I picked up the beer and stared at the minnow. It was flopping around in the narrow confines of the bottom of the glass. I can tell you that there is no joy in chugging a beer with a minnow in it, and it took me two tries to get it down. I erred in my original approach. Certainly no one would try to swallow a three-inch minnow sideways, but it is equally incorrect to attempt to down one tail first. They tend to want to swim right back up. This is why your northern pike breaks its prey's back, and turns him head first before swallowing him.

Most of the Otter Street boys downed their minnows on the first attempt, but one fellow, a big, mean-looking giant of a man in worn farmer clothes, couldn't keep either the minnow or his dinner down. There was a big to-do made of this.

"You puked your minnow."

"So I puked it. Nobody should eat a live thing. It ain't right. It's sick."

"You puked your minnow, you puked your minnow."

Mark and I were reconciled. Neither of us had puked his minnow, an obvious and certain measure of our intelligence. We played pool, then found ourselves back in the trucks, swerving and sliding out over the lake toward Oshkosh. We were downing green hornets at a pretty furious pace, stopping now and again to stand out in the barren, windswept night and yellow the snow.

Yanking my hand out of my pants, I ran toward the door, scattering the two huskies, and sprinted down the hill to the tip-up flag, which was swaying in the wind over my northern hole on Lake Nagawicka. Very gently, I pulled the tip-up out of the hole. Nothing. Suddenly the line began running out at a furious pace, and this, I knew, had to be the beginning of the second run. I pulled back on the line, and the force at the other end simply pulled it from my hand. The tip-up itself slid rapidly over the snow and wedged itself sidewise into the hole. Then, a split second later, the entire device shuddered, and a crack shot up the side of the pole.

The fish had taken all the line, and set the hook itself. I grabbed the tip-up, and pulled at the line, finally getting some slack. The fish was coming back, and I pulled the line in by the yard. When he took it out again, I held tight with both hands. It burned and cut as the fish ran, but now he was beginning to tire. We worked that way, man and fish, for over half an hour, and the line was frozen red with my blood. I was alone and my hands were coated with ice. The fish, I realized in one awful moment, could kill me.

But now I had him within feet of the hole. He shot by once, twice, three times, a huge dark shadow, six, maybe seven feet long. He was diving deep, and circling, trying to cut the line on the jagged edge of the bottom of the hole. I gave him line, then worked him back. There was a moment when he was only a foot below the ice, his massive head just below the hole. Quickly I twisted the line around my right hand, which I held to my chest, and fell back onto the snow, pulling the fish up with the whole of my weight.

This next happened in an instant, but the particulars are immensely vivid in my mind's eye. The northern was a quarter of the way out, wedged tight to the sides of the eight-inch hole *by the very bulk of his body*. The head was above the ice to the gill line, and it was green—green in the way that only primitive things can be—and there were large white blotches at the back of the head, as if the fish were unimaginably old.

My line had snapped, and there was nothing more I could do. The wind was strong and already ice had begun to form on the fish. I moved closer, tired and hurt, and this moment lives with me. A northern pike has a long flattened mouth, and the eyes are set close together on a ridge resembling a brow. It is a fish that can look you directly in the eye. What I saw there was a hatred more palpable than time itself. But what caused me to stagger, all at once weak in the knees, was the realization that there was intelligence in those cold green eyes, that the evil of its hatred was focused on me, *that the fish recognized me*.

The great mouth gaped open, and there was a sound, not loud but high-pitched and piercing, like a siren cranking up to wail. The fish jerked once, twice, then slid slowly, very slowly back into the hole. The siren shifted in pitch, higher now, triumphant. In that last split second, I saw deep into the fish's mouth, past the rows of inward-curving teeth to something that frightened me more than I care to think about.

It was an old ten-inch plug. There was still some white on the body of the plug, and a speck of red at the top. Three treble hooks were spaced along the bottom.

This is a true fish story and I dedicate it, respectfully, to the memory of Gene Shepard.

THE
RAGGEDY
EDGE

FEAR
OF
FRYING

We have always depended on the kindness of
rangers.

DEATH VALLEY HIKERS FOUND SAFE BUT
TIRED, read the front-page headline in the *Death
Valley Gateway Gazette*. Since the article was
about me and a good pal—and it's the only time
I've been front-page news, anywhere, ever—I found the
unstated assumptions, uh, distressing. Even in the *Death
Valley Gateway Gazette* a man tends to read his clippings
compulsively, and this story, by implication, might have
been titled HALF-DEAD DUMBSHITS IN THE DESERT.

According to the article,

> An aerial search of the rugged desert and
> mountain areas between Badwater in
> Death Valley National Monument and
> Mount Whitney in the eastern Sierras
> located two overdue hikers on Wednesday
> (June 20th).
>
> Rangers found the pair, a writer and
> photographer from *Rolling Stone* magazine,
> to be in "good but fatigued" condition due
> to exhaustion from the rugged hike in tem-
> peratures well over the 100-degree-Fahren-
> heit mark. . . . [The journalists] started their
> rugged trek from the lowest elevation in

the continental United States, approximately 282 feet below sea level, and plan to conclude their journey to reach Mount Whitney, the highest point, at an elevation of 14,375 feet above sea level.

[Chief Ranger Dick] Rayner considered the rescued hikers to be "extremely fortunate" and cautioned monument visitors on the hazards of summer hiking and backpacking in extreme Death Valley temperatures.

THE ABSOLUTE PIT

I am as low as a man can get in the United States, and I am slowly sinking lower. Death Valley, 550 square miles of it below sea level—all scalding salt flats and dunes—is surrounded by mountains: by the Amargoasa, the Panamint and the Last Chance ranges, which rise from four to eleven thousand feet above the valley floor. These mountains catch what rain the westerly air current didn't drop on the Sierras, and water rolls down the mountainsides into the valley, where it immediately evaporates, leaving the accumulated mineral residue of chlorides, sulphates, and carbonates.

Not all of the water is lost, however. Some of it skulks in a steaming, muddy bog that lies just under a brittle salt crust out toward the center of the valley. Somewhere near the lowest point in the continental United States, the salt crust refuses to support the weight of a man; it takes the boot to the ankle, then the leg to the calf, the knee. Walking becomes a crack-splash affair, and the sharp, crystalline salt crust scrapes and cuts the shins. The bog below is a musty-gray combination of hot mud and salt that clings to boots and legs like hot clay. First the valley chews up your legs, then it rubs salt in your wounds.

There are rumors that "in some places in the middle of the bog, the soft salty area in the bottom of the valley, a team of horses or a man walking have been instantly sucked down out of sight." This bit of cheerful information comes from Daniel Cronkhite's well-researched book *Death Valley's*

Victims. The author acknowledges that the story may be apocryphal and goes on to quote Old Johnnie, who told of "finding a dead man's face looking up at him out of the ground. 'He was a Swede with yellow hair, and he stared at the sun. He sank standing up.'"

This is a report to brood upon when walking across Death Valley around two in the morning with a photographer from *Rolling Stone.* You want to crack-splash through the steaming mud about thirty feet apart, so that if one should go down, the other can more efficiently panic and go lurching off into the desert night, hands in the air, screaming and gibbering.

When the photographer, Nick Nichols, and I reached what we supposed was the nadir of life in the United States, the absolute pit, Nick also discovered that he had dropped his strobe, "back there." He began trudging along our back trail, muttering malign imprecations and leaving me standing knee-deep in hot, salty mud. There was no place to sit down, unless I wanted to take a scalding mud bath, and the Van Gogh stars spun madly overhead. The desert sky was impossibly clear, and I could make out the colors of various stars and planets, so that, glancing up, I felt as if I were stranded in space.

Thick, muddy water was draining back into our posthole footprints—it was a sick sort of squishing sound—and the dead of a Death Valley night swallowed up Nick's receding light. Alone, in the darkness, I stared down at the unbroken salt crust of the valley floor. There were innumerable pillars of salt standing in inch-high clusters. Some formations, like certain tropical corals, took on the shapes of crystalline flowers, and they wound about in baroque curlicues, snaking across the floor like endless meandering rivers.

The mountains—waiting to reveal themselves in the light of the rising moon—whispered to one another in warm, gusting breezes that swept across the valley. The hot salt crust of the valley floor, under the cold light of swirling stars, emitted a faint glow, like the radium dial of a watch. The world was an ocean of salt and sand, so flat the eye saw a ridge, nuclear white, that rose on all sides.

I stood stock-still, wondering if I was sinking any deeper. The hot mud had been knee-deep on me, or so I thought, but now my legs felt braised to midthigh. It seemed hard to breathe out there, alone, in the middle of the night. I felt slightly faint and realized that in this condition I could very well commit philosophy.

"DEATH DESTROYS A MAN, BUT THE IDEA OF DEATH SAVES HIM" — William Forester

Every life offers certain challenges that require grit, intelligence, spirit, spunk, careful planning, and nifty interpersonal skills. Try cashing an out-of-state check in New York City on a Sunday. Buy a used car from a friend of your brother-in-law. Ask for a promotion. Or a divorce.

Few of the challenges we face every day, as a matter of course, are physical, however, and a growing number of people seem to feel that lack keenly. Some have taken up individual sports as a kind of antidote to physical stagnation. People run marathons, they compete in triathlons, cycle the breadth of the country nonstop, or attempt to get their names in the *Guinness Book of World Records* by doing cartwheels across the state of Nebraska.

My problem with most athletic challenges is training. I am lazy and find that workouts cut into my drinking time. The thought of a new personal best no longer fills me with ambition or a burning desire to win. I need incentives.

Consequently, every once in a while, I like to flirt with some physical challenge in which the price of failure is death. Amazing how easy training becomes in such a situation, how carefully one plans, how intently the mind focuses.

Over the past decade, I've jumped out of quite a few perfectly good airplanes—"When the people look like ants," my first instructor said, "pull the chute; when the ants look like people, pray." I've been diving with tiger sharks on the Great Barrier Reef and have crawled creepy damp through caverns half a mile below the surface of the earth; I've run some nasty rapids, climbed a few mountains, traded bolts of red cloth for food in the Amazon basin, and surfed my kayak through ice floes on waves thrown up by calving tidewater glaciers.

A number of magazines have actually paid me to do these things, to realize a lot of adolescent fantasies. These stories want to write themselves, and the work seems effortless. Research, for instance, in a situation where shoddy research can be deadly is scintillating. On location, and at risk, the senses are bombarded, and the world seems to vibrate with color and sound and life. Impressions are hard edged, settling permanently inside the brain, where at odd and frequent intervals they combine to explode in star showers of adrenaline-charged images and ideas. Writing the subsequent article requires a good deal less head banging than, say, analyzing the national deficit. We are talking about adventure here, about fear recollected in tranquility. And fear—we've all felt it—is unforgettable.

One day last year I spoke with my editor about self-imposed physical risk in the natural world. In a nation where signs in the national parks warn visitors not to fall over the lip of a cliff, there is a sense of something sadly lost. Survivors of people who step out into space and go hurtling tragically off the tops of cliffs can file, and win, lawsuits. The Park Service feels obliged to install guardrails and erect signs explaining the concept of gravity.

Nothing is safe in a world where lawyers define what is dangerous. As it happens, a growing number of people have discovered that they enjoy a view unencumbered by guardrails and warning signs. These folks feel that they have enough sense not to fall off the nearest cliff. In point of fact, many of them search out spectacular cliffs for the sole and specific purpose of seeing them without plunging to their doom.

There is a whole industry that caters to the impulse. What I've been doing out in the jungles or in the Arctic is called "adventure travel" these days. My colleague Dave Roberts recently described the growth of the adventure-travel industry:

A 1979 estimate . . . postulated some 2,000 tour operators worldwide [outfitters who supply river rafts, climbing gear, et cetera] . . . a figure which is certainly already obsolete. Another estimate, from 1980, suggests that 2 million Americans have participated in an adventure-travel trip—with rafting, backpacking, and skiing leading the way. Yet public perception of this incredible growth has been lacking, and travel agents themselves have lagged behind their own clientele. The ASTA *Travel News* . . . issued this caveat: "Travel agents had better be prepared to book adventure whether they like it or not."

What I proposed to *Rolling Stone* was a series of articles about various natural challenges, taken to extremes, and written for the edification of adventure travelers and armchair adventure travelers. In one part of the series, I'd personally walk from the lowest point in the continental United States to the highest point. It was not an original idea—lots of peoples have maps and can see that these two extremes are separated by a mere hundred or so miles. It is certainly not impossible. Perhaps a dozen men and women of my acquaintance could make this trek at a dead run. But adventure is relative. I knew next to nothing about the desert, and unless I got into some kind of shape and learned a lot, real quick, death was one of the more extreme consequences.

THE INDIANA JONES OF PHOTOGRAPHY

"I know what you did," Nick Nichols raged. We were kneeling on the floor of a hotel room in San Francisco, and topographical maps of Death Valley were spread out on the floor. The bed was littered with desert-survival books, wide-brimmed hats, long-sleeved shirts, heavy cotton jeans, homemade turbans, backpacks, cookstoves, canteens, and cameras. "You were sitting in some editor's office in New York and came up with this, this . . ."

"Idea?"

"This insanity. You can't propose a story on the girls of Tahiti. Oh, no. Or the four-star restaurants of France. Or the grand hotels of Europe. You come up with this, this . . ."

I could tell Nick loved the idea. Together we have made something of a living working the adventure-travel beat. We've trekked through sections of the Amazon and Congo basins; studied and lived with mountain gorillas in the Virunga volcanoes of central Africa; swum in the pool under Angel Falls; flown with the air force into the eye of a hurricane; and made the first rainy-season ascent of Arthur Conan Doyle's "Lost World," Mount Roraima, in Venezuela.

Nick has made rafting descents down white-water rivers in Pakistan, cycled partway across China, rappelled nearly a mile down the face of a cliff in the Arctic—a world free-fall record that maybe ten people in the world know about—photographed fire dances in Suriname and been arrested in Zaire for reasons that have yet to be explained. *Photo* magazine calls Nick Nichols "the Indiana Jones of photography."

We studied the maps for a while. The Park Service officials we contacted had actively discouraged the hike. We would be trekking through a blast furnace, they said. Late June was deadly in the valley. Why didn't we hike from Mount Whitney down to the ocean?

Trekking from the highest point to a pretty low point, we said, seemed to lack the proper emotional resonance. Chief Ranger Dick Rayner sighed and said that we'd have to file an itinerary with him and that we'd have to have a support vehicle, a four-wheel-drive rig driven by a third party. If we failed to reach the vehicle at the proper points and times, the driver would report to the rangers and a search party would be dispatched.

Frank Frost, a Northern California photographer, agreed to drive the support vehicle, and we were in business. Dick

Rayner had said that natural springs in the valley were undependable and fouled with diarrhea-producing giardia. It was best to stash water, to bury it in plastic jugs. We should plan on two gallons a day, minimum.

Nick and I formulated a set of rules. It was okay to make our packs as light as possible by burying food along with the water. We'd avoid roads and bushwhack cross-country as much as possible. Since the Park Service required a support vehicle anyway, it was okay to pack it full of cold water and iced beer.

"This one ranger I talked to," Nick said, "he told me that a couple of groups a year try this trek, and they've had to rescue a few of them. The guy said he had been in Death Valley for several years, and he never knew anyone who made it. Ninety percent of them, he said, quit the first day. He said it was psychological. Either that or poor planning."

"We're pretty psychological," I pointed out.

Nick didn't reply. He was studying a copy of *Death Valley's Victims,* looking at the photos of desiccated corpses baking out on the valley floor.

"We're going to die," the Indiana Jones of photography said.

HOT DAMN

We managed to slog through the crusted, steaming bog before dawn, according to plan, and found the water and food Nick had buried. Our campsite was Tule Spring, on the valley floor, at the foot of the Panamint Mountains. We pitched the rain flies from the one-man tents we carried and settled down for a long, mindless sleep. The tents would provide shelter from the sun: we had tested them out on the grass at the Death Valley Visitors Center, in the village of Furnace Creek. The temperature inside the tents had been twelve degrees cooler than the outside air.

By eleven that morning I felt like a side of beef, and my skin was the color of medium-rare prime rib. The pores on the back of my hand were the size of quarter, or so it seemed, and dozens of tiny but cruel dwarfs were building

a condominium inside my skull. The thermometer registered 128 inside the tent. The record high temperature in
the United States is 134, recorded on July tenth, 1913, in
Death Valley. If it was 12 degrees hotter outside of the
tent—140 degrees—I was dying through the hottest American day on record.

But I found the temperature outside was only 113. It
didn't make any sense. I laid the thermometer down on the
ground, next to my boots, and the mercury pegged at 150
degrees. The thermometer wasn't made to measure temperatures any higher. What we'd failed to consider, Nick and
I, is the fact that gravel and sand—like white cement high-
ways under the summer sun—get hot. Real hot. A lot hotter
than grass or even the air itself. The Indian name for Death
Valley, Tomesha, means "ground on fire." In 1972, a record
ground temperature of 201 degrees was recorded on the
valley floor.

Instead of protecting us from the 113-degree outside air,
the tents were concentrating the 150-plus-degree ground
temperature and literally baking us. Nick and I moved outside. We sat on foam pads, under lean-tos we had made with
space blankets. With the noonday sun directly overhead,
the blankets provided perhaps two square feet of shade. It
was now 121 degrees. Hot air, rising off the superheated
sand and salt, scalded our lungs. Sleep was impossible.

"The tents were a dumb idea." Nick said.

"Poor planning," I muttered.

Then we didn't say anything for nine hours.

I could feel the hot air rising all around us. The laws of
physics demand that heavier, cooler air should fall from the
heavens, and that is what happens in Death Valley. It falls,
comes into contact with the ground, becomes superheated,
and rises. The mountains surrounding the valley allow no
air to escape, so that as the day wears on, the upper levels
of air—which have made several passes over the ground—
are not really cool anymore, only less hot than air at ground
level. In effect, the valley is a giant convection oven.

All this rising and falling air whistles across the valley
floor in gusting waves of arid wind that suck the moisture

out of a man's body the way a hand wrings water from a sponge. You sweat, of course, but you do not feel sweat on your body in Death Valley, even at 121 degrees. The killing convective wind will allow no moisture to form, but all that rapid evaporation is a cooling process, so the wind feels good, almost pleasant, as it desiccates the body. And that is why people who die in the desert are often found naked, lying face down on the skillet of the valley floor.

Some victims have been found with a quart or two of water in their possession. Apparently, they intended to save the water until they felt they really needed it. Staggering, suffering from dehydration or heat exhaustion or heat stroke, they fell unconscious, and the ground on fire killed them in a matter of hours. Other victims, too weak to walk, simply fell to the sand and couldn't rise to their feet. In 1973, Death Valley killed three people this way.

Unpleasant thoughts. Huddled there in my small square of shade with the circumstances of various tragedies stumbling slowly through my mind like terminal winos, I began dreaming of the Man in the Freon Suit. What a guy! In Death Valley, certain legends exist and have the ring of truth about them because everyone knows them, everyone repeats them, and they are so poetically morbid as to live in memory, whether one wills them to or not.

Such is the tale of the Man in the Freon Suit. I heard it my first day in the valley, at Furnace Creek, a tale eagerly told concerning an unfortunate inventor who constructed a kind of space suit, using the tubing and coils of an old Frigidaire. The man ventured out into Death Valley, wearing his air-conditioned suit and pulling a battery behind him in a small wagon. The suit malfunctioned, however: it apparently began pumping out great blasts of freezing air. According to legend, the man couldn't remove the suit. Perhaps his fingers had frozen beyond the point of movement. At any rate, he was found lying on the floor of Death Valley, lying there on the baking 180-degree plain, frozen solid.

Many people knew the story, though no one was quite sure when it happened. Most folks put the tragedy some-

time around 1950. One person thought he remembered the
man's name: John Newbury or Newhouse or Newton.
Something like. Poor son of a bitch.

In point of fact, the story of the Man in the Freon Suit
was first reported by Dan De Quille in the July second,
1874, issue of Virginia City's *Territorial Enterprise* under the
headline SAD FATE OF AN INVENTOR. De Quille's story concerned a "man of considerable inventive genius" named
Jonathan Newhouse who had constructed a "'solar armor,'"
which consisted of a hood, jacket, and pants, of "common
sponge," all about an inch thick. "Under the right arm," De
Quille reported,

> was suspended an India-rubber sack filled
> with water and having a small gutta-percha
> tube leading to the top of the hood. In order
> to keep the armor moist, all that was neces-
> sary to be done by the traveler as he pro-
> gressed over the burning sands, was to
> press the sack occasionally, when a small
> quantity of water would be forced up and
> thoroughly saturate the hood and the jacket
> below it. Thus, by the evaporation . . . it
> was calculated might be produced any de-
> gree of cold. Mr. Newhouse went down to
> Death Valley, determined to try the experi-
> ment of crossing that terrible place in his
> armor.

According to De Quille, Newhouse was found the next day,
about twenty miles into the desert,

> a human figure seated against a rock. . . .
> His beard was covered with frost, and—
> though the noonday sun poured down its
> fiercest rays—an icicle over a foot in length
> hung from his nose. There he had perished
> miserably, because his armor had worked
> but too well, and because it was laced up
> behind where he could not reach the fasten-
> ings.

The story was reported as news worldwide, and the boys in the newsroom at the *Terminal Enterprise* must have had a good laugh over that one. De Quille, like his contemporary Mark Twain, could tell a story so patently false that truth smirked out from around the edges.

In my mind's eye, I could see the foot-long icicle, blue white under a molten sun. Slowly, the thing began to grow, and it floated dumbly out into the shimmering salt pan of the valley floor, where it stood like a massive religious icon, a monolithic icicle plunged into the heart of Death Valley.

By nine that night it had cooled off enough to walk. Neither of us had slept for over forty hours. Worse, we had lain our boots on the ground to dry. The boots had been wet and caked with muddy salt. The ground on fire had baked them into weird, unfootlike shapes. Mine seemed to weigh fifteen or twenty pounds apiece. The canvas and leather felt like cement.

We hammered on the boots with rocks, cracking away the caked adobe.

"Leaving the boots on the ground," Nick pointed out, "was dumb."

There was poor planning involved, all right. The next water stash was only five miles away, at a place where a scrubby bush grew beside a rocky four-wheel-drive road. Unfortunately, in that area there had been a number of springtime flash floods. Water had thundered down the mountainsides in several temporary rivers, and each wash, in the light of our headlamps, appeared to be a four-wheel-drive road. We couldn't find the water. Poor planning.

The evaporative wind had cranked up to about forty miles an hour. This was serious. We retraced our steps, searching for the stash, walking like a pair of Frankenstein monsters in our adobe boots. We both were developing severe blisters, but there was no stopping now. Finding the water was more important than some little excruciatingly crippling pain.

About 2:30 that morning we stumbled over the water and

food. We had been out on the Valley floor for twenty-six hours, in temperatures sometimes exceeding 120 degrees. My feet looked and felt like I'd been walking across hot coals. We both carried extra boots, but walking over ground on fire makes feet expand. Mine looked sort of like big red blistered floppy clown feet. My second pair of boots simply didn't fit, not even a little bit. Another bit of poor planning that meant I'd have to walk forever in cruel shoes, limping pathetically.

We'd made too many mistakes, Nick and I, and the errors had compounded themselves exponentially, so that we had completely lost the will to push on. In the distance, seventeen miles away, we could see the lights of Furnace Creek. We doctored our feet—break the blister, apply the antiseptic, coat with Spenco Second Skin tape—and discussed complete capitulation. In our condition, with blisters and thirty-pound packs, we could probably make two miles in an hour. It would take six and a half hours to walk to Furnace Creek just to surrender.

On the other hand, the next stash was three miles away, in the Panamint Mountains, at an elevation of 2,300 feet. Say, four hours to cover eight miles, and give it another hour for each 1,000 feet of elevation. The stash was about six and a half hours away. It would hurt just as bad to give up as to push on, and it would be ten or fifteen degrees cooler at 2,300 feet.

Still, if blisters and exhaustion kept us from reaching the rocks before noon, that could be fatal. We decided to gamble and headed for the high country, hoping the idea of death could save us.

INTO THE FIRE

We were perhaps 1,500 feet up into the Panamints, walking up a long, bare slope littered with sage. There was no shade anywhere on the slope. We had miles to walk before the rock would rise above us and provide some protection from the sun. Quite clearly, neither of us could survive another day crouched under a space blanket.

Nick was wearing shorts, and I could see the muscles in

his thighs twitching spasmodically. It was only two hours until sunup. There was a full moon that night, and in its light I suddenly saw, sloping off to my right, a long, narrow valley. In that valley, almost glittering in the moonlight, was a town full of large frame houses, all of them inexplicably painted white. The houses seemed well maintained but were clearly abandoned. There was nothing on the map that indicated a ghost town here in Trail Canyon.

"Jesus, Nick, look." I pointed to the ghost town, perhaps 250 feet below us.

"What?"

"We can hole up down there."

"Where?"

"Down there."

Nick stared down into the valley for a full thirty seconds. "You're pointing to a ditch," he said finally. "You want to hole up in a ditch?"

I squinted down at the ghost town. Slowly, it began to rise toward me. The neatly painted white houses became strands of moon-dappled sage in a ditch perhaps five feet deep.

"I been having 'em, too," Nick said.

Nick wouldn't say what his hallucinations were like. I had to coax it out of him.

"Graveyards," Nick said finally. "I been seeing graveyards."

An hour and a half later we sat to rest. To the east, over the Funeral Mountains, on the other side of Death Valley, the pale light of false dawn had given way to a faint pastel pink. The sky suddenly burst into flame, filling the high canyons with a crimson that flowed down the ridges and flooded the valley floor with blood. Then the sun rose over the Funeral Mountains, fierce and blindingly hot, like molten silver, and its white heat scattered the crimson, so that for a moment the full weight of the sun lay glittering and triumphant on the great lifeless salt pan below. It was still cool—perhaps 85 degrees—but, within a matter of hours, the temperature could rise to 120 or more.

It was the first time in my life I'd ever found a beautiful

sunrise terrifying. It was like seeing a huge mushroom cloud rise in the distance, that sunrise.

THE POST CARD OF THE RESCUE

In the rocks above the bare sage slope, we found a narrow S-shaped canyon, where we lay down to sleep. Throughout the day, the sun chased us around the bends of the S, but there was always shade somewhere. We shared the canyon with a small, drab, gray sparrowlike bird that seemed to be feeding on some thorny red flowers that grew in the shade. I loved Death Valley. It was, as the ranger said, psychological, this place. It slammed you from one extreme to another. My heart seemed to expand inside my chest, and I could feel tears welling up in my eyes. I turned away from Nick, and we sat like that for a time, back to back.

"Nice here," I said finally. "Comfortable."

"Birds and shit," Nick agreed. His voice was shaky.

We slept for twelve hours, ate at nine that night, then slept until six the next morning. The swelling in our feet had gone down after twenty-one hours of sleep, and we could wear our extra boots. I felt like skipping. By noon that day we had reached an abandoned miner's cabin where we had stashed six gallons of water.

"How do you feel?" I asked Nick.

"Real good."

"Me too."

"We're going to make it," he said.

"I know."

It was cool enough to cook inside the cabin, and Nick was whipping up one of his modified freeze-dried Creole shrimp dinners when we heard the plane.

It was moving up the slope, circling over the route we had given Dick Rayner, and we couldn't believe they were looking for us now that we felt like gods of the desert. It was still twenty-four hours to the first checkpoint. Why were they searching for us? I laid out a yellow poncho so the rangers could spot us. Beside the poncho I arranged several dozen rocks to read "OK" in letters ten feet high. The plane

came in close and dipped a wing. The pilot looked like
Rayner. He circled twice more, then flew back down Furnace Creek.

It was an odd sensation, having them out spending tax-
payers' money searching for us. I felt like some boy scout
had just offered to help me across the street.

APOTHEOSIS

We had, it seemed, acclimated to the desert. It was easier,
now, to walk during the day and sleep in the cool of the
evening. We took the Panamint Valley at midday in temperatures that rose to 115 degrees. The next day, climbing
another range of mountains, we came upon a series of en-
closing rock walls that reminded us of our good friend the
S-shaped canyon. It rose up into the mountains, and there
was a small, clear creek running down the middle of the
canyon where green grass and bulrushes and coyote melons
and trees—actual willow trees—grew. Ahead, water cas-
caded over some boulders that had formed a natural dam.
The pool beyond the boulders was clear green with a golden
sandy bottom. It was deep enough to dive into, and the
water was so cold it drove the air from my lungs like a
punch to the chest. Above, several waterfalls fell down a
series of ledges that rose like steps toward the summit of the
mountains.

The same sun that had tried to kill us in Death Valley
offered its apologies, and we lay out on the rocks, watching
golden-blue dragonflies flit over the pool. It was 111 degrees, and we were sunbathing.

The next day we made twenty miles overland. The day
after that, almost thirty. We crossed the salt flats of the
Owens Valley in the middle of the day, roared into the town
of Lone Pine, registered with the rangers to climb Mount
Whitney, and reached the summit in a day and a half. It is,
perhaps, the easiest pretty high mountain in the world to
climb: a walk up.

About forty people made the summit that day, but only
half a dozen of us camped there. I was using the stove to

melt snow for drinking water and shivering slightly because my summer sleeping bag wasn't keep me entirely
warm. Nick was shooting the sunset over the headwaters of
the Kern River far below.

"My fingers are numb," he said. "It's hard to focus." The
thermometer read sixteen degrees.

"Yeah, well, you know what they say."

"What do they say?"

"If it's not one thing, it's another."

"Nice view, though," the Indiana Jones of photography
said.

THE KINDNESS OF RANGERS REVISITED

When we walked into Dick Rayner's office, I had a copy
of the *The Death Valley Gazette* under my arm. The chief
ranger agreed that, yes, according to the plan we'd filed, we
hadn't been late. What had happened, he said, was that
Frank Frost, in the support vehicle, had climbed to the top
of a mountain with a commanding view of our route and
had spent a day scanning the trails with high-powered
binoculars. It was the day we had spent sleeping in the
S-shaped canyon. Frank couldn't find us anywhere.

He reported to the rangers, who had immediately set out
to save our lives. The foul-up hadn't been anyone's fault
really, and I suppose I was glad that the Park Service em-
ploys men like Dick Rayner who are willing to leave
an air-conditioned office to save a couple of nincompoops
like us.

Still, I couldn't help zapping him a little. "The article
says we were more than twenty-four hours overdue. I
mean, look at our trip plan. We still had twenty-four hours
to the first checkpoint."

Rayner said, "I didn't write the article."

"They quote you directly, though. You say we were in
'good but fatigued condition.' "

"Well, we saw your footprints across the valley," Rayner
said. "That's a tiring walk. And we could see you were in

good condition when we flew over. So: 'good but fatigued condition.' "

The chief ranger seemed a little embarrassed. He recounted some of the rescues he'd participated in, and one of the deaths he knew about. Rayner seemed to be saying that he'd just as soon nobody walked across Death Valley in the summertime. It was his job to discourage such treks—to put guardrails along the cliffs—and he apparently felt that newspaper articles about half-dead dumbshits in the desert were something of a public service. He was a good man who just purely hated the idea of people getting hurt in his park.

"Would you do it again?" Rayner asked.

I glanced over at the Indiana Jones of photography, who was smiling in a manner that made him look somewhat psychological. "We could change the rules," he said. "No stashes. We walk from spring to spring and carry portable water purifiers. Badwater to Tule Spring to Trail Canyon . . ."

Dick Rayner seemed intrigued. Certainly against his better judgment, he pointed to the map on his desk and said, "There's a spring here that would get you into the canyon in better shape."

VERTICAL CAVING

I t is like no night on the face of the earth: in this cave the darkness is palpable and it physically swallows the brightest light. The air underground smells clean, damp, curiously sterile. It feels thick, like freshly washed still-damp velvet, and I am about to rappel down a long single strand of rope into the heart of all that heavy darkness. This is the second deepest cave pit in America: the drop is four hundred and forty feet, about what you'd experience from the top of a forty-story building. If you took the shaft in free-fall you'd accelerate to one hundred and some miles an hour and then—about six seconds into the experience—instantly decelerate to zero miles an hour. And die. Wah-hoo-hoo over and out. With six bad seconds to think about it.

Contemplating those six seconds sets the mind slithering through some dank and chilling chambers. The worst of it happens at the precipice. There you are, hooked into the rope, ready to back off the cliff and slide down into the darkness of the abyss and it feels like some mushy daytime soap "On the Brink of Forever." Suppose a horde of bats comes belching out of the pit—damn nasty screeching rabid little suckers. They could get caught in your hair, bite your ass, interfere with your concentration. And God only knows what other horrors may lurk in the depths so few have penetrated. Monsters out of H. P. Lovecraft's fevered dreams. Listen, and you can hear them down there in the darkness, scheming, conspiring, gibbering with blood lust. (Probably just the sound of running water, probably just a

241

small falls somewhere in the darkness.) Ah, but it feels like
a place for bubbling sulphur pits, for lakes of fire complete
with damned souls screaming in eternal torment. Oh,
Dante would love it here on the lip of Incredible Pit, deep
inside Ellison's Cave under Pigeon Mountain just outside
Lafayette, Georgia.

All black fancy, generated out of primal fear, this train of
thought. Better to contemplate the expedition as a whole:
Ellison's Cave is simply the most spectacular vertical caving
experience in America. It is rated as one of the most physically taxing and technically difficult wild caves anywhere.

A lot of people who don't go into caves have theories
about why other people do. There's talk that gets all fuzzy
and Freudian around the edges, a lot of thumb-sucking
nonsense about figurative returns to the womb that makes
cavers seem just a tad, oh, psychotic. The truth is simple
enough: certain people go into caves because most folks
don't. The urge is called exploration and everyone understands it to one degree or another. We were, all of us, explorers from our first breath, in a time our world expanded
in wonder.

The physical act of exploration is still possible. The forests may be gone, and land is replete with shopping malls
and fast-food outlets, but drop half a mile into the earth and
there is a pristine wilderness of danger and challenge and
alien, almost obscene, beauty. There is wonder left in the
world.

The order cavers impose on this wonder is called making
the connection. A connection has been made when a person
manages to crawl, climb, slide, or swim from one cave entrance and exit through another.

The connection is the stated goal, just as making the
summit is the mountaineer's goal. And just as each mountain presents a series of unique challenges, so does each
cave. Ellison's is a kind of Everest of American caving. The
primary obstacles to be overcome are two large pits: holes
in the ground, deep below the surface of the earth, each of
them large enough to contain a forty- or fifty-story building.

Dropping these natural shafts on a single rope may be an act of exploration, but there's more than a tad of terror vibrating in the core of the wonder. Consequently, standing in the darkness, on the Brink of Forever, I check my rig for the fifth or sixth time. Yes, yes, everything just so. Seat harness—A-OK. Carabiner—locked. How's the rope? Is it threaded properly through the rappel rack? There is a right way to do this and a wrong way. The wrong way is called a "death rig."

I've got a bag hanging from the seat harness and it contains all the things I'll need for the projected twelve to twenty hours it should take us to make the connection. Check out the contents: a spare light, some candles, lighters, warm clothes in a plastic bag to keep them dry, some spare bits of hardware, a couple of roast beef sandwiches. Yes, sir, dropping down to the ninth level of hell and bringing along a lunch.

The folks who have brought me here are pros, experts, and it seems wise to seek their counsel at the Brink. "Am I death rigged here or what?"

Kent Ballew gives my rappel rack a cursory glance. "Looks good to me," he says. Looks good? What does he mean, looks good? Lots of things look good to Kent Ballew. Women with pouty mouths look good to Kent Ballew. Fast cars look good to Kent Ballew. Do I really want to spend the last six seconds of my life thinking about what looks good to Kent Ballew?

"You mean I'm in solid," I persist, "not death rigged?"

"That would be my considered opinion," Kent says, since he has determined that I require a degree of formality and certitude in this matter.

And so I walk backward to the edge of the pit, lean back on the rope I've rigged into, and begin falling out into nothing. It is as if my intention is to do a back flip into the pit.

arry "Smokey" Caldwell, arguably one of the most astute and inventive vertical cavers in the world, felt my life was worth a week's training anyway. Vertical caving, as practiced by Caldwell and his cohorts, is not a skill someone picks up in a day. Single rope technique (SRT) is an elegantly esoteric art, and my guess is that the people who are any good at it can be counted in the hundreds. Smokey runs a business—Pigeon Mountain Industries in Lafayette, Georgia—that caters to these folks. PMI manufactures the specialized rope used in vertical caving, and it sells the various bits of hardware needed to literally walk up a rope. The techniques Smokey and men like "Vertical Bill" Cuddington pioneered translate well to endeavors beyond the realm of sport. PMI sells rope and gear (and sometimes expertise) to fire fighters, mountain rescue teams, and the military. Indeed, my partner in training with Smokey was John VandenBurg, a fire fighter from Ontario, Canada. He would use his training to save lives—to rescue people on the top floors of a burning high-rise, for instance—and I would use mine to explore America's deepest caves.

Smokey started us off on a simple outdoor cliff—a sixty-foot drop called the Eagles Nest—and soon enough we progressed to sinkholes, large pits open to the air. My favorite was called Valhalla, though Kent Ballew, an employee of PMI, found it spooky in the extreme. Kent is the kind of guy who can do a bootlegger's 180 degree turn on a Chattanooga street, dead sober, and then discuss the matter with an officer of the law in such a way that he gets off with a stern warning. Kent, you sense, is a man who lives a life full of stern warnings. Like most hard-core cavers, he finds calculated risk a life-affirming activity.

And that is why what happened a few years ago in the pit called Valhalla upset him so badly. Some cavers had rappeled into the 260-foot pit and were waiting there, under an overhanging rock the size of a 18-wheel truck. The overhang protected them from falling rocks displaced by cavers above, and it was entirely wise for them to be sitting there. But the rock gave way, and the two cavers were crushed beneath its unthinkable weight.

Smokey and Kent were on the team that recovered the bodies. They had to dig under the rock, and what they found there has haunted Kent Ballew ever since. "Valhalla used to be my favorite pit," Kent told me. "I used to do it twenty times a year or more. Now it's like the pit's turned hostile. Those guys did everything right and the pit killed them."

We did Valhalla on a weekend. Perhaps fifty spectators were watching when Kent Ballew began his descent. He backed over the lip and, it seemed, just let go. It looked like he had come out of the rope, like he was falling, and several people screamed. This is the way Kent rappels, and he relishes screams of terror from concerned onlookers.

I followed him down. The brake bar rack used for these long rappels is an elongated horseshoe-shaped device. The rope is threaded through six crossing bars and the bars may be slid close together to create friction and thus slow the descent. Spread the bars out for a Kent Ballew–like full-tilt rappel.

Valhalla was surrounded by foliage at the top. Inside, it was a symphony of sculpted, soaring rock, and I wanted to take my time. Bright summer sun filtered through the trees surrounding the pit, and a dozen shafts of slanting light fell inside the pit in pure operatic overstatement.

The PMI rope we were using was specially designed for long rappels. It consisted of a braided outer sheath that protects the load-bearing inner core from abrasion. The core was composed of twenty-two parallel strands of splice-less nylon. This static kernmatle type of construction meant the rope did not spin, and had very little stretch. A mountaineering rope, by contrast, is designed to stop a falling climber and must stretch to cushion the shock that occurs when some plummeting unfortunate reaches the end of his tether.

This is not to say that PMI rope has no stretch at all. At

the bottom of a pit like Valhalla, for instance, when you stand and take your weight off the rope it pulls up a few feet. This upward pressure makes it difficult to get the rappel rack off the rope. For this reason it is a good idea to lift the legs and rappel until you are almost sitting on solid ground. Which is what I was doing—cruising to a sit-down landing in this open to the sky pit—when I saw the copperhead snake coiled directly below. At such times, one doesn't reflect that the only way a snake could get to the bottom of the pit would be a fast and fatal 260-foot fall. The copperhead was curled in striking position. I grabbed the rope, pulled myself up, and said "wok!" in the manner of a man who has stepped barefoot onto something squishy and foul and possibly alive. Ballew, who had put the dead snake under the rope, thought this was among the more humorous things he had ever seen. I discussed his sense of humor with him, and the discussion was in the nature of a stern warning.

Still, we left the snake there for photographer Nick Nichols, who was next on the rope. Nick has been photographing caves for a dozen years and is well known in the speleological community. Because caves, as opposed to sinkholes like Valhalla, are perfectly dark, it is impossible to get an idea of their dimensions with one light. Nick's genius is to illuminate the caves with light—with a combination of old-fashioned flash guns, flares, radio-controlled strobe lights, and great white hot magnesium explosions. Cavers accompany Nick—he gets them to carry his gear—into the deepest and most inaccessible caves because he will provide them with photographs of a place they have been to but have never really seen.

Because I was with Nick, Smokey and Kent saw to it that we hit the deepest cave pits in the Southeast. This process of rappeling down and climbing back up without attempting to make a connection, is called "yo-yoing the pit." One day we yo-yoed the 282-foot-deep Mystery Hole just outside Chattanooga, once thought to be the deepest cave pit in America. There had been a death in this cave as well. Back in 1959, 18-year-old Jimmy Shadden had attempted to de-

scend into the Mystery Hole on a frayed ski rope and fell
to his death. The rope, it was found later, had a breaking
strength of 270 pounds. (PMI's $7/16$-inch rope has a maximum tensile strength of 6,800 pounds.)

There is a waterfall in the Mystery Hole, and a caver
named Buddy Lane has devised a clever dam so people no
longer have to descend and ascend through the freezing
spray. We dammed the falls and rappeled down into the
darkness of the Mystery Hole. Buddy Lane, who accompanied us on this one, stayed up top to let the water drain out
of the dam once the rest of us were on the floor of the pit.
It came crashing down, 280 feet, and the bottom of the pit
was a roaring chaos of howling mist for over five minutes.
Ballew said a word of prayer for "ski-rope Jimmy" (whom
he regarded as a friendly spirit), Buddy Lane redammed the
waterfall for us, and we began climbing up the rope in the
dark.

Ascending is a complicated process. The first essential
item needed for a long rope climb is a seat harness. This, in
its simplest form, is a long strip of heavy nylon webbing
that is wound about the waist and legs and tied off. A carabiner—an oblong metal ring that snaps open on one side—
is clipped into the seat and hangs just below the belly
button. If the seat harness is properly tied and fastened, you
could clip the carabiner onto a stout hook in a wall and
simply sit there.

Single rope technique, as practiced by the best vertical
cavers, involves the use of mechanical devices called Gibbs
ascenders: these are little metal gadgets that slide easily *up*
the main rope. Put your weight on a Gibbs and it will bite
down and hold with dull metal teeth, which do not damage
the rope.

The bottom Gibbs is attached to a loop of webbing worn
on the right foot. You could wear a second Gibbs on your
left foot, and hook it into the rope just above your right foot.
The problem with this is that you will never be able to lift
your right foot above your left. Consequently, you will end
up lifting your body weight only on your left foot.

What you really want to do is walk up the rope, lifting

one foot above the other so that each leg alternately carries
your weight. To do this, you need to rig a "floating cam,"
which is a Gibbs worn just off the left knee. A foot loop
drops from that Gibbs to your left foot. A length of elastic
cord fastened to a harness around your chest pulls the knee
Gibbs up the rope when you lift your left foot.

In this way, you can walk up the rope. There are two
more devices that make the process easier. The first holds
your upper body in toward the rope. Because you are really
only attached to the rope at the left knee and right ankle,
it is necessary to hold yourself in to the rope with your
hands so you don't fall over backward. Rather than use arms
at all, you can wear a chest harness with a small wheel in
it. The wheel, which is set in a small metal frame, is positioned over the breastbone. You run the rope through the
wheel and it will hold your chest into the rope so you can
climb no-handed.

A device that allows you to rest and also provides an extra
measure of safety is a "top Jumar." Like a Gibbs, the Jumar
is a metal ascender that will bite and hold when it feels
downward pressure. The Jumar is attached to the rope at
about eye level. A length of webbing connects the Jumar to
a carabiner on the seat harness. As you climb, you slide the
Jumar up the rope. When you are tired, you simply sit in
the seat harness and the Jumar holds you.

It took a week for me to begin to feel comfortable working this rig and for Smokey to decide I was ready to try
Ellison's Cave. "You've been to the chapels," Nick told me,
"now we're going to the cathedral."

ost of the caves in the southeastern section of the
United States are limestone formations. In the distant past, the area was a vast sea, and in this sea
various creatures lived, absorbed calcium com-
pounds from the water, and when they died their
calcareous skeletons formed beds of limestone. In
time, the sea retreated to the east as the land rose and the

Appalachian Mountains formed at a tectonic wrinkle point. Much of the new land consisted of vast outcroppings of limestone that broke and twisted, that folded in on themselves, that were, in fact, a place where caves bred and multiplied.

Limestone is the mother of caves, and surface water the father. Rainwater seeping through topsoil absorbs carbon dioxide and so forms carbonic acid. Limestone is soluble in this weak acid, which will find cracks and fissures in the broken humped-up rock of the old sea bed. In time—given the capacity of acidic surface water to melt rock—the fissures became canyons, the cracks became pits. Rainwater can, over the centuries, carve out great halls. Underground waterfalls form immense pits with smooth vertical walls.

The land itself is so honeycombed with meandering underground passages that many drainages in Kentucky and Tennessee and Georgia and Alabama do not contain rivers. The water simply moves underground. When the water table falls, the stony courses of these underground river systems are left dry.

Rainwater still seeps into the dry passages: into the double oval passageways shaped like keyholes, into the grand ballrooms. It falls over the lips of pits. Because there is no green plant life in the depths of a cave, there is no carbon dioxide in it either, which accounts for the alien "clean" odor of most caves. In a cave environment, the weakly acidic surface water wants to reach chemical equilibrium, and carbon dioxide, so recently absorbed in the green world above, is suddenly released in the lifeless stone passages below. Limestone that had once been in solution becomes solid, and fantastic formations are created.

In a large room, over time measured in centuries, a single persistent drip can form a stalactite, those odd stone icicles that hang *tight* to the ceiling. The corresponding formation, a stalagmite (you *might* walk into one), grows up from the floor. Small sheets of water flowing down the side of a wall can form flamboyant multicolored stone draperies, and water running along the floor of the cave leaves flowstone deposits that look like a river frozen in stone.

These formations are like nothing seen on the surface of the earth. They have an alien sculpted beauty that suggests some strained, ancient, and unhuman intelligence at work. Sometimes, in the near silence, you can hear that intelligence speak in the sound of distant running water. It sounds vaguely like the mumbling of human voices and it generally comes from below, from deeper. . . .

Because there isn't much life in caves, they lack the familiar odors of life and death. Near the entrances you might find some nesting birds, a few spiders, some salamanders. These common creatures don't penetrate much past the twilight world of the entrances. But deep in the caves, in the absolute darkness, is where you find white eyeless crickets carrying antennae—longer than their own bodies—which they use the way blind people use canes. There are bats hanging in some of the passageways, bats hanging in great gray furry masses. Drops of water collect on their bodies so that a light shone upon them backscatters bright and silver with a slight otherworldly prismatic rainbow effect. Sometimes, in the permanent ponds and lakes, you may find white albino fish, and where the eyes would be on these fish, there is only smooth white flesh.

To see these things, these odd creatures, these revelations in stone, is reason enough to venture into caves. The impulse is called tourism, and there are plenty of commercial caves open across the United States where people may safely scratch that itch in some comfort and safety. But the urge to explore, to go where no man has gone before, takes hard-core cavers into a world of wonder where the words *comfort* and *safety* are no more than cruel jokes.

True, wild caves sometimes contain passages in which a tall man can walk upright. More often, passages are a tad low, and people must walk the equivalent of several city blocks bent over at the waist. Since rocks and stalactites projecting from the ceiling can deal a nasty blow, it is wise to walk looking forward and above, with the head rolled back slightly on the shoulders. Cavers call this comical means of locomotion a Groucho walk. Some passages require a squatting duck walk and others a belly crawl. This last can be painful: often the floor of the passage will contain a small cold stream flowing over a bed of excruciatingly sharp rocks.

And then there are passages that seem impossible, little holes in the rock not much bigger around than a long-playing record. Here it is necessary to put the arms through first, like a diver; it is necessary to expel all the air from the lungs, to wiggle through, snakelike. Getting caught in such a hole is a panicky, claustrophobic situation. Even the best cavers sometimes have to be "talked through" bad holes. "Hey, Frank"—and here you speak calmly, reasonably, in a kind of a whisper—"maybe if you got your right foot up a bit, you could push against a rock I see. Be through in a second. No problem. No hurry. You got it, buddy. . . ."

There are dangers in wild caves that are not matters of common sense and simple intuition. In passages where bats congregate, for instance, they leave nasty little lakes of droppings. Lightning has a habit of streaking into the mouths of caves, striking guano accumulations and causing them to explode.

Aside from exploding bat shit, cavers can be injured by falls, cave-ins, falling rocks, or by the wet cold that drains the body of heat. Get lost in a cave and you don't have to worry about starving to death. The damp cold will kill you first. You can watch it happen, actually see the onset of hypothermia in a cave where the year-round temperature may stand at fifty-five degrees. Just hold your hand up and shine a light on it: five streams of steam rise from your fingers. One caver who was trapped for over forty hours in a Kentucky cave told me she couldn't stop doing this as she waited, hoping to be rescued. "I was watching myself die," she told me.

Drowning is quicker and not uncommon. Since the caver doesn't know what the weather is outside, he must constantly look for and mark rooms with high and accessible ledges. A big thunderstorm can fill the passages with rushing water. Even in the highest rooms, doomed cavers have watched helplessly as the water level rose to their legs, their chests, their necks. In the end they died with their lips against the cold stone of the ceiling, died knowing that this was the last breath they would ever take.

Cavers consider such dangers problems to be overcome: they see them in the way mountain climbers see ice-covered rock and unstable avalanche chutes. And while the mountaineer strives to reach the summit, the apotheosis of the sport is to make a first ascent.

Most people have some sense of what that means—a first ascent—but few understand the caver's drive to make the first connection in a newly discovered cave. New caves are often found today by cavers who "walk the ridges," looking for holes in the ground or places where small rivers disappear. Generally, the river will reappear somewhere below, perhaps on the other side of the mountain. Clearly then—unless there are two streams—the river flows through the mountain. Which means there are passages leading from the high entrance to the lower one. The purpose of exploration is to map the cave, to avoid both getting lost and having time and the damp cold of the cave suck the life out of your body, to climb over great piles of fallen rock, to wade through pools, to belly crawl and Groucho walk your way from one entrance and then exit through another.

It may take dozens of trips to make the connection. Sometimes a passageway may "go," may lead to more passages. Sometimes two hours' worth of belly-crawling misery ends when the passage squeezes down to nothing. Because passages sometimes fold in on themselves like strands of spaghetti, it is often possible to apparently dead end, only to find a tiny hole leading from one series of snaking passages to another. Very thin cavers are often sent ahead to see if such a hole "goes." Small slender women who don't suffer from claustrophobia are valuable in this regard. They are among the "stoutest" of cavers.

In the past thirty years, cavers, especially in the Southeast, have been presented with new and seemingly insoluble "problems" in some of the most spectacular of the newly found caves. In Fern Cave, in Ellison's Cave, there are huge pits the caver has to negotiate in order to make the connection. In the absolute blackness there is no way to accurately judge the depth of these pits—a beam of light shone down them is simply swallowed up by the eternal darkness—but a rock dropped into the abyss of Ellison's Fantastic Pit takes just under seven seconds to hit bottom. The physics of the situation suggest a drop of 550 feet, about half of what you'd get from the top of the Empire State Building.

Rope ladders were too heavy, too difficult, to Groucho walk and belly crawl through holes. And they tended to spin under a caver's weight. Ski rope was the suicide's solution to the pits, and mountaineering rope spun so badly that early cavers became nauseated in only a few feet. What cavers needed, in order to make the connection, were new methods, new techniques. Single rope technique—the use of specialized rope, rappel racks, and mechanical ascenders—was the answer.

During the time these techniques were being developed—from 1967 through 1981—there were eight fatalities among accomplished vertical cavers. Four were the result of problems with the seat harness, two happened when the caver slipped at the lip while off the rope, one occurred when the rope pulled out of its anchor, and one person death rigged himself.

Since the caving community is a small one, accounts of these deaths spread quickly, and the hard-core vertical caver, in consequence, tends to be more safety conscious than one might first suppose. A small magazine, *Nylon Highway*, published by the "vertical section" of the National Speleological Society, caters to this hard core and contains reports on accidents as well as offering safety hints and accounts of new pits. It also lists records for the "classic" one-hundred-foot rope climb, which now stands at under thirty seconds.

In the last half dozen years, the technique that was developed for the purposes of exploration—and modified to save lives—has become a sport in and of itself. A number of cavers now simply yo-yo the pits with no thought of further exploration, and some of these fanatics have taken their dirty underground sport out into the light of day. Last October, I accompanied my caving friends to Yosemite Na-

tional Park where we yo-yoed the half-mile-high face of the
mountain called El Capitan. That, however, is not the longest rappel ever made. In 1980, a team that included Nick
Nichols and Kent Ballew yo-yoed a 3,200 foot drop off Mt.
Thor, on Baffin Island. That accomplishment is the longest
single rope rappel ever made—PMI supplied a mile-long
rope for the effort—but the *Guinness Book of World Records*
refused to sanction the record. The editors felt people
might die trying to outdo the cavers.

SRT, however, was developed in caves, in complete darkness, for the purposes of exploration in an underground
wilderness, and this fact was what brought me to Georgia
and Ellison's Cave. Discovered in 1912, the cave was virtually ignored until the winters of 1968 and 1969 when Della
McGuffin and Richard Schreiber decided to push a few
passages. In so doing they discovered the two deepest free-
fall pits in America: Fantastic Pit, at 600 feet, and Incredible
Pit, at 440 feet. A caver making the connection in Ellison's
must negotiate both pits.

Five of us—Nick Nichols, Kent Ballew, Smokey Caldwell, myself, and Jim Youmans, an Atlanta high-rise
contractor—rappeled about eighty feet into a vegetation-choked sinkhole high on the west side of Pigeon
Mountain. It was a place of sloping dirt walls and
copperheads that brought us to a 100-foot-long horizontal passage leading into Ellison's Cave proper. The passage ended in a tight steep canyon called the Stairstep
Entrance: another short rappel. At the bottom there was a
long belly crawl: a nose in the water crawl so painfully
difficult that it is called The Misery. Happily, some enter-
prising cavers long ago dug through a wall of breakdown—
a mound of rock that had fallen from the ceiling of the
cave—and created a jaunty walk-through passage straight to
the lip of Incredible Pit. The passage there is very narrow,
and people stand single file, waiting their turn on the rope,
which is anchored into the rock at several different points.

I had had a small crisis of courage on the lip, but now, secure in the fact that I hadn't death rigged myself, I was taking my time, enjoying the view and feeling an eerie dreamlike calm: this can't be real. I tightened the bars on my rack in order to slow down. A hot shot like Kent Ballew can take this 440-foot drop in about five minutes. I wanted to make my descent last, to spend half an hour savoring Incredible Pit. The walls, scoured by centuries of acidic falling water, were smooth, like the barrel of a shotgun. There was a monumental symmetry to the pit that sent the soul spinning: it was a cathedral crafted of stone and darkness.

At times, the rope hung so far from the wall that there was nothing to be seen but a shimmering twilight at the periphery of my light. At such times it was possible to feel something of what astronauts must feel on spacewalks: a sense that you have never been so alone, so exhilarated.

In time I could see my light reflecting off the calm pool at the bottom of Incredible Pit. I hung off there for a time, took a flashgun from my pack, and waited for Kent and Smokey to get on the rope. They would position themselves at certain intervals, then we would all turn off our lights and Nick would open the lens on his camera. At a signal, everyone would flash, and, in the development of time, we'd have a photographic idea of the enormity of the pit. And so we hung there for half an hour or more, coordinating flashes for different shots, then dropped onto the floor of the cave. We had another twelve hours of hard travel in front of us until we hit Fantastic Pit.

I recall moving through a world of spaghetti passages snaking every which way. The maze rose to a high walk-through passage, and from there it was just under a mile, as the bat flies, to Fantastic Pit. There was a lot of climbing and crawling and sweating so that when we stopped, the cold began working at us and it was better to move than sit.

Five or six hours later, square in the gut of the mountain, I was led down a keyhole-shaped passage about ten feet high. Off to the right was a clear, almost transparent formation that dropped about three feet from the ceiling, and there were glassy bubbles in it. It looked like ice, as if it might melt, and it is called the North Pole for that reason. Some of the ice had fallen to the floor. I found it tasted like Epsom salts. "Looks like a chandelier, doesn't it?" Nick Nichols asked me. "I mean, if there was ever to be a chandelier in here, this would be it. I think this is the most beautiful cave formation in the South. Maybe in the country."

It may be, but just past the North Pole is a passage that leads down to a room completely filled with spun glass and crystal-clear needles and cotton candy. These Epsomite flowers bloom in Angel's Paradise, a cavern about ten feet square and five feet high. Because there is no way to get to these exquisitely delicate formations without dropping Fantastic or Incredible Pit, they are little visited. Even so, curious cavers carry dust in with them, the dust coats the delicate structures, and the rule is: "if you've seen it before, don't go again." I was directed to the cavern and given fifteen minutes alone, in Angel's Paradise. It was a pristine underground wilderness, and for the nonce, it was mine alone and I felt dizzy with fatigue and privilege.

Nearby there were great striated walls, and it was possible to see where the mountain had moved, where the walls had grumbled and slid, one against the other, in an area called the Slick and Slides. After that, the passages got smaller and more profuse, like an anthill on about three different levels. We emerged into a dry sandy streambed, ate some lunch, then moved down a narrow passage and climbed over what Nick called "this horrible thing," which was a slick, muddy rock that blocks the tunnel. About eight feet up the Horrible Thing there was a small opening you take head first. If you can get up. I needed help getting up the Horrible Thing, and I was thinking about how helpless I really was in the face of such obstacles—how perfectly dead I'd be alone here—when I tumbled eight feet down the other side of the damn Horrible Thing and found myself on the floor of a room 250 feet long and 600 feet high.

Tag Hall is the floor of Fantastic Pit, the deepest dome pit in America. The pit itself is a beautiful oval and its floor is smooth, pebbled, almost perfectly flat, as if groomed.

Smokey had rigged two ropes earlier, and they hung from a balcony 510 feet above. Nick started first, Smokey followed while Kent Ballew and I climbed the second rope. I found I could climb about 40 or 50 steps (40 or 50 feet), kicking out with each step to help the Gibbs ascender bite into the rope, before I needed to push the top Jumar up the rope and sit, breathless, in my seat harness. Below, I could feel a rhythmic jerking on the rope as Kent climbed.

At the 400-foot level, there was a boulder the size of a small house hanging from the smooth bore of wall. My instructions were to sit there and wait for more instructions. Nick Nichols was up top already, working on a picture. It took some time, preparing the shot, and I must have sat motionless for fifteen minutes, feeling again the odd liquid sensation of being suspended, alone in space, at peace, serene in a hostile world. I was sweating profusely in the chill, and my entire body was leaking heat, was literally steaming. The smooth ovoid walls that enveloped me shimmered and glittered in the shafts my light threw into the steam, which was the stuff of my own life. There was a sense of a connection made, an Angel's Paradise of the soul to be savored.

And then we switched off our lights, set off the flares and flashes, not to mention a magnesium explosion on the floor of the pit, all for Nick's camera. Fifteen minutes later, I pulled myself over the lip of the balcony, fifty stories above the pebbled floor below.

We were almost out: from there it was a simple misery to belly up a streambed, claw up over another horrible thing, then crawl on our hands and knees for fifteen minutes until we got to another fixed rope slung off a wall eighteen feet high. Having just spent an hour climbing 510 feet, gearing up for this climb was a pain in the ass, which is why Smokey calls it the Nuisance Drop. At the top, we found ourselves in the Rectum, a round upward-sloping passage of slippery and unpleasantly suggestive mud, which empties into the Warm-Up Pit: a 125-foot rope climb. At the top of the pit is the Agony, a 1,500-foot belly crawl. This is the natural exit but, some years ago, cavers discovered a stand-up passage leading up a stream bed to a small hole that they dug out, forming a new exit. This exit bypasses the Agony and is called the Ecstasy.

So we walked out of the Ecstasy fifteen hours after bypassing the Misery. We had dropped Incredible and passed under the North Pole. We had sat for a time in Angel's Paradise, braved a couple of horrible things, struggled up the throat of Fantastic, and made the connection with something we knew with our first breath and have not entirely forgotten.

TIME
AND
SPEED
AT THE
RAGGEDY EDGE

N
W ✦ E
S

I have a strange vision: I see Albert Einstein on skis. I see those deep, haunting eyes behind yellow goggles, the errant, absentminded mien, hair bursting out from under an idiotic tasseled wool cap; I see Albert Einstein on skis with old beartrap bindings. He is wearing some motley admixture of motheaten woolens, not entirely chic, you understand, but there he is on the bunny slope, burning up his first run, tearing down the hill, lickety-split, just about as fast as a child can walk. Pipe stem arms are windmilling this way and that—whoaaaaa to the right, whooooo to the left—until the frail old body finally settles into that Samurai warrior stance everyone assumes on the first run.

Here's Albert Einstein at the bottom of the hill with a tanned instructor saying: "Okay, Al, now what I want you to do is try to get your weight forward a little. . . ."

But Al is scratching his head through the old woolen cap with the dangling tassel. The eyes are far way, the awesome mind at work. He was a minute and a half on the slope, but he *felt* as if he lived a full hour through his senses. The world expanded inside his chest and time swam slowly by, as if through a sea of custard. Skiing, Albert Einstein decides, generates his intensity in three dimensions . . . at the expense of the fourth. Of course, he thinks, everything is relative, and it's just a theory, but what if a man could ski fast enough to stop time dead? Energy would equal, what, mass times . . .

"This time," the instructor is saying, "we're going to try something pretty complicated. It's called the snowplow turn. . . . Hey, Al! You still with us, buddy? Earth to Al . . ."

Al is not paying strict attention to the instructor. He is thinking that it's pretty damn funny the way time has no dominion over a man skiing the raggedy edge.

We've all experienced it: some spate of events that poleaxed time.

It seems to start in the belly. Remember the last time you were driving along the freeway, no cars out front, none behind, nobody in sight anywhere. It's just you and the radio and some vague daydreams about taking a shower with the one you haven't seen in too long and suddenly RIGHT BEHIND YOU there is a great blast of sound, as of some massive juggernaut bearing down on you from behind, some eighteen wheeler out of control and howling in rage and warning . . . where is it? where is it? . . . and you feel an instantaneous jolt in the belly that snaps your spine straight. Suddenly, without thinking about it, you can see all directions at once: to the empty road ahead and the empty road behind, to the total lack of vehicles on all sides. And slowly, yes, you come to understand that the intrusive sound comes not from the road, but from a highballing freight train that runs parallel to the freeway.

That feeling is gone from your belly, you are covered with a fine glaze of sweat, and your hands shake a bit on the wheel. The jackhammer inside your chest begins to sound more like your old familiar heart. How long did that all take: ten minutes, fifteen, half an hour? No, probably less

than five seconds all told: less than five seconds from full
alert to anticlimax, with no time at all elapsed between the
scream of the train and the jolt in your belly.

It's a chemical reaction, pure and simple, that cripples
time in your mind. Each of us possesses adrenal glands, two
penny-sized hunks of specialized meat perched atop each
kidney, and it is the inner ten percent of this gland, the
medulla, that controls, among other things, our perception
of time when the body is at stress. The adrenal medulla—
given properly stressful situations—secretes adrenaline and
noradrenaline. Both hormones pump the body up to full
capacity: they increase respiration, make the heart beat
faster, and pump the blood away from those areas that don't
need it (like the belly) and funnel it to those that do (like the
hands).

nly recently have scientist been able to differenti-
ate between the effects of adrenaline and noradrenaline. In a typical rat torture study,
psychologists have discovered that you can scare
rats stupid with a sudden and obscenely loud blast
of noise, a noise like the howl of a highballing
freight train. Rats that are scared at random intervals exhibit high levels of anxiety, and their blood is found to
contain extraordinary amounts of both adrenaline and
noradrenaline. But rats blasted by sound at regular intervals exhibit less anxiety. They seem to be able to prepare
themselves for the regularity of terror, and their blood
shows low levels of adrenaline and high levels of noradrenaline.

Noradrenaline is the good stuff. Adrenaline is associated
with fear and anxiety, while noradrenaline affects those
systems in the brain that are concerned with emotion: especially euphoria, well-being, and alertness. A man or woman
can increase levels of noradrenaline in the system by sub-
jecting the body to the stress of sustained exercise. Runners
who are able to push themselves for half an hour or more

sometimes experience "runner's high." The constant stress on the body has set noradrenaline sloshing about in the brain. These runners talk about a kind of euphoria, about a feeling of well-being, and a near-supernatural alertness, a perception of our world so intense, so encompassing, that time is no longer of the essence.

Cross-country skiers and racers, of course, regularly experience runner's high, but downhillers often describe similar sensations. The feeling is most often associated with a kind of stress we define as danger, or perceived danger: call it fear. Ski long enough at the limit of your abilities, and time slips into low gear.

The trick here is training. Sure, that once-impossible slope is still scary—it will get the anxiety-producing adrenaline pumping—but practice reduces adrenaline levels and diminishes terror. Like rats subjected to regular sound-blasting, the trained skier should exhibit higher levels of the good stuff, of the noradrenaline, which produces both euphoria and that preternatural alertness that begins to coagulate time itself.

Filmmakers have known that slow is fast since at least 1954. Before that, directors tried to suggest supernatural speed by filming a sequence in fast motion. I am think of F. W. Murnau's 1922 classic, *Nosferatu*, with Max Schreck starring as the most horrid Dracula ever. Schreck, rising from his coffin, the long fingers, gnarled in front of his splendidly terrific face as if they were talons, is enough to send the faint-hearted running blindly out of the theater. But the scene in which Nosferatu's black horse-drawn coach makes supernatural time along a mountain trail generally draws laughs from modern audiences. Fast motion is funny. Horses run ridiculously. Cornering is jerky. Fast motion is Chaplinesque. Subjectively, it just doesn't feel right.

In 1954, Akira Kurosawa tackled the problem of filming incredibly fast action in *Seven Samurai*. When the bandits rode into that fictional sixteenth-century village, the seven samurai chopped 'em up in slow motion. And it worked.

Other directors began to catch on: ah so, they seemed to say in unison, *slow is fast*.

In 1969, Sam Peckinpah used slow-motion techniques in *The Wild Bunch*. The final slaughter in a Mexican village, circa 1913, is a symphony of violence, and like most deadly violence, it happens with a rapidity so intense that the most horrifying sequences are realized in slow motion.

In the seventies, the idea that slow is fast came to television in two successful series: "Kung Fu" and "The Six Million Dollar Man." Inching into the eighties, a series called "The Incredible Hulk" presented the physiologically sound idea that a man under enormous stress might call on unimagined wells of strength. Like those women you read about who lift Camaros off their trapped babies, the Hulk only tore down buildings when that mother, Necessity, dictated. And he did it in slow motion.

These filmic techniques work because everyone has suffered through some degree of strong stress. Everyone knows, at least subconsciously, that time seems to slow down when we endure intense experience. Our bodies remember: slow is fast, slow is strong.

We don't actually think: hey, let's maximize regularized stress to stimulate the old noradrenaline secretions, get high, and watch time decelerate. What we do is push it right to the raggedy edge because it's fun, because it makes us feel good.

What we do is think: I can ski this slope. We think, I'll really burn up the hill this time. What we do is take calculated chances because they make us feel good.

I'm at the top of a good run called Pierre's Knob, at Bridger Bowl outside Bozeman, Montana. It's a little after four and the lifts are scheduled to close at 4:15, but if I tear down the knob and cut over to the middle lift down the short, steep expert slope called White Lightning, I can probably make one more run.

Now, I know this is a dicey situation. I've been skiing straight since ten this morning, with no time off for lunch. My legs are a little shaky. The big sky is glacial and gray, and it's getting difficult to see the bumps. This, I know, is the time of day when people get hurt. They get hurt doing exactly what I am doing. They get hurt skiing right up to the edge of their ability when they are tired and it is late and the light has gone bad on them.

No matter. Here I am, blasting down Pierre's Knob— best run of the day, I'm really burning—building up a head of steam for the short flat before White Lightning and ohoh, a little shot in the belly because I almost lost it there . . . but, yes, I've got it back, I'm in control and I can see all the way to the lip of White Lightning. My mind's eye can see the way I'll take it. No stopping at the top to read the slope: I'll just bang right over the lip in a shower of snow and be down to the lift before caution can assert itself.

The run is so steep that you can't really see it until you are right on top of it, and I am contemplating the line I'll take in my mind as I roar up onto the lip. Time begins inching toward freeze-frame because something is terribly wrong here. Something is dangerously askew. Ah, there it is, right on the lip of White Lightning: the top of a small bush or tree is sticking four or five inches up out of the snow. I have the leisure to notice that it looks like a juniper and to reflect that they are sturdy little suckers. Microseconds inflate into minutes. It is plainly evident that I am going to hit that juniper. I am already skiing the raggedy edge. I am going to crash and burn unless I can somehow adjust for treacherous vegetation.

Time, fortunately, has run up against a sea of noradrenaline and is struggling against it like a mastodon in a tar pit. I'll just put all my weight over onto the right ski like this; and I'll lift the left ski over the juniper. Plenty of time: the bush is approaching at a single frame a second. Slow motion city. There is time to feel the wind on my face, to realize that it will probably snow this night. I am looking at the juniper, but I can see the lift below and half a dozen people waiting in line. I know that I will make the last run. I have all the time in eternity to lift my left ski. . . .

Except that execution trails perception. The inside tip of the lift ski doesn't quite clear the juniper. My forward motion causes the unweighted ski to swivel savagely, and the back edge bangs into the calf of my right leg. There is the sound of a snap, but I know it is just impact, and not a broken bone: I am tipped forward. I am about to fall. Golly, this is taking a long time. You can achieve the same sensation by standing on the bottom stair and leaning slowly, slowly forward until you lose your balance. Here it comes—Jeez, I'm halfway down White Lightning, flailing all the way, and all the people in line below are looking at me—and that's it, I'm going down. Head first.

This, I reflect casually, promises to become even more unpleasant. I make first contact with the ground. Skis pop off and drag behind on the straps. Ass over teakettle one more time. Snow inside my parka. Everything is happening in slow motion: this is the agony of defeat writ large. I am coming slowly over on the third revolution and have no choice but to bite snow. I wonder if there is some formula to calibrate how long a body weighing two hundred pounds will slide on a 20-percent slope, given the friction of a nylon parka—whoops, over one more time—and I come to rest at the bottom of the hill. Just slide right into the last position in the lift line.

"I'm okay," I announce to the world at large. No one has asked me. They are all too busy laughing. I have provided an example of comedy skiing at its best. But I made it. I'm the last person on the lift this day.

And I am not in pain. Adrenaline, noradrenaline, and another substance secreted by the body in times of stress or pain—betaendorphin, the chemical structure of which resembles morphine—all combine to numb pain. In a ten-minute ride to the top of the mountain, these substances begin to be reabsorbed. What this means is that the body's natural painkillers have worn off. What it means is that I come off the lift and collapse, feeling like I've been trampled by a lot of fat people riding elephants.

It takes over an hour to side-slip down the mountain. The sun has set, snow is falling, and the world has entered another ice age. Time and motion, at last, are one.

ADVENTURES
IN THE
ENDO ZONE

They're up there now, on the ridge above the Bridger Bowl Ski Area, risking their lives, catching clean air, running the avalanches and the Orgasms, banging chutes, kicking the snow loose, packing it down, controlling the danger, stabilizing the slope. Most of those who ski below don't even know they exist, the powder hounds and pinheads, the air patrol and chute divers. Up above the beginners and intermediates and merely expert skiers, the Bridger Bowl extreme skiers are pounding down nearly vertical avalanche chutes whose very names suggest insane degrees of difficulty: Psychopath, Madman's, Cuckoo's.

They embrace the concept of terminal wipeout and broken bones, of the face wash and the endo—not to mention the possibility of being buried alive under several tons of snow—like voracious lovers. The skiing can get kinky on the ridge overlooking Bridger Bowl. The runs that aren't named for psychological aberrations invoke the pleasure of sex: Mr. Creamjeans, the Tits Traverse, Tease Me Dear, and the Orgasms, which everyone calls the O's.

And if they weren't on the ridge, these extreme skiers pounding up and down in their own psychopathic or pornographic frenzy, those of us confined by the limits of our ability to lower slopes would be exposed to one of the more unpleasant forms of death, white and cold, thundering down from above.

The theory of geographical determinism supposes that

the physical environment of a people influences its institutions and culture. This theory might hold, for example, that in America slavery was largely confined to the South because climate and soil conditions there conspired to produce labor-intensive crops, like cotton, while Northern agriculture was best suited to family farming. This may or may not be so—it seems a pernicious idea to me—but there is little doubt that the natural world determines the sort and quality of athletes. Does anyone doubt that there are more and better surfers currently living in Hawaii than in Kansas?

In Montana, one small ski area, catering primarily to locals, produces some of the finest specialized extreme skiers in the world. Impossibly steep slopes falling through shoulder-width canyons of rock will produce both broken bones and excellence. "Fear," as Coleridge said, "gives sudden instincts of skill."

The hill that gets all that adrenaline pumping is Bridger Bowl, located just outside Bozeman, Montana. The mountain is particularly prone to avalanches because of its verticality. While most ski areas are located on mountains with rounded tops, Bridger rises sharply to a narrow ridge. To get a sense of the mountain, imagine that the floor of your mouth is the bowl. The ski lifts begin at the root of your tongue and stop at the gum lines. Above the groomed slopes are the jagged teeth of the ridge.

The bowl is sheltered from the wind, and the only place it really blows hard is up on top of the ridge. Snow sweeps up over the back of the mountain and forms a huge overhanging cornice that shadows the vertical cliffs below. For the most part, it is dry, powdery snow that falls here—called cold smoke—and it fills the canyons and forms pillowlike slabs on the steep slopes below the cornice.

The pillows spawn avalanches. Given a bright warm day, for instance, the snow will form a sun crust. New snow atop the crust will have a different crystalline structure, due to inevitable differences in water content, rate of fall, and temperature. it is the interface between snow layers that causes problems. As falling snow compresses, the crystals round out, quickly losing their star shape. Now, with a great slab of new snow sitting atop a bed of icy ball bearings, which in turn is balanced atop hard sun-crusted snow, the pillow is unstable, and any little thing—a loud noise, a skier moving silkily over the surface—can cause hundreds of tons of ice to begin rolling downhill.

Several years ago, one of the high pillows slabbed off on a warm spring day long after Bridger had closed for the season. The avalanche rumbled down into the bowl, pushing the air before it so that half a dozen one-hundred-foot-high Douglas firs were bent nearly double with the howling force of hurricane-level winds. When the mass of snow rolled by the trees, the wind stopped, at once, as it never does under ordinary circumstances. The trees snapped upward so violently in the sudden calm that they broke off about halfway up. You can see these fifty-foot-high stumps about three-quarters of the way down the mountain. They provide an uncomfortable feeling of claustrophobia under the Big Sky, a sense of massive weight hanging precariously above.

No one has ever been seriously injured in an avalanche at Bridger Bowl since it opened in 1954, and this is because the ski patrol is particularly sensitive to the danger. Every morning at first light, before most of the day's skiers are even awake, seven to ten members of the patrol walk the ridge, knocking down the snow that overhangs the cornice. They toss hand charges—two and a half pounds of dynamite—into the pillows that form fifteen to twenty feet under the ridge.

Meanwhile, other patrol workers fire a seventy-five-millimeter recoilless rifle into larger, lower pillows. The mounted gun throws a high-explosive plasticized tracer that knocks loose spectacular avalanches.

Joel Juergens, the twenty-nine-year-old director of the Bridger Bowl ski patrol, calls this sort of work "control." After substantial snowfall, "a dump," Juergens will examine the twenty-four-hour pattern of winds and eyeball the slopes for areas of potential danger. "If there are areas of instability," he explains, "we deal with them."

Still, because of the mountain's unique shape, there is one
area the ski patrol can't stabilize between first light and the
time the lifts open. Down under the cornice, below the
steeply sloping pillows of snow, there are dozens upon dozens of short, steep, narrow canyons, the sort of avalanche
chutes climbers and skiers call couloirs. Snow builds up in
the couloirs over a season: enough snow to rumble down
into the lower pillows and kick loose an avalanche on unsus-
pecting skiers smoking down the groomed runs below. Because there are so many of these chutes, with so much snow
piling up in them after each storm, the patrol can't possibly
deal with every one of them, every day.

The couloirs are areas of instability, and they are controlled by the unpaid and unstable persons who call them
Madman's or Psychopath or the Orgasms.

"I suppose I've been in over fifty avalanches," Tom
Jungst said. Tom was telling me about avalanches on our way up to the top of the mountain. Beyond the highest lift, there was a trail to
the lowest point of the ridge. It was four hundred
feet, straight up, and we had to walk it, carrying
skis over our shoulders and kicking steps into a wall of snow
that rose so vertically I didn't really see the top until I was
almost on it. Each shin kick into the snow provided a little
place to stand, a platform to launch the next kick. This
wasn't skiing: it was twenty minutes' worth of hard mountaineering.

I am a recreational skier, most comfortable on advanced
intermediate slopes, and as such, I had no business being on
the ridge. However, I was with Barney Hallin, a captain of
the air patrol, and two chute divers, Jungst and Steve Ault,
who all swore that they could get me down "in one piece."
The ski patrol checked us out before we started up the trail.
We had to have designated partners and carry avalanche
beepers. A sign at the bottom of the trail said that the ridge
was hazardous: so steep that rescues are extremely difficult.

What the sign really meant is that folks are pretty much on their own up above the groomed slopes.

We crested the ridge, where the wind hit us like a symphony of rage and the land dropped away on both sides, forever. The expert slope below in the bowl actually looked gentle; my favorite intermediate run was a white flatland prairie. Wind-driven snow iced my beard so that I imagined I looked like a tough guy in a cigarette ad.

Tom Jungst and I checked out the Walkman-sized beepers. We set them for "transmit." If the snow swallowed either of us, we'd switch to "receive" and search for the other, by sonar. The louder the beep, the closer the crushed and suffocating skier. At the point where the beeping is loudest, a searcher should take the basket off one of his poles and poke around for the buried buddy. Tom told me where I could find a "rescue stash," with shovels and evacuation sleds.

Jungst said he'd guide me on an easy traverse of the ridge, where the avalanche danger was minimal. Even so, he thought I ought to know what to do in the event that something slabbed off and rolled over me.

Experience has taught Tom that the best thing to do in an avalanche is to "go with the flow." Don't fight it. Try to swim to the surface, get yourself oriented, and get your skis pointing downhill.

These aren't the wet, heavy avalanches you get in California or the East: it's not the sort of moving snow that sucks you down into it and imprisons you with its weight. The powder at Bridger is generally soft and light. If the avalanche doesn't get much above Tom's head, he can generally ski it. "In a slough or slide like that," he said, "you want to turn out of it. Get away from it, off to the side. The best angle to take is forty-five degrees, downhill." Tom has skied so many avalanches that he and partner Jim Conway refer to this maneuver as "doing a forty-five."

In the chutes, however, with stone walls rising sixty and one hundred feet on either side, it is impossible to do a forty-five. At first the snow is only knee-deep, and it shoots by you, pushing at your legs, sliding on its ball bearings while you're scraping along on the same surface on the abrasion of skis. Keeping the boards under you in moving snow is a knack that can only be learned by surviving a dozen or more light powder avalanches. "Most of these chutes narrow down quite a bit in places," Tom told me. "The snow piles up there." I got the impression that it was a little like standing in a locked room during a flood that would crest at the eight-foot level. "It'll get up to your neck," Tom explained, "and probably lift your skis up above the hard surface. You want to spread your arms out, keep your hands above it, and you should be able to float on it, with your head up above the surface. When the chute widens out, the snow level will drop, your skis will hit solid snow, and you can do a forty-five."

The cold smoke that falls on Bridger is so light that it doesn't stick to slopes much steeper than fifty-two degree. Several of the chutes below the pillows get a bit more vertical than that. After a particularly big dump, these chutes are filled with a few tons of powder trembling on the brink of an avalanche that will empty the couloir in a sustained boreal thunder. But, just for a few hours, yesterday's bare, rocky canyon is skiable.

"Won't the first person through knock loose a slide?" I asked Tom.

"That's why you want to be the first person through," he said. "After the slide, you can't ski that chute anymore." He and Conway take these chutes together, one behind the other. "Mostly," Jungst said, "the slide catches us at the narrow spot. If Jim's leading, I can usually see his head above the moving snow. All of sudden, he does a forty-five, and I know exactly where my skis are going to hit."

In effect, Jungst, Conway, and other chute divers like them are controlling the slopes, doing away with areas of instability. This is the reason the ridge is open to extreme skiers. "These guys do a large percentage of our control," Joel Juergens had told me. "The more people who ski the ridge, the more stable our snow pack." Juergens said that perhaps 250 people a day ski the top of the mountain: the exertion of the walk, the expense of the avalanche beepers, and the hazardous nature of the slopes keep numbers down. "These are all good skiers," Juergens said. "We only have to make a couple of rescues a year up there. Only a very few of the very best ski the steepest chutes. There's two guys, we call them the Chuteski Brothers: the steeper and narrower the couloir, the better they like it." The Chuteski Brothers sounded an awful lot like Tom Jungst and Jim Conway.

Only a small fraction of the ridge runners used the mountain's verticality to fly.

Barney Hallin is one of those who like to jump. Call it flying. The Montana distance-hang-gliding champion, Barney loves the howling chinook winds that devil the eastern Rocky Mountains because they are perfect for "body flying." This is a sport that requires a steady seventy-mile-an-hour blow. In a hard chinook, Barney can be found atop one of several high hills, hovering over a cliff, flying, held up by the caprice of the wind alone.

On the ski slope, Barney likes to catch "big air, clean air," and the verticality of the ridge is perfect for the sort of ski soaring he likes, which mostly takes place ten feet or so above the snow.

I side-slipped a hundred yards down the shallowest section of the cornice and dug a sit-down position on the slope. Above, Barney edged up to the cornice, and I could see the tips of his skis projecting over a perfect perpendicular cliff that dropped about fifty feet before edging out into a long, steep slope. There was a small wisp of cloud between myself and the tips of those skis.

Barney wanted to take the cliff in "free fall," but he just couldn't help himself: he popped it, which is to say he put some leg into the jump in order to catch more air. It was fifty feet of good clean air, and Barney took it nicely, falling free against the face of the cliff with his skis folded back under him. In the history of the world, most people who've

fallen this far—it's about the distance you'd plummet from
a five-story building—have waved their arms and screamed
all the way down before getting disagreeable bits of themselves into inaccessible cracks and crevices in the rock or
pavement below. If Barney were to land on a flat, he'd break
his legs, at the very least, but he expected to touch down
where the mountain began to edge out under the cliff, in a
place where the slope would rise up gently to kiss his skis.

This was his first run of the day, and Barney didn't know
what the snow would be like—he probably shouldn't have
popped it—and he landed in crud, an unexpected wind
crust. His skis cracked through the crust into a soft slush
below, and the hard upper layer of snow, the crust, yanked
at his legs. Barney looked like a man trying to sprint
through several shin-high strands of barbed wire. He
pitched forward, and Tom Jungst, standing beside me,
edged into position. If Barney began a long fast slide toward
the cliff a quarter mile below, Tom would ski an intersect-
ing traverse and throw a block tackle into his friend. This
is one good way to stop an uncontrolled slide up on the
ridge.

Barney, falling, tucked his head into his shoulder. He
didn't care to plow up a thousand-foot-long furrow with his
face. His speed and the rolling motion put him in danger
of cartwheeling down the slope, doing an "endo," tumbling
ass over teakettle all the way to the cliff. But Barney had
fallen before, lots of times, and the kinetic computer in his
muscles figured in the steepness of the slope, the condition
of the snow, the terrain below—all this in an instant too
short to calibrate—and he threw the skis over the top of his
head, like a swimmer churning into a tumble turn. Properly
oriented downhill, on a slope so steep Barney was very
nearly standing up, it was only a matter of cocking the
ankles slightly, catching an edge, and popping back up to
the safety of skis. This maneuver is impossible on the shallow slopes I frequent, but Tom Jungst said that it is the
thing to do on extreme terrain. "If you fall," he said, "the
thing that is going to save you, short of a block tackle, is
getting back onto your skis."

Tom couldn't really describe how he decides what shoulder to roll on in order to get back up. "If you've fallen a lot," he told me, "you say, 'Oh, one of these,' and your body just takes over from there."

Barney, not shaken in the least, cut into a giant slalom turn the moment he was up. He began "arcing it out," hitting a high-speed rhythm down the face of the mountain, moving on a slight angle to his left to avoid the cliff below. He disappeared into a stand of trees where he would have to pick up speed by narrowing down the arc in order to "weasel through." High-speed tree runs on steep slopes have proved fatal on many slopes. Imagine driving into a Douglas fir at thirty-five miles an hour. You could total your car. Hit the same tree at the same speed without the protection of a car's steel envelope, and you total your karma.

I was up and moving along the least-steep section of the traverse, finding a new position where I could watch Barney come blasting out of the trees, picking up maximum speed. He dove straight down the sort of slope I'd call a cliff, then popped it, hard, at the top of a ripple on the face of a mountain. The roller was shaped like a wave, a large oceanic swell, and Barney might have skied it easily, never losing the safety of the snow, but he wanted to catch some air.

Knowing precisely when to pop a roller is an art. It isn't like going up for a basketball at the tip. You want to roll your hips forward and get out over your skis. Time it wrong, go straight up, and the tyranny of physics rolls you backward in such a way that you're looking up at the sky through your skis. Competitive divers call this maneuver a gainer. Barney Hallin calls it "doing an upside-down Volkswagen." He knows of one man who broke his neck in this way, simply by mistiming his pop at the top of a roller.

Barney didn't suck up into a tuck. He took the roller like a ski jumper, leaning forward over his skis so that he could get wind under him and use his body as an airfoil. He caught another forty feet of clean air.

Below the roller, there was another wave of white, a

knoll, which is distinct from a roller because of the relative
steepness of the downside slope. Barney popped the knoll
for his biggest air of the day. He caught one hundred and
fifty clean feet of it, soaring about twelve feet above the
slope, flying over a couple of small trees and the photographer below. He might have popped it differently and gotten
a full thirty feet of height, but there is a danger of stalling,
of rolling back into a neckbreaking upside-down Volkswagen, when you go for the sky rather than distance.

Far below, I could see a spot of color that was Barney
Hallin. He was arcing down the apron, a long, wide, talus
slope where powder accumulates in absurd profusion after
a big dump. Most folks who ski the ridge take the same
relatively easy traverse I was on to the apron and the sensual caress of waist-deep cold smoke: powder that slows
them enough to take a slope that would be suicidal, for
most, in icy conditions.

Unlike Barney Hallin, who is interested in the physics of
flight, the powder hounds who ski the apron at Bridger
Bowl value the aesthetics of rhythm. They glory in skiing
virgin snow, in being the first to mark the powder with the
signature of their run. Their track should follow the fall
line and not be jagged with stops or, God forbid, pock-
marked with falls. The turns should be tight and symmetri-
cal. Following a good powder run, the skier can see his
rhythm written in one sinuous line upon the face of the hill.
This is figure skiing, a form of self-expression in snow. The
most artistic of the powder hounds use skis the way a
painter uses a brush.

A few times a year, a blizzard will dump five or six feet
of cold smoke on the apron, and the most avid of the deep-
powder hounds hit the ridge wearing snorkels. "They use
them to ski powder that's over their heads," Barney explained to me. "Someone skiing like that, all you can see is
a rooster tail coming down the clean powder; maybe the
flash of color of someone's hat. Every time you breathe in
powder like that, you suck in a lot of snow. It gives you one
of those headaches you get when you've eaten too much ice
cream, too fast." Experienced deep-powder hounds position

the snorkel behind their heads, so they suck in less snow and have milder ice-cream headaches.

"Actually," Barney said, "I think most of them wear snorkels so they can tell someone else they did it."

In several respects, Bridger Bowl is not particularly unique. There are good powder slopes at many other Rocky Mountain ski resorts. The tree runs above Jackson Hole are probably hairier than anything at Bridger. A few American mountains offer more verticality: Jim Conway has skied some of them, including the north face of Longs Peak, in Colorado, and Maroon Bells, outside Aspen. The most famous, and deadly, extreme ski runs in the world are located near Chamonix, in France. During the two weeks Jim Conway spent skiing there last year, four skiers died.

The athletes of France literally ski down the face of mountains. "It takes massive balls," Conway told me. "One fall and they're dead."

Because the snow above Chamonix tends to be wet, it sticks to steeper slopes. The hottest skiers of France, men like Patrick Vallençant, manage to run sixty-degree faces. The technique most often used is called a windshield wiper turn. It involves one hop-around after another, and the skier is always looking down the fall line over one shoulder or the other. "The thing about the French," Conway told me after his trip, "for them, it isn't considered difficult unless the run is death-defying. Consequently, they're more daring than we are at Bridger. On the other hand, they're more cautious in terms of technique, because a single mistake can kill them."

What makes the ridge above Bridger unique is the number and narrowness of the avalanche chutes. There are nests of couloirs all over the West, but you have to climb half a day or rent a helicopter to get to them. At Bridger, the chutes can be had for the price of an avalanche beeper and a tough twenty-minute climb. This accessibility has spawned a kind of specialized excellence.

Like river rats, the chute divers at Bridger are interested in making first descents down the most difficult couloirs. Once when Jim Conway and Tom Jungst were scouting the ridge for new chutes, they noticed a ski patrolman following them, from a distance, like an inept spy. The guy seemed nervous about something. Conway downclimbed into a couloir he had always passed by before because it seemed to narrow down and fall over a cliff. (Downclimbing is a combination of rock climbing and side-slipping.) Part way down the chute, Jim saw a way of skiing it.

"Hey," he shouted, "this goes."

Apparently, Conway had discovered one of the patrolman's favorite runs, and the man screamed at them in anger and frustration. Tom named the chute for the words they heard hurtling down on them from above. You Fuckers remains one of his favorite runs.

Each couloir offers its own set of problems. Skiers have to downclimb into You Fuckers. On Tease Me Dear, they resort to the esoteric sport of tree jumping. The run is actually a ridge between two chutes with a drop-off on either side. It starts off with six nice, tight powder turns: get too wide on those turns and you go screaming off the cliff. The run seems to end at another steep drop-off of thirty or forty feet. There is, however, a tree that grows just below the cliff. Jungst and Conway discovered that they could lean out over the drop, grab one of the branches, and lower themselves to the ground by falling through supporting branches. Below there is another run of five or six tight powder turns, ending at another cliff where there is another good jumping tree. And so on. Tease me, dear.

Some couloirs narrow down to shoulder width in places, some have boulders strewn across the fall line. Each one is special. While the extreme skiers of Chamonix can be compared to rock climbers who work big walls, the chute divers of Bridger do what amounts to bouldering, which is to say they ski runs of intense difficulty but short duration where a fall is not fatal. The sport is not nearly so dangerous as the

French variety, and technique, rather than brute survival, is the goal. People who merely windshield wiper through a couloir at Bridger are not respected.

"Everyone has his own ideas about technique," Tom Jungst told me. "There's one group we call the stable-gorilla family. The best skier is a guy who's built like a linebacker, and he skis in this massive, straddle-legged style. There's a petite woman who skis with him, and she gets down some pretty radical chutes the same way. So you watch them, and after a while you realize that sometimes, in some chutes and some snow conditions, stable gorilla is the way to ski."

Jungst and Conway prefer a more graceful, fluid style. "It's a takeoff on World Cup skiing," Conway told me. "It's carving into the turns, knowing when to release the edge and get the energy out of your skis so you can make the tightest turns possible. You finish one turn, dive downhill, and immediately transfer your weight to the new outside ski. While diving, you apply a subtle pressure to the outside ski. As it comes around to the fall line, you angulate your hips and knees, which applies more pressure to the ski and gives it a reverse camber. If you release right, the energy in the ski should snap your legs around. The upper body is leaning downhill as the skis cross in front of you. Simultaneously, you should be diving downhill again."

Tom Jungst, like many of the chute divers, is a former ski racer. He placed in the top twenty in NCAA Division I slalom two years running, but he now thinks ski racing is "very tame." To get up for races, Jungst would "go to the top of whatever mountain I was on and ski the wildest thing imaginable: a chute, a tree run. I'd come into the start of the race rushing on adrenaline, exploding with energy." Soon enough, Jungst gave up racing for the ridge. "Standing above a chute is a strange feeling," he told me. "I'm usually extremely calm and most interested in details like snowflakes and pine needles. Then I focus on the run I am going to create." Jungst thinks mental imagery and visualization are essential to a good run. "I see myself and every move I will make beforehand." When Jungst dives into the chute, "My eyes don't focus but take in everything as a whole." As in ski racing, "Things come at you far too quickly to make conscious decisions." When the boulders and walls and drop-offs explode into the field of his vision, Tom Jungst is not really there. He sees himself as from above, like a disinterested spectator.

L isten, forget about technique and visualization: the best way to get down the ridge is my way. Ski the shallowest sections until your speed gets uncomfortable, then bail out. Try to fall across the slope and dig up a lot of snow so that you can roll out and slide slowly down the mountain. This exercise in world-class cowardice earns about one hundred vertical feet per slide.

I was dug in below the chute Tom Jungst called the Fourth Virtue. From the top, the chute looked like a cliff, but there was snow on it, and I couldn't believe that the incline was only a little over fifty degrees. There was room for two narrow turns before the chute narrowed down to twice shoulder width and veered off to the left. Sunlight glittered off sheer ice in the throat of the couloir.

I took a wide traverse around the chute, slid down below it, and sat in the snow, waiting for Jungst. He came barreling out of the narrow turn and banked off snow piled against the wall, because using the terrain is important to him. Tom planted his pole, sprang into a turn, and side-slipped slightly through an icy patch before carving into his next turn and a dive that took him beyond the looming walls of the canyon. He was heading directly for a pile of crusted snow deposited by yesterday's avalanche. Jungst snapped into a tight turn. The slope was so steep, he purposely bounced his inside shoulder into the snow, which cut his speed so that he skirted the upper edge of the mound of avalanche crud.

Steve Ault came down next, and I could hear him grunt with the effort his grace was costing him. He scraped over the ice, caught an edge, did a shoulder roll, and came back up on his skis just in time to plant, hop, and windshield wiper once to avoid the crud pile. A small slide—a layer of snow perhaps six inches deep—rolled down behind Ault.

We gathered at the top of the long powder slope called the apron. It was the gentlest slope I'd seen all day, and I tried to ski it with a little dignity. On the fifth turn I took a header, did a one-hundred-yard endo, twisted my knee, and broke the binding of my left ski. The words "no business on the ridge" kept echoing in my mind. While fear may give sudden instincts of skill, it doesn't give skill itself. Just so. Pain gives sudden instincts of our limitations.

My knee was swelling against the fabric of my pants, and I decided that, should I decide to ski ever again, I'd confine myself to lower slopes. Let the psychopaths stabilize the ridge for me.

Barney Hallin, on his second run of the day, was barrelling down the apron above. He stopped where I lay in a pile of pain and offered what he must have imagined were words of encouragement. "Hey, I think it takes a lot of guts for a beginner to try to ski the ridge," he said. Then he was gone, skiing so beautifully that a wave of goose flesh rippled up my back.

THE
SURVIVAL GAME
Ultimate Tests in a Simulated Wilderness

Bob Gurnsey stood stock-still, listening, his big Nel-Spot pistol at the ready. According to his map and compass, the blue flag station had to be a couple of hundred yards away, somewhere in among the closely spaced maples, birches, and poplars. There were eleven other men somewhere in the hundred-acre tract of New Hampshire forest. All of them needed a blue flag as badly as Gurnsey. All of them carried Nel-Spot pistols.

Gurnsey moved to a stone wall and vaulted it. He landed lightly on his hands and knees, the pistol on the ground under his right hand. He wasn't alone.

"Now hold it *raht* there."

The words came out in a soft, syrupy south Alabama drawl, and they pierced through to Gurnsey's heart like a cold sword. He was dead, wasted, out of the game.

Gurnsey looked up into the barrel of a Nel-Spot held by R. D. "Ronnie" Simpkins. The gun was huge, immense, bigger than a .45, and Gurnsey could see that Simpkins was holding it rock-steady, drawing a bead directly on the bridge of his nose—dead square between the eyes. Gurnsey knew Simpkins by reputation—he hunted turkeys and could call all kinds of game birds up to his gun using a device he made from a crumpled snuff can and a diaphragm. (Simpkins, always a gentleman, referred to the last item as "a family saver.") Gurnsey never doubted that the turkey hunter would pull the trigger. He looked down toward the gun under his hand. If Simpkins faltered for a minute, if he moved the gun a little lower, Gurnsey would roll and fire. He was willing to take a hit anywhere but the face.

"Ah'm watchin' your eyes and you don't even want to think what you're thinkin'," said Simpkins. He never wavered. "Take your hand off the gun, real slow." Gurnsey did as he was told. "Now move away from the gun."

As Gurnsey inched away from his Nel-Spot, Simpkins lowered his own. Then, in a swift, unexpected motion, Simpkins lurched forward. He struck Gurnsey on the stomach with the palm of his free hand. That hand came away red, bright red, and there was a larger spot of color smeared across the belly of Gurnsey's camouflage suit.

Gurnsey looked down at the red streak in disbelief. He had been wasted by hand, eliminated from the game by a man whose gun, quite obviously, didn't work.

I received my invitation to the first annual Survival Game sometime last April. I accepted, but too late, as it turned out—all twelve positions in the contest filled quickly. Evidently I wasn't the only one who felt the unmistakable urges of the competition.

The invitation said the game had been devised with "your participation in mind, in order to make this world a better place to live." There were five pages of rules, but in essence the game seemed to be a grandiloquent version of capture the flag. A hundred acres of New Hampshire wood were to be divided into four quadrants: blue, red, green, and yellow. Somewhere within each quadrant was a station hung with twelve flags corresponding to the color of the quadrant. The object of the game, as explained in the letter, was to capture a flag from each station. The first player to emerge from the woods and arrive at one of two home bases in possession of the flag from each of the four quadrants would be the winner.

It was, all in all, a simple-enough orientating exercise, until you took the Nel-Spots into account. These large pistols are manufactured for marking cattle during calving season. They shoot small pellets of dye powered by a CO_2 cartridge. The guns are (somewhat) accurate up to about thirty yards. Any of the twelve competitors could fire at any other. A player marked by dye was out of the game.

The last page of the letter was an answer form with two boxes to check. The first box was an acceptance. The second read: "The idea of this thing terrifies or horrifies me. Or both. I think you're all a bunch of sickies."

This turned out to be the response from a number of people who chose not to play. In general, negative responses came from cities, especially New York, and the organizers were often labeled "macho" (at the very least). Several women had been invited to play, but for various reasons they said they were unable to compete. More elaborate responses, both written and verbal, contained such words as "sick," "twisted," "perverted," "puerile," and "fascist."

The men behind all this—the organizers of this mayhem—were writer Charles Gaines and a New York stock trader named Hayes Noel. For years, Noel had contended that in such a simulated survival situation a city boy, whose nerves are raw, whose responses are quick, might hold an advantage over a good woodsman whose tranquil life has left him unable to cope with more visceral human challenges.

The game had merely been a matter of discussion until photographer George Butler discovered the Nel-Spots in a farm catalogue. "The guns made the game possible," Gaines told me. "The dye pellets raise a welt, but if you are wearing safety goggles, as we require, they cause no serious injury. Secondly, the guns are much more symbolically weighted than, say, a thrown tomato."

It was, of course, that very symbolic weight that generated the firestorm of negative response. It was that same symbolic fact that got the animal juices flowing in each of the competitors.

On the morning of the competition everyone assembled at Charles Gaines's home. Each entrant had chosen to wear full camouflage gear. (The rules insisted that each player wear only a single layer of normal-weight clothing, perhaps because an over-zealous competitor had made a suit of foam padding after ascertaining that dye pellets invariably bounced off the foam without bursting.) Aside from the camouflage, each competitor wore a heavy holster containing the ominous-looking Nel-Spot. God knows what the neighbors thought. It looked as if Gaines and his cohorts were on their way to invade Dominica. The competitors were dispersed separately, in various parts of the woods, and all were started at ten sharp.

As a nonplaying observer, I stumbled onto the first sustained Nel-Spot fire fight a half hour into the game. Gaines and Simpkins were banging away at each other when Simpkins lost the charge on his CO_2 cartridge. Just then, Gaines hit him fairly with a pellet that didn't burst.

"You got me."

"No, you're not marked." The writer stood three feet from the turkey caller. "Give up," Gaines said. "I don't want to shoot you at this range. It'll leave a welt for a month." Simpkins, who knows Gaines for the savage competitor he is, assumed the writer's gun had jammed. He turned and escaped into the deep woods. Gaines stood there with a perfectly functioning pistol. "You learn a little about yourself in this game," he told me later. "I guess I'm a little softer than I like to think."

Of course it was Gaines's lack of killer instinct that allowed Simpkins to eliminate Bob Gurnsey later with the hand-held dye pellet. The game carried its share of fate.

Different competitors had different strategies. Hayes Noel, for instance, was doing very well, proving his point about city boys by making the most of being a good runner in excellent condition. His idea was to sprint from flag station to flag station and depend entirely on his reflexes and marksmanship, when the noise he made drew another competitor into his range. He had three flags and was on his way to the last when somebody wasted him.

Other players, notably Bob Carlson, a doctor from Alabama who eliminated two players he had bet on heavily to win, blasted away at any and all comers.

That was exactly what G. Ritchie White wanted to avoid. A registered professional forester, White was clearly the best of the competitors with a map and compass. His strategy was to move slowly and silently, using the contours of the land to hide himself. Where another player might run parallel to a creek bed on the straightest line between two stations, White took the more arduous and circuitous ridge route. White planned to engage no one in a shooting battle. It was the winning strategy.

White emerged from the woods unmarked, holding four flags, two hours and fifteen minutes after the contest had begun. "I hunt deer," he told me, "and you have to concentrate. But there is an extra dimension in this. The idea of being hunted in return. You have to concentrate on every sound, every movement. I was mentally exhausted after the first hour."

The results of the game were probably inconclusive, but it was instructive to see how people react in a survival situation—even a mock survival situation. Certainly the two city boys in the competition had done remarkably well—better, perhaps, than country boys might have done in a competition that involved a New York subway map and cashing a check in Manhattan on a Sunday.

"I believe in competition for its own sake," Gaines told me later. "I also believe that we have very little real wilderness left anymore. The outdoors, then, is a backdrop, a screen for what you want to project upon it. You either give in to the concept that there is no more challenge in the outdoors, or you throw your own projection on the woods. I mean, if you climb ice or run rapids, you impose your own rules. And you do this to pull out responses similar to real survival situations."

Gaines was probably right, at least for those of us who enjoy this constant testing and attendant adrenaline rush. It is a way of finding out who you are, and even those who object to the concept of the game, to its emotional weight, look for the same kinds of answers—by whatever means available. I know for a fact that quite a few of those who said they found the idea "sick" spend twice-weekly sessions with a man who says "uh, yes, uh-huh, and how do *you* feel about that?"

It also seemed to me, in the aftermath of the game, that there was something vaguely funny about it, something humorous in a cosmic sense. The invitational letter had ended with a quote from Menander, a Greek: "A man's fate is but his disposition." True enough, until one is maimed by a runaway pie truck or struck by lightning, or buried beneath thirty tons of concrete when a hotel walkway collapses in Kansas City. The game, it seemed to me in its aftermath, was just another way of whistling past the midnight graveyard that exists in all of us, an image one may find frightening or funny, depending on his disposition.

Menander lived about 300 B.C., and is considered one of the first full-blown comedians in dramatic history.

SHIVA WINKED

Being a Reverential Account
of Wild-Water Rafting
in the Foothills of the Himalayas

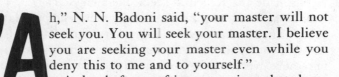

"**A**h," N. N. Badoni said, "your master will not seek you. You will seek your master. I believe you are seeking your master even while you deny this to me and to yourself."

A day before, rafting on a river that drops out of a snow field in the Himalayas, I had been thrown out of the boat in a rapid where I spent some time tumbling underwater in nature's frigid spin-and-rinse cycle. This was followed by a fast rush through a couple more downriver rapids that featured numerous unpleasant collisions with boulders of varying sizes and unvarying solidity. The successive impacts necessitated some predictably unsuccessful attempts to breathe underwater. My life had not passed before my eyes, but somewhere in the middle of the third rapid, cartwheeling along ass over teakettle, caroming off rocks, the phrase "holy shit, this is serious" began ringing through my mind. It was high noon and, even deep underwater, I could see the bright mountain sun above. It shimmered on the surface of the water, nuclear bright, and I fought toward it, feeling the surface retreat from me even as I swam. It was like a bad dream, a real tooth-grinder, and I longed to rise to the light, to breathe, to break through to the other side, the other side of the sun.

Now, thirty hours later, sitting in a hotel restaurant, there was a lingering congestion in my lungs, and I felt as if someone had taken a baseball bat to my entire body.

N. N. Badoni, a sweet shop owner in this north Indian town of Dehra Dun, suggested that I might consider my swim a religious experience. N.N. was an avid trekker and devout Hindu.

I am not much of a fan of the Hindu religion, associating it as I do with the pestiferous weenies known as Hare Krishnas whose panhandling presence in American airports results in such mind-boggling exchanges as "We're giving away copies of this book: it's five thousand years old."

"Five thousand years?" Stunned disbelief. "It looks brand-new."

My experience with holy types in India thus far, I told N.N., made the Krishnas seem like a class act.

N.N. agreed that some of the holy men who populate the subcontinent like rats in a grainery were undoubtedly transparent frauds and despicable money-grubbers. Still, he felt there were teachers of spiritual distinction: teachers who did not come to you. They were men you searched for in your soul. And when you found them, you would know. He mentioned a pair of swamis, now deceased, whose teachings had enriched his life.

I nodded politely, and N.N. bought me another beer. He was of the priestly Brahmin caste and did not, himself, drink. N.N. had provided research for Gary Weare's book *Trekking in the Indian Himalaya*, and had spent many years studying the Garhwal region north of Dehra Dun, where I had just been. Located in the lush Himalayan foothills that rise above the blistered plains of northern India, the Garhwal is considered the Abode of the Gods, and is replete with Hindu pilgrimage sites: Gangotri, near the source of the sacred Ganges river; Yamunotri, at the head of the Yamuna river where pilgrims boil rice in the hot springs below the temple to the goddess Yamunotri so that they may eat the "food of the gods;" Kenarnath, the divine resting place of the god Shiva; and Badrinath, the home of the god Vishnu. The Garhwal is the holiest and most sacred area in all of India.

I had been rafting the Tons, one of the innumerable glacier-fed rivers of the Garhwal. It is a little-known tribu-

tary of the Ganges, and at its source are the snowfields of
the 20,720-foot-high mountain called Bandarpunch, the
monkey's tail. The Tons is considered holy to Shiva, one of
the most complex of the Hindu gods. Shiva blows hot and
cold: he is at once Shiva the Beneficent and Shiva the
Avenger. In the homes along the Tons, there are small
altars where candles burn below bright printed posters of
the ambiguous god. Here is Shiva carrying, in his four
hands, a trident, a deerskin, a drum, and a club with a skull
at the end; Shiva with a serpent around his neck; Shiva
wearing a necklace of skulls. The streak of blue in his hair
represents the Ganges, for it is Shiva who brought the Holy
River to earth, breaking its fall from heaven by allowing it
to trickle through his matted hair. Shiva is usually depicted
as having a third eye in the middle of his forehead. When
the extraneous eye is closed, Shiva is pacific, and the figure
symbolizes a search for inward vision. When the third eye
is open, Shiva the Wrathful rains fire and destruction upon
the earth.

N.N. said that these tales of the gods weren't necessarily
the literal truth of creation. They were a way of *thinking*
about creation, life, and the meaning thereof.

It is a commonplace observation that India, and northern
India in particular, has been a hotbed of innovative spiritu-
ality since the dawn of civilization. Hindus, Moslems, Jain-
ists, Sikhs, Buddhists, Christians, exist side by side and all
react one upon the other so that over the centuries, it has
become religion—colorful, earnest, variegated—that de-
fines the country. Indians, as a people, are intoxicated with
religion, and even a visitor of sharp and jaundiced opinions
is likely to be tumbled willy-nilly in the torrent of spiritual
concerns.

N.N. was right, of course. My little swim in the Tons was
an exercise in perceived mortality. Food for compulsive
thought. I couldn't, for instance, shake this terrifying religious image. It is Shiva as I had seen him in the posters,
Shiva the Pacific, the inward-looking. Suddenly, the third
eye snaps open and there is piercing fire, nuclear white, and
final.

I thanked N.N. for the beer and the conversation then hobbled off to my room. When you begin to imagine strange three-eyed gods winking at you, it's time to regroup, reconsider, change your religion, even finish the last beer and go to bed.

Delhi is the capital of India, and its administrative center, New Delhi, is often described as a city of gardens. Unfortunately, I had come to this otherwise graceful city in the worst of times, which is to say, during the month of May. Afternoon temperatures rose to 110 degrees and would hold there for another month until the cooling rains of the monsoon. Dust, fine as talc, floated over everything and colored the sky a dull whisky brown. In the countryside, whirlwinds swept over the baking plain and, at a distance, it was impossible to tell the sky from the earth.

Delhi's heat, in the month of May, tries men's souls. In 1986, on May thirteenth, a man named Gupta killed his wife because he believed she was sleeping with another man named Gupta. Eight persons—members of a wedding party who had asked for some water at a temple—were injured in a fracas with temple keepers who believed the water would be used to mix alcoholic drinks. A civil servant who had not been promoted at the dairy board killed himself and left a note excoriating his superiors.

There was a Santa Ana tension in the still, burning air of the city, but May and June are also months of snowmelt in the Himalaya, the months the foothills erupt in wildflowers, the most auspicious months for a pilgrimage to the cool beauty of the sacred Garhwal.

Sixteen of us were camped in a lush meadow, by a wide eddy on the Tons river, in the Abode of the Gods. There was a scent of rhododendrons in the air, and the temperature, at four in the afternoon, stood just shy of 80 degrees. The river valley was narrow, 400 yards across, and the hills rose steeply and spirelike on either side, obscuring a glittering ridge of the high Himalaya to the north. There were leafy alders on the meadow. Deodar pines, like lodgepole pines, forested the higher slopes. It was a young river valley, recently cut in geological terms, and the Tons, fed by spring snowmelt, was running high and fast.

It was our first day on the river, and Jack Morrison laid it out for his nine paying passengers. Jack is the president and chief guide of White Magic Unlimited, a rafting and trekking outfitting business out of Mill Valley, California. He had made a first descent of the river five years ago. The original plan had been to raft the more well-known Yamuna River, of which the Hindu scriptures say: "No mortal mocks her fury; no mortal stops her onward flow." But the Yamuna had struck Morrison as a pretty tame ribbon of water—about class II whitewater: "rapids of medium difficulty with clear, wide passages"—and he didn't think American mortals would be willing to travel all the way to India for a gentle float trip. Hiking east, over an icy ridge, he came upon the Tons. It was his dream river, the river he could build his company around.

As Jack spoke, local people from the nearby village of Mori gathered about. The children came first, followed by old men, and finally, men who seemed to hold positions of authority in the village. They wore clean western-style clothes in subdued colors. Women did not come into our camp. They sat on the ridges in tight little groups, and occasionally the wind would carry the tinkle of giggles down into the meadow where we sat.

This would be the fourth time the river had ever been

run, Jack said. The trip was really "a commercial explora-
tory," which meant there would be a lot of time spent
scouting the rapids ahead and deciding on strategy.

There was plenty of big water, but what set the Tons
apart from other big-water rivers Jack knew—he mentioned the Bio Bio in Chile and the Zambesi in Zambia—
was the "consistency" of the white water. "It is one rapid
after another," he said, "almost eighty miles of class III and
IV and even class V rapids. The whitewater sections are
separated by one hundred yards or less of flat water, which
are probably moving at five to seven miles an hour." Class
V rapids are defined as "having extremely long, difficult,
and violent rapids that follow each other almost without
interruption . . . plenty of obstacles, big drops, violent current and very steep gradient." The obstacles and drops on
the Tons meant the rafts would have to do a lot of evasive
maneuvering in heavy water. It was a very "technical"
river.

The major danger, of course, was being thrown from one
of the rubber rafts or having it flip. A person might be held
down for some time in a big hole, might be thumped up and
down in a circular motion—"Maytagged"—but the more
deadly situation would be to be swept through several con-
secutive rapids. "On most rafting rivers," Jack said, "there
will be a quiet pool at the end of a rapid." On the Tons,
however, the rapids were "closely linked," and even the
strongest swimmer could be swept from one rapid to another. "The water is cold," Jack said, "it's all spring snowmelt now, and the longer you're in it, the more it saps your
strength. Swim too many rapids, and you'll be too weak to
make it to the bank. If you go in, do everything possible to
get out after the first rapid."

Such was the nature of our pilgrimage.

Aman feels a fool. Here I was, sitting under one of the alders, trying to read a book entitled *Hindus of the Himalayas* and getting absolutely nowhere because I was surrounded by a hundred or so Hindus of the Himalayas who wanted to know what I was reading.

The book, an ethnography of the region by Gerald Berreman, said that the plains Brahmins consider the people of the hills to be rude bumpkins. They live in this most religiously significant area of India, but according to Berreman, they engage in "frequent meat and liquor parties . . . are unfamiliar with scripture, largely ignore the great gods of Hinduism, marry across caste lines," and do other things that made me think I'd enjoy their company.

I read that passage to a man named Ajaypal Rana who declared it "blasphemy." His tone was mild, unconcerned. He might just as well have said the passage was "interesting" for all the passion in his voice. I read on. "Says here that people 'conceal these activities' and they 'project behavior indicating adherence to the accredited values of society.' "

Mr. Rana smiled and asked if our rubber rafts were inflated with helium. "Just air," I said. My friend seemed disappointed by the technological poverty of this arrangement.

The night was just cool enough for the thinnest of sleeping bags, and I had laid mine out under one of the leafy alders, in a field of calf-high marijuana and mint. The breeze felt like velvet, and the stars swirled above in the clear mountain air. Far to the south, the sky flickered electric blue as heat lightning shimmered over the baking plain of the Ganges River.

We had talked for several hours, the Hindus of the Himalayas and I. There were men with obvious physical handicaps among the villagers, but they had been teachers or farmers or tailors. There were no beggars among the hill people.

Which had not been the case in Delhi. On the streets, the heat pounding down from above then rising up off the concrete kept battalions of beggars working feverishly. There was no shade, no place to sit, and so the horribly mutilated hopped or rolled or lurched along, hands (or what passed for hands) out, beseeching looks on their faces. The novelist and travel writer V. S. Naipaul, a West Indian Hindu who wrote two brilliant books about his travels in India, the land of his grandfather, found the sheer numbers of beggars particularly distressing. In *India: A Wounded Civilization* he wrote: "The very idea of beggary, precious to Hindus as religious theater, a demonstration of the workings of karma, a reminder of one's duty to oneself and one's future, has been devalued. And the Bombay beggar, displaying his usual mutilations (inflicted in childhood by the beggar-master who had acquired him, as proof of the young beggar's sins in a previous life) now finds, unfairly, that he provokes annoyance rather than awe. The beggars themselves, forgetting their Hindu function, also pester tourists; and the tourists misinterpret the whole business, seeing in the beggary of the few the beggary of all."

There had been, in Delhi, a young man, nearly naked but for a white loincloth. He was lean and dark, starkly muscled, and his right leg had been amputated just above the knee. He saw me—an obvious tourist—across a wide boulevard choked with the chaotic late-afternoon traffic that, in India, is a form of population control: that day, in Delhi alone, three died in accidents and seventeen were injured. The man came for me, threading his way nimbly through the cars, hopping on one bare foot and a crutch fashioned from the branch of a tree. I was amazed at his dexterity, the athletic fluidity of his movements.

The beggar hit the sidewalk, and just for a moment I saw triumph in his face, and a kind of joy. But as he fell into hop-step beside me, the light died in his eyes and he stared fixedly with a wet and pathetic spaniel-eyed beggar's gaze. "Alms," he said.

I am a man who habitually doles out spare change to winos, I suppose because I see the possibility that I might, one day, total my karma and find myself sitting in alley behind a tattoo parlor, swigging muscatel from a bottle in a paper bag. But this idea of sins in the previous life resulting in the mutilation of children by beggar-masters and misery pimps—I would not, I decided, perpetuate this system. I would not, as a matter of principle, give money to beggars.

"Alms," the one-legged athlete moaned.

I stared through him and silently chanted the mantra that makes beggars disappear. "You are invisible. . . ."

He hopped along by my side for three city blocks—"you are invisible"—then peeled off and made for the other side of the street, playing picador with the taxis.

I kept replaying the encounter in my mind and it was keeping me awake. His misfortune wasn't his fault. Giving him money: the penny or so he wanted, would it be such a sin? I thought: it would be like standing on the brink of hell and tossing in a wet sponge.

The first day out of Mori was the easiest. There were rapids without a lot of rocks. The people had gathered by the hundreds to see us off. It is a romantic conceit, but I had rather hoped they might regard us with awe. "Crazy brave fools risking watery death for naught but glory . . ." That sort of thing.

As it was, we had severe competition because a band of Gujars, seminomadic Moslem herdsmen, had come in that morning. I heard them driving their cattle along the trail above our meadow and saw them in the pale light of false dawn: fine tall people with aquiline features, shouting and laughing on the hillside above. The women wore intricately patterned pant-and-tunic combinations and covered their heads with colorful scarves of bright red or green. The older men dyed their beards red. All the males, men and boys, wore red skull caps embroidered with golden thread and topped by a red pom-pom on a braided stalk.

There had been Gujars among the Hindus the night before, but this was a special group. Their clothes were finer and brighter, the women wore more bangles, their cattle were fatter, and their dogs were bright-eyed and well fed. They were, I learned later, show-biz Gujars.

The group, about eighteen of them, set up in a meadow not far from us, and the people of Mori abandoned us for the Gujar show, which was undoubtedly more interesting than watching people load rafts all morning. The Gujars had with them several dusty black Himalayan bears, sometimes called moon bears for the white or orange-yellow crescent on their chests. The bears were controlled by a long rope that ran through the nose and out the mouth, but they seemed to respond to verbal commands. There was "sleeping bear," who lay on his back with his paws in the air, "smoking bear," who sucked on a six-foot-long stick of bamboo, "disco bear," who danced, and "hugging bear," who gently embraced a local child. The people of Mori laughed, threw coins to the Gujars, and strolled back to watch us cast off.

And so we paddled out of the eddy, caught the current, and went spinning down the Tons, crazy brave fools who would risk watery death but who were, demonstrably, no more interesting than your basic dancing bear. The Gujars had stolen our thunder and destroyed a romance. "Stupid damn hats," a man paddling beside me said. "Makes 'em look like nitwits."

Two days later, we hit Main Squeeze, the first really nasty rapid. It was hellishly technical. The river narrowed down to thirty feet, and, naturally, a bridge spanned the Tons at the point of its greatest fury. The water thundered between rock walls in wildly irregular waves that clashed, one against the other, throwing spray ten feet into the air. Just before the bridge, the river rose up over a rock—a domer—then dropped four feet into a hole. The hole was six feet long, and at its downstream end, a wave four feet high curled back upstream.

We wanted to hit the hole dead on, power paddle into the curling wave, punch through, jog right to avoid the tree trunk pylon for the bridge, duck under the bridge—Jack Morrison said he'd never seen the Tons so high—then hit hard to the right. Ten feet past the bridge, the river widened to fifty feet, but a rock thirty feet wide cut the Tons into two ten-foot channels. The left channel was shallow and rock strewn. We would need to pull hard right as soon as we passed under the bridge.

There were three boats. Seven of us were in the paddle boat: three of us on each tube with paddles and Jack Morrison manning the oars from the frame in the back. Jack called out orders—"paddle right"—and muscled the bow into the line we'd chosen. We had spent two hours scouting Main Squeeze and we ran it smartly in thirty seconds.

Those of us in the paddle boat were getting cocky, impatient with all the scouting Jack thought necessary. We were a strong team and we worked well together. Why couldn't we just R and R: read the river and run? There was some grumbling about this matter.

A tributary I couldn't find on the map—local people called it the Pauer—emptied into the Tons, effectively doubling its volume, just before the town of Tiuni. The river below gathered force and the gradient steepened until the Tons was dropping one hundred feet every mile. It was a wild ride, the Tons below Tiuni. There were, for instance, five major rapids just below the town, with no more than twenty yards of flat water in the whole run. Occasionally we hit a hole out of position and people were thrown from the boat— "swimmer!"—but we managed to right ourselves and scoop swimmers out of the water without stopping.

A mile downstream from the town, we passed a dozen or so men sitting on the rocks beside a six-foot-high pile of burning sticks. We were paddling hard, dodging rocks, and punching through curlers, but there was time enough to see the body on top of the funeral pyre. A yellow sheet covered the torso to the shins and flames licked at the bare feet.

The ashes would be dumped into the Tons and they'd flow into the Yamuna, which empties into the sacred Ganges. There, in those holy waters, the soul of the departed might achieve *moksha:* liberation from the cycle of being, from the necessity of being reborn.

At the moment, however, the physical body was being consumed in the burning flame of Shiva's open third eye.

On the second to last day, the river entered a long narrow gorge. The cliff walls that rose on either side were an oddly striated travertine that looked like decorations on some alien and inhuman temple. We had come seventy miles, dropped almost three thousand feet, and the river had spent much of its power. There were long flat-water floats where the river was so quiet we could hear the chatter of monkeys and the calls of cuckoos. The land, which upstream had looked like a steeper version of the northern Rockies, now took on a more gentle, tropical rhythm. Palm trees grew at the edge of the cliffs, and their roots dropped eighty feet into the nourishing water of the Tons.

There were waterfalls here and there, and once, floating languidly under cobalt skies, we passed through a falling curtain of mist that stretched one hundred feet along a mossy green cliff wall. It was warmer here, 85 degrees, and I raised my face to the cooling water. The sunlight was scattered in that silver curtain—each drop a prism—so that for a moment what I saw was a falling wall of color that shifted and danced in the breeze. The mist had the scent of orchids in it, and I wondered then why it was that anyone would want to be liberated from the cycle of being.

There was big trouble the last day. The Tons had lately been so flat and friendly that the last series of rapids were a major surprise and are, in fact, called Major Surprise. I followed Jack and his boatmen as they scouted the noisy water: there was a hole, a pretty good curling wave, a house-sized rock, and a small waterfall called a pourover. We needed to skirt the rock, punch through the hole, and pull left in order to hit the pourover at its shallow end, which would give us a drop of about four feet.

Major Surprise ate us alive.

I recall hitting the hole and punching cleanly through the curler. But we didn't get left, not even a little bit, and the boat rose up over a domer so high that I found myself looking directly into the sky. We tipped forward—the drop was eight feet—and the boat seemed to hesitate momentarily, like a roller coaster at the summit of the first rise. This, I told myself, does not bode well.

The first thing a person notices underwater in the turbulence of a big hole is the sound. It's loud: a grinding, growling jackhammer of unrelenting thunder. You do not register temperature and, if you are being Maytagged, you have no idea where you are. It's like catching a big ocean wave a bit low: there's a lot of tumbling involved, not to mention a sense of forces beyond human control.

The river took my swimming trunks. It ripped the tennis shoe off one of my feet, sent me thudding against unseen rocks, shot me to the surface dead center in the middle of the hole, sucked me down again, and batted me around for a period of time I was never able to calibrate. It didn't seem *fair*. I couldn't even recall falling out of the boat: the entire situation was unacceptable.

Some time later I came to the surface and the hole was behind me. The river ran right, between a large rock and a canyon wall. A person could get wedged in there, underwater. I swam left, and suddenly felt myself being hurtled down a smooth tongue of water toward a series of peaked waves of the type boatmen call haystacks. It was like being sick, like vomiting. After the first painful eruption you think, good, that's all over. But almost instantly your stomach begins to rise—oh, God, not again—and that is the way I felt being sucked breathless into the second rapid.

While I was zipping along underwater, trying to get my feet downstream to ward off rocks, the other members of the paddle boat team were enjoying their own immediate problems and proving Jack Morrison's contention that we were taking the river entirely too lightly. John Rowan and Martha Freeman had been sucked to the right and managed to pull themselves out after the first rapid. Jack and Billy Anderson held on to the boat, which was still stuck in the hole and being battered by the upstream curler wave. Sue Wilson and Douglas Gow were somewhere out ahead of me in the second rapid.

I surfaced and spotted Gow in the flat water between that second and third rapid. He was ten yards downstream and he didn't seem to be swimming at all. His helmet was missing. I thought he might have been Maytagged rather badly, that he might be unconscious, and I am proud to say that I swam to the man who needed help. (Actually, Gow had taken off his helmet because it slipped down over his eyes and he couldn't see.)

"You okay?" I called when I was within arm's reach. Gow practices emergency medicine in Australia and is used to reacting calmly in tense situations. "Fine, thanks," he said, and then—oh, God, not again—I was pulled down into the third rapid.

There was, in time, a sense of water moving more slowly. Sunlight shimmered on the flat-water surface, which seemed to recede even as I swam toward it, but then there was air and a handhold on the rocky canyon wall. Presently, Morrison and Anderson came by in the boat and fished me out of the river. I lay on my belly on the floor of the raft and spit up a quart of yellow water.

We were somewhere else then, pulled up onto the sand at the left side of the river. Sue Wilson and Doug Gow were

gasping on the bank. Someone gave me a pair of swimming
trunks to wear. This did not seem to be an important matter. I lay on my back, on the floor of the raft, looking at the
sun, and there was a moment when it seemed to darken
slightly, but I did not lose consciousness. I thought of
Shiva's blinding third eye, of a long lewd wink.

I went to Rishikesh, the holy city on the banks of the
sacred Ganges, just in case.

The river runs through a wide, rocky gorge there, and
every day pilgrims by the thousands cross over a suspen-
sion bridge that spans the Ganges and leads to the temples and ashrams of Rishikesh, to what the guide books
call "the abode of saints and sages." To get to the bridge,
you have to walk down a wide staircase set against a white
cement wall. There are large rectangular boxes sculpted
into the wall, and sitting in these boxes are the most unfortunate, the most horribly mutilated beggars in all of India.

Either they lived in those boxes, or they were carried
there each morning, because it was clear that none of them
could walk. As I passed, they called out to me, called out in
the most theatrically pathetic and heart-rending tones:
"alms, alms, ALMS . . ." I made them invisible and passed
on to the abode of saints and sages.

A wide cement walkway ran along the ridge top and, in
the formal gardens on either side, sacred cows grazed on a
variety of colorful flowers. Beggars didn't seem to be allowed here, near the temples, but holy men lined the walkway. There were more sadhus and gurus and anandas and
babas and bhagwans and rishis and maharishis than a guy
could shake a stick at. A man in a white loincloth with
yellow sandalwood paste on his forehead offered to bless me
for a rupee. I gave him the eight cents, just in case, and he
held out his palm to me, like a policeman stopping traffic.

Under a tree set in the center of the walkway, a thin dark
man lay on a bed of nails, a collection bowl for donations
by his side. He wore a skimpy loincloth that revealed a thin

appendectomy scar that angled up from his groin. Nailed to the tree was a large frame containing four photographs. The first three showed the same man lying on his bed of nails in front of what I took to be various holy places. The fourth was him reclining in a pile of thorns.

Farther down toward the main concentration of temples I stopped into an herbal medicine shop where, according to a leaflet I was given, they sold "chandra prabhavati," which was said to "cure piles . . . rheumatic pains, gonorrhea, syphilis, and spleen complaints." I asked to buy some mahavrinraf oil, which "checks the fallings of hair, invigorates the nerves, and removes brain fag." They were fresh out of mahavrinraf oil.

Some earnest young people—three or four Indians and a like number of Westerners—urged me to follow them to their ashram. "Let's go," I said brightly, but something in my attitude—brain fag maybe—put them off.

There were steps that led down to the holy river, and places along the bank to bathe. A bath in the Ganges is said to wash away a pilgrim's worldly sins. The river was swift and cold, hard to swim. I got myself out into the teeth of the current and let it carry me several yards. It felt good, going with the flow like that.

Passing back over the bridge, I stopped in front of the boxes in the wall and allowed myself to finally see the beggars. "Alms," they cried, and I gave them alms. I stood there tossing wet sponges into the fires of hell, just in case.

Later that night, in Dehra Dun, I met N. N. Badoni. He told me that the soul seeks its master. I told him about the Tons river.

TIM CAHILL is the author of two previous books, *Buried Dreams* and *Jaguars Ripped My Flesh*. He is a columnist and founding editor of *Outside* magazine and a contributing editor for *Rolling Stone* magazine. Mr. Cahill has recently completed a fifteen-thousand-mile trip in a stock pickup truck from the southernmost point in South America to Prudhoe Bay, Alaska, and is at work on a book about the journey. He lives in Montana, in the shadow of the Absaroka Mountains.

VINTAGE DEPARTURES

___ *One Dry Season* by Caroline Alexander	$10.95	679-73189-X
___ *Fast Company* by Jon Bradshaw	$6.95	394-75618-5
___ *Maple Leaf Rag* by Stephen Brook	$7.95	394-75833-1
___ *A Wolverine Is Eating My Leg* by Tim Cahill	$9.95	679-72026-X
___ *Coyotes* by Ted Conover	$9.95	394-75518-9
___ *In Xanadu* by William Dalrymple	$9.95	679-72853-8
___ *Bad Trips*, edited by Keath Fraser	$12.00	679-72908-9
___ *Samba* by Alma Guillermoprieto	$11.00	679-73256-X
___ *One for the Road* by Tony Horwitz	$6.95	394-75817-X
___ *Video Night in Kathmandu* by Pico Iyer	$12.00	679-72216-5
___ *Running the Amazon* by Joe Kane	$9.95	679-72902-X
___ *Navigations* by Ted Kerasote	$7.95	394-75993-1
___ *Making Hay* by Verlyn Klinkenborg	$5.95	394-75599-5
___ *In Bolivia* by Eric Lawlor	$8.95	394-75836-6
___ *The Panama Hat Trail* by Tom Miller	$6.95	394-75774-2
___ *All the Right Places* by Brad Newsham	$9.95	679-72713-2
___ *In Trouble Again* by Redmond O'Hanlon	$8.95	679-72714-0
___ *Into the Heart of Borneo* by Redmond O'Hanlon	$7.95	394-75540-5
___ *The Village of Waiting* by George Packer	$12.00	394-75754-8
___ *The Road Through Miyama* by Leila Philip	$9.95	679-72501-6
___ *Iron & Silk* by Mark Salzman	$10.00	394-75511-1
___ *From Heaven Lake* by Vikram Seth	$5.95	394-75218-X
___ *In the Shadow of the Sacred Grove* by Carol Spindel	$8.95	679-72214-9
___ *The Voyage of the Sanderling* by Roger D. Stone	$12.00	679-73178-4
___ *Fool's Paradise* by Dale Walker	$7.95	394-75818-8
___ *You Gotta Have Wa* by Robert Whiting	$10.95	679-72947-X

Available at your bookstore or call toll-free to order: 1-800-733-3000.
Credit cards only. Prices subject to change.